THE CHANGING
CULTURE
OF AN
INDIAN TRIBE

By Margaret Mead

WITH A NEW INTRODUCTION
BY THE AUTHOR

Capricorn Books New York

TO MY MOTHER

EMILY FOGG MEAD

WHOSE STUDY, THE ITALIAN ON THE LAND,
WAS ONE OF THE PIONEER STUDIES OF
CULTURE CONTACT IN THE
UNITED STATES

FOREWORD

This is a pioneer study in a neglected field. Many years of patient research have been given to recording and understanding what aboriginal cultures were before and during the early period of contact between Indian and white, with scarcely a thought as to what has happened since. Naturally such studies were undertaken to satisfy curiosity rather than to be useful, but even so they were the first necessary steps to a study of culture change as presented in this book. Further, it is because this initial task has been so well done for the Indian tribes of the United States that the way is now clear to study the Indian in our midst instead of the Indian living a free life in forest and plains. Thus the author of this volume could approach her chosen problem well equipped with an intimate knowledge of white culture on the one hand and on the other a well-organized body of data respecting the old tribal culture which ultimately came into collision with white culture, the result being the situation in which the tribe now finds itself. No one seems to be satisfied with the outcome, Indian or white. According to popular belief, the Indian has met with little short of disaster at the hands of the whites, his health, family life, and mode of getting a living are all believed to have been smashed by the steam-rollerlike advance of white culture. Such statements may be too sweeping, in that attention is fixed upon the most tragic phase of the adjustment instead of upon the whole cycle of contact, for if the history of any American tribe is scanned, it appears, that, for the most part, the first period of contact was to the Indian a season of prosperity. The first whites were traders rather than settlers; they brought new and useful objects for which the Indian could exchange furs and food. At once the Indians became producers of surplus goods, they broadened their outlook and many tribes increased in population and power. Later came the encroachments of settlers and diminishing natural resources, leading to a struggle in which the Indians were subdued by force and confined to reservations. Perhaps more than half of these died during this time of stress, while the remnant, in almost total economic and social collapse, entered upon a period of sullen passive resistance, attempting, as far as possible, to rehabilitate in isolation their old aboriginal life. Yet, after a time, adjustments began to be made; a slow increase in population set in and, with varying success, each tribe muddles along as a social and economic dependent of the nation in charge.

A complete study of the Antlers would entail a searching inquiry in each of these successive periods of white contact, a program now under way among some neighboring tribes. Dr. Mead, however, undertook a more restricted examination of the tribal woman as she reacts in the present period of white contact. One reason for this restriction was that to date we know a great deal more about the Indian man than about the woman. Further, some preliminary observations suggested the assumption that the complicated situation in which the tribe now functions might bear less heavily upon the Indian woman than upon the man, but should this assumption be found unjustifiable, a study of the contemporary Indian woman might still be worth while as a contribution to the study of woman in general. Also, it is but fair to say that this study was projected from the plane of scientific curiosity solely and not with a view to reformatory or ameliorative developments. The results, if they stand the test, may give some insight into the present Indian situation which in turn may serve those who must make administrative judgments. If so, well and good, but it can scarcely be expected that such a pioneer attempt will go far in this direction. Many other tribes must be studied exhaustively and in other national settings before one can feel sure of the cultural factors involved.

For one thing, the author gives us a picture of an Indian tribal community as she saw it during her visit, accompanied by suggestive comments and interpretations. The fundamental situation in this tribe is not far to seek. It strives to maintain the old ideal, that food and other necessaries are for immediate consumption and distribution at the hands of him who calls, and at the same time to carry on in the midst of a nation-wide intense economic individualism. To maintain a community in which the accumulation of goods is regarded as anti-social and integrate the same with contemporary white culture is to try to harmonize two incompatible institutional systems. The usual white policy is based upon the concept that under a reservation and land allotment program the tribe may so adjust its culture as to form a block of individual land holders, retaining their social solidarity and at the same time operating in the white economic system as self-supporting producers. Perhaps this is one of the most difficult social problems a people can face, but it does not follow that a solution is impossible. We suspect that further studies will reveal some tribes well on the road to a solution, though the picture of the Antler tribe as given by the author places them at the critical stage of the necessary transition. However all this may be, we are indebted to the author for pointing the way to a promising field for social research.

CLARK WISSLER

New York
June, 1932

ACKNOWLEDGMENTS

The field expenses of this investigation were most generously contributed by Mrs. Leonard Elmhirst's Committee in 1929, in a grant to the Department of Anthropology, of the American Museum of Natural History, for an investigation of family life and the social setting in a selected tribe of American Indians. For the opportunity to make this study and the time and clerical assistance necessary for this analysis of the results, I am indebted to the American Museum of Natural History. I am particularly indebted to Dr. Clark Wissler for direction of the research and for patient and illuminating criticism of my conclusions. I owe special thanks to Miss Bella Weitzner for editorial supervision of the manuscript.

To those members of the Indian tribe, the identity of which I have cloaked with the tribal alias of Antler, and whose personal identities I have hidden beneath fictitious names, who made me welcome in their homes and at their dances, I wish to express my appreciation for all their friendliness and consideration.

MARGARET MEAD

AMERICAN MUSEUM OF NATURAL HISTORY,
New York City, July 20, 1931

CONTENTS

CONSEQUENCES OF RACIAL GUILT
INTRODUCTION: 1965

The Relevance of This Study to the Modern World

We live in a period in which demand far outruns disciplined knowledge and the number of those who can make accessible even the knowledge we have is insufficient. Thirty-five years ago, the study of cultural change was an important background concern of anthropology. Today it is an essential requirement for social action.

The seriousness of the situation can perhaps be measured by the contrast in our awareness then and now. In 1930, this study was regarded as having relevance, at most, for our policies toward American Indians or for the specialized problems of governmental contacts with primitive peoples. Today, a principal plot enacted on the worldwide political stage derives from the clash between the guilt of those who have combined technical superiority with a sense of racial arrogance and the assertion of the rights of those who in different ways have experienced that arrogance. In the past, those who were technologically more advanced, numerically stronger, or better organized for attack overcame less advanced or weaker groups —killed, enslaved, or drove out the men, appropriated the women, and attempted to transform the children. Today, within our growing ethic of human brotherhood, this age-old historical process has been transmuted into a monstrous act that requires retribution, restitution, and repeated acts of atonement.

This ethical doctrine, shaped by conflict, is expressed in a great variety of ways, especially in the attitudes that inform anti-imperialism, anti-colonialism, the demand for Civil Rights, and the obligation to provide technical and scientific assistance to emerging modern nations.[1] It is an expression on a world scale of the doctrine that has become a guiding element in United States policies toward the Indians of North America. And this book is one record of the disastrous effects upon the Indians themselves of a doctrine that has grown out of the conflict between ideas of racial guilt and racial rights to restitution.

---

[1] Margaret Mead, "The Underdeveloped and the Overdeveloped," *Foreign Affairs,* Vol. 41, No. 1 (October, 1962), 78-89.

It is true that in the course of culture contact, enormous shifts in power and wealth occur. But the doctrine of the responsibility of the successful to make atonement to those whose rights have been denied is a new synthesis of modern findings on evolution, a more rigorous interpretation of Christianity, and contemporary thought about the right to political self-determination. The belief that those who in the past have won are inevitably in the wrong—the belief that is the key to anti-colonialism—is founded on a repudiation of the kind of culture change in which the gun has replaced the bow, the steam engine the draft animal and the outrigger canoe, and the organized state the small tribal group. Beyond this, it is a belief that sheds a glorifying light on the defensive fighting of the losers. And it has acquired a spurious reality because in the last three centuries the winners so often have been white men who have suffered from a sense of racial superiority and have barefacedly claimed as theirs all the institutions of the ancient world that, in fact, they had acquired through culture contact and military or missionary subjugation.

This association of racial superiority with successful superordination and of conversion with partial subjugation arises from man's capacity to symbolize and, in so doing, to transform members of his own species into non-men, predators or prey. Later, when feelings of guilt overcome those who have participated even indirectly in this symbolic process of dehumanization, situations arise in which the victims are, in a new sense, victimized. And we have the plight of the Indians I have called "Antlers." For attempts to give massive, inappropriate technical assistance have only served to paralyze whatever efforts the Antlers have made to move into the modern world. Racially based restitution has the effect of perpetuating the very wrongs it attempts to atone for and correct.

This study, looked at from our present viewpoint, should help to illuminate some of the ethical and social consequences of misplaced racial guilt. For to accept responsibility on the basis of race for the actions of predatory members of one's own group is as nonsensical as it is for members of an exploited group to accept responsibility on a racial basis for the ignorance or defenselessness of those who were exploited. *The* American Indian, *the* white man, *the* Asian, *the* African, and *the* American Negro, in whose name so many passionate speeches are being made, never did anything—neither inflicted nor suffered wrong. Each of these is a figure of speech, and the error lies in our still unbroken habit of grouping whole peoples in this way by race or nation and of attributing to actual people traits of "racial" superiority or inferiority that only fit the generalized figures we ourselves have created. The wrongs that were done were not suffered by *the* American Indian, but by individuals, members of particular tribal groups; and these wrongs were committed not by *the* white man, but by specific white men (and by specific members of other races also) who, acting within the accepted modes of behavior of their time, took what superior force and superior technology made available to them.

It is unlikely that we should be able to prevent the dislocation of many human lives even if technological change were entirely to replace military conquest and political maneuver in a more organized world. Technological change inevitably leads to the destruction of older ways of life. Yet, given any choice, there are few peoples who prefer stone to steel tools, who insist on walking when motor transport is available, or who prefer the flicker of oil lamps when electricity is there to light the darkness. In transitional societies, the beauty and harmony of age-old adaptations are disturbed, more members of the society are disturbed, and the broken patterns of their ways are far less aesthetically satisfying. But if all the members of the larger society, both those who benefit by and those who suffer from the changes that are taking place, regard themselves and one another as members of the same human race, this can provide for a sense of mutual responsibility in which all have a part to play in creating a new integration. Where a consciousness of common humanity underlies action, the situations that have doomed the descendants of the earlier settlers of this country to long, imprisoning misery need not occur.

The Antlers are a culturally deprived people today. But this is not because they lost their land or because the buffalo were decimated when the use of guns made obsolete their old hunting techniques. Their cultural deprivation has its source in the treatment accorded them by Euro-American settlers who regarded them first as racially distinct and then as inferior and who failed to share with them the whole dignity of membership in our technologically superior culture.

The answer to cultural deprivation resulting from culture change is a responsible, lively effort at cultural supplementation for every culturally deprived individual, without regard for race and with a full appreciation of the cultural context of each individual's life. It would be tragic if our misguided efforts to make economic and political restitution for the sufferings endured because of acts of racial arrogance in the past resulted in the perpetuation of older beliefs about "race" in the attitudes of other men toward other groups in the future.

METHODS USED IN THIS STUDY

Ethnological descriptions, in common with other types of historical study, retain their value over time. In this they are unlike experimental studies that use rats, guinea pigs, or human beings to generate data. A good experimental study seeks to eliminate all that is irrelevant to the particular piece of research; the less necessary it is to think of the experimental subjects as rats with species characteristic behavior or men with complex life histories, the better it is for the task at hand. And once a hypothesis has been tested, there is no need to take further account of the particular subjects. Later advances in theory will make a return to this experiment unnecessary.

The situation is a different one in natural history and in human history. A precise description of the nest-building activities of a pair of robins is valid, however undeveloped the science of ethology may have been when the observations were made. And where human behavior is concerned, a precise description stands forever as a unique record of a given people in a given place at a given time. No other people will ever repeat specifically what these people did in this place, at this time. Were their actions to go unobserved and undescribed, our record would be the poorer. And once the description is set down, materials exist for later analysis as new theoretical developments provide new concepts and new tools and methods and as new social situations raise new questions that require new scientific answers.

For earlier work to retain its usefulness, however, it is essential always to restate the conditions under which the observations were made and recorded so that its specific relevance within the contemporary context will be clear. Traditionally, anthropologists have been trained to recognize (though they must also be continually reminded) that every anthropological account includes the anthropologist himself, that all statements must be interpreted in the light of what was known at the time they were made, that all methods must be judged within the framework of methodology that was available, and that every estimate of the behavior of an identified group made by a fieldworker must be set against the background of his own experience in the study of other groups by the same methods.

This investigation differs in many respects from any other fieldwork I have done. Its duration was very brief—from June to October, 1930. Both my husband and I had made two earlier, intensive studies of living Oceanic cultures, in each case using the language of the people. Among the Antlers, where we were dealing with a broken culture, we used English. Given the shortness of the field period and the presence of three English-speaking generations, this seemed the more appropriate solution. My husband used interpreters in working on the details of the old culture which he was reconstructing, but as my work dealt with the present I used Indian English.

The conditions of work and the lack of the language precluded research on little children. Since it was summer and the schools were not in session, my only visit to an Indian boarding school took place at the end of the fieldwork. Photography, which had not yet been elaborated into a research tool, was ruled out by the need to protect the anonymity of individuals and of the tribe as a whole. In 1930, there were no tape recorders. Projective techniques, some very primitive forms of which I had developed in my earlier studies, had not yet been elaborated as tools for probing individual versions of cultures in transition. Like other anthropologists doing fieldwork then, I depended on paper and pencil methods of recording. Though tools now are available that provide far greater objectivity and far more beautiful data, just such paper and pencil methods of recording remain the chosen tools of many anthropologists doing fieldwork today.

The method of Event Analysis that we had developed in our fieldwork in Manus in 1928 had to be adapted to the very different mode of life among the Antlers. In a compact New Guinea village, one could see what was happening and later one could interview the participants about the details of an event. In contrast, among the Antlers, who lived scattered over a large reservation, we could observe very few actual events and instead had to depend on accounts given us by others. Nevertheless one must differentiate clearly between accounts of events in the lives of known persons, where the actors and the narrators are alive and known, and accounts of events recorded from the memories of the old, where the actors remain unknown. Traditionally, students of broken cultures have worked with a few identified informants on whom they have depended for the reconstruction of events that took place long ago. Our established preference for working with contemporary events in the lives of people whom we knew individually meant that I spent a great deal of time identifying and observing the individuals about whose lives I learned verbally among the Antlers. This is, I think, a good example of how previous work on a living culture affects the approach of the anthropologist to the problems posed by a broken culture. Most Americanists have had the reverse experience of working first on a broken culture, where they know they are working against time in their dependence on the fading memories of old men and women and feel that they are cut off from any possibility of observing events of the kind described to them.

I had one advantage that students of culture contact in other parts of the world often lack. I had at my disposal excellent earlier studies, one written by a missionary and another a collaborative work by a highly gifted Indian and a dedicated white investigator. Furthermore, my training under two American Indian specialists, Franz Boas and Ruth Benedict, and research on Polynesia had equipped me to use old missionary and explorer sources. In studies of culture change, it is essential for the student to have training in the handling of various types of documents, a kind of training few students today receive except in the somewhat overspecialized field of ethnohistory.

I brought to this research on the Antlers a willingness to include within the field of my observation of a "primitive" people representatives of the white world and an understanding of the over-all governmental structure. In those days, no matter how many generations of contact lay in the past, it was the fashion to treat each primitive people as an independent group whose culture had been contaminated by "traits" they had borrowed from other cultures and whose lives had been damaged by the exploitative behavior of the carriers of the invading or superordinate culture. Research on American Indian cultures included discussions, for example, of the effects of the "fur trade" or of the "introduction of the horse," and passing reference was made to the Indian agent's location on the reservation simply as a geographical marker. But for the most part, day-to-day interaction between the encysted enclaves of Indians and members of the surrounding white communities was either ignored or treated as an external event like the weather.

The first real evidence of the emergence of a new viewpoint that gave weight to both sides of a culture contact situation came only in 1935 with the publication of a first report by the Social Science Research Council's Subcommittee on Acculturation[2] and with the appearance of a paper by Gregory Bateson, in which, using techniques that anticipated cybernetic methods, he included both groups within an analyzable system.[3] For my own awareness of the problem

[2] Melville J. Herskovits, "Social Science. A Memorandum for the Study of Acculturation," *Man*, Vol. 35, No. 162 (October, 1935), 145-148.
[3] Gregory Bateson, "Culture Contact and Schismogenesis," *Man*, Vol. 35, No. 199 (October, 1935), 178-183.

I owe a special debt to my mother's study, "The Italian on the Land," [4] which I watched her make when I was four. In her research, she treated Italians as future members of the society into which they had migrated and regarded the nature of that society as relevant to their lives. I also knew and appreciated the work of Christie MacLeod who, in writing *The American Indian Frontier*,[5] had taken into account the interrelationships that shaped Euro-American culture contacts. It is interesting that Felix Keesing, whose first work was with Polynesians who had been able to exact from the invading white settlers some respect for themselves,[6] also, in his research on the Menomeni,[7] undertook a study of American Indian culture contact at about the same period as this study was made.

In another publication, I have made a brief attempt to bring this research up to date. Here I prefer to leave it as it was written thirty-five years ago. One statement only should be added: As yet nothing has stemmed the deterioration or altered for the better the past misery described in this book.

A series of momentous events separates the present from that past—the Great Depression, the New Deal and the inauguration of federal relief programs, World War II, the long period of postwar affluence, and the growing recognition that cultural deprivation is a major problem that we must meet if we are, indeed, to move toward a great society. For American Indians these changes have had their chief impact through alterations in the policies of the Bureau of Indian Affairs, fluctuations in governmental attitudes toward Indian dependence, attacks on and defense of the Peyote church, new land claims and new law suits, the attempt to establish a movement through which all American Indians could find a sense of Indian identity, and the development of various programs of technical assistance under such headings as soil rehabilitation, stock reduction, irrigation, and resettlement.

Yet, fundamentally, the conditions described in this monograph prevail today. Where American Indians continue to live on reservations in circumstances in which they are provided with income

---

[4] Emily Fogg Mead, "The Italian on the Land: A Study in Immigration," *Bulletin of the Bureau of Labor*, No. 70 (Washington: Government Printing Office, 1907), 473-491.

[5] William C. MacLeod, *The American Indian Frontier* (New York: Knopf, 1928).

[6] Felix M. Keesing, *The Changing Maori*, Memoirs of the Board of Maori Ethnological Research, Vol. 4 (New Plymouth: Thomas Avery, 1928).

[7] Felix M. Keesing, *The Menomeni Indians of Wisconsin, a Study of Three Centuries of Culture Contact and Change*, Memoirs of the American Philosophical Society, Vol. 10 (Philadelphia: American Philosophical Society, 1939).

without work or in which the possibilities for work are so insufficient that the entire group lives in extreme poverty—with the result that the group is doubly stigmatized by race and by the effects of poverty—their cultural and economic deprivation has worsened with the years. Those individual Indians who have been able to seize some opportunity to enter the majority culture—who have obtained an adequate education and have made a career in the modern world—succeed as other Americans do, on an individual basis. But others remain tied through their self-definition to a childhood way of life that binds them to the reservation. And still others retreat before outsiders' definitions of them as alien in race and, therefore, alien as human beings. Where by definition Indians are set apart and exist, in their relations to the world, not as individuals but as an undifferentiated group, they do not share in modern American culture. Emotionally bound to an archaic identity that has acquired racial associations, American Indians represent one of the major intractable groups among the culturally deprived. The descendant of Scotch-Irish immigrants, however culturally deprived he may be, has only to escape from the confinement of Appalachia in order to enter American culture as an individual. But the preoccupation with race that persists into the present holds back the individual Indian who attempts to move into the modern world and sends the half-decided back to a life where distorted memories of the past serve both as an alibi and as a protective shield against the harsh realities of the present.

BACKGROUND OF THIS STUDY

In the winter of 1930, when Dr. Clark Wissler, the Chairman of my department in The American Museum of Natural History, asked me to make an exploratory study of the position of American Indian women, I was not at all eager to undertake this task. All of us were fully aware of the importance of recording dying cultures and the few living primitive cultures that still could be studied in a distant place like New Guinea. My anthropologist husband and I had established a rhythm of fieldwork, write-up, and return to the field, as quickly as possible, for as much fieldwork as funds allowed. Plains Indian cultures were already broken cultures. The buffalo were gone. The old hunting grounds had been planted over. Living on reservations, Plains Indians no longer formed autonomous functioning societies in which one could study the large in the small or gain a new understanding of alternate cultural solutions to human problems. I believed quite firmly that first things should come first. Studies of culture change and of basic human psychology will always be feasible. But once the living, isolated, small cultures have disappeared, they will never recur. This picture has changed since we can think about the possibility of isolated space colonies where new variations of human culture may once more develop. But the basic problem remains. Once we have assimilated all the isolated terrestrial primitive societies, whose cultures carry on the patterning of the Stone Age period in man's evolution, we shall never again be able to take this path into the past or study alternate solutions to an earthbound life.

In my original introduction I wrote:

The whole contribution of ethnology to sociology lies in the possibility of comprehending and describing a complete culture, and the interrelation and functioning of its parts. Such descriptions of primitive societies have the added value of contrast, of mores worked out through long periods of isolation, which serve as controls to our observation of societies within our Indo-European culture pattern. If, in addition to description of the marriage regulation or inheritance usage, the sociologist and social psychologist is to accept findings upon the role of the individual, the interaction between cultural conditions and personality, the degree of conflict or need of adjustment in the lives of any sex or age group, he must accept one further premise; he must accept homogeneity in lieu of number of cases. . . .

The study of transitional primitive culture is in a most unstrategic position. Such cultures provide neither the homogeneous routinized background upon which the ethnologist depends for the validity of his conclusions nor the large number of cases by means of which the statistical sociologist attempts to control the complexity of his material. Let me particularize. These communities are small in number, at least to all practical purposes, because they must be studied through ethnological field methods, that is, through intensive individual work. They present all the usual obstacles with which primitive society confronts attempts at exterior objective treatment. They are suspicious, on the defensive, prone to lie about relevant details such as status of parents, number of marriages, number of abortions, number of days which they have worked. They are usually not only unwilling, but incapable, of providing reliable quantitative data.* They do not know their ages, age of maturity, or age at death; often the

---

* And there are not enough of them to provide the statistician's refuge—the hope that the numbers who lie in one direction will be statistically counteracted by the numbers who lie in the other.

relative ages of spouses cannot be ascertained. Conventions re-
garding adoption and subsequent ignoring of real paternity, or
name avoidances, or taboos on the name of the dead, render
statistical treatment of genealogies impossible. Their criteria of
reality very usually differ so markedly from our own that native
evidence on any point can be accepted only after it has been
systematically sifted with the pertinacity and reservation of
judgment required of a detective. To these obstacles is added in
varying degree, depending upon the tribe in question, the language difficulty. The investigator has either to devote months to
learning the language—an expenditure of effort justifiable among
a primitive people but of more questionable economy when that
culture has disintegrated—or rely upon English with the margin
of misunderstanding which this necessitates.

Added to all these drawbacks, these barriers to quantitative
investigation which make the statistical sociologist so critical
of the ethnologist are all the conditions which make the ethnologist doubtful of the sociologist's conclusions upon our society, no matter how bulwarked by large numbers of cases those
conclusions may be. The homogeneity of a true primitive society
is gone. The integrity of the cultural background is gone. Parts
of the culture which once reinforced and articulated with each
other in a smoothly functioning whole are gone. The old economic base has been removed, or the native religion has been
destroyed; the government has eliminated polygamy, suppressed
war parties, made sorcery a crime, or outlawed maternal descent.
The student finds not an organic social background but an odd
collection of traditions, once integrated, now merely coexistent.
So among the Plains Indian tribe which forms the subject of
this study, the old cultural discords persist, without their former
outlets in war or vendetta. The old exogamic rules and abhor-
rence of clan incest remain, without the rule of residence and
costume which formerly made the avoidance of such incest a
simple matter. Matrilocal residence, once a well controlled device
by which men of property and prestige added additional hunters
to their households, has become, with the abolition of hunting,
a way in which young men avoid all economic responsibility and
a barrier to early marriage among girls of propertied families.
The student cannot rely upon testing his conclusions about the
functioning of any one aspect of the old culture by following
out its reverberations in other cultural departments.

The student lacks not only an integrated culture but also
the typical individual, the product of the routinized social atti-

tudes of a primitive society. The complex conditions arising from
culture contact, rapid change, intense conflict between the standards of the different generations, varying social experience, different degrees of bilingualism, all combine to produce the type of
variety of personal choice and personal adjustment characteristic
of complex, heterogeneous societies. One might go through the
tribe deviously collecting the reasons why the twenty women between the probable ages of twenty and thirty had left their husbands, and get twenty different explanations, varying from the
fact that the husband had contracted syphilis in the war, that he
had deserted his wife for a woman from another tribe for her
money, that another man in the tribe had seduced her by promises
of a big car, that her husband was in jail for drunkenness, that
the baby had died and he had blamed her, or that they had parted
to avoid being stigmatized as quarrelsome. The last two reasons
are traditional cultural ones. From such an inquiry, it is possible
to deduce the conclusion implied in the selection of the group,
that marriages in this age group are unstable. So, by the way, are
marriages in all the other age groups. If this were a primitive
society, it would be possible to refer the instability of marriage
to its place in a coherent, understood scheme. If it were even as
stable as the society of contemporary Ohio, the investigator might
point to the divorce laws as one feature definitely contributory
to divorce, when Ohio statutes were compared with those of
other states or with earlier Ohio conditions. The investigator in
primitive society would find marriage instability following traditional lines of loyalty to kin, residence difficulties, attitudes toward barrenness. Whether he questioned five natives or was fortunate enough to question fifty, the chances would be high that
the reasons given by them would agree closely with each other,
would be intelligible in general social terms. But the addition of
cases in a transitional culture means merely the multiplication of
difficulties; the more subjects questioned, the larger the number
of different answers that will be received. A numerical approach,
at best meaningless, because in a tribe of one thousand odd, there
would never be enough cases, simply reveals the complexity and
difficulty of the situation.

We return, then, to the question of the possible value of such
a study, and for analogy must turn to clinical description of
human pathology. While it is possible to oppose, say, a bulk of
statistical data on the normal to a bulk of statistical data on the
feeble-minded child, because of large numbers of cases of each
sort, statistical treatment of cases of Schilder's disease or cases

of double personality is impossible. The psychiatrist presents each case in detail because of its power to illuminate our knowledge of the physiology of the brain and of the human mind. Each case of double personality adds something to the scientific knowledge of double personality; it adds far more to the scientific knowledge of personality, of human drives, and the mechanisms by which these drives can receive satisfaction in fantasy.

The study of human societies in peculiar conditions of disequilibrium serves, I believe, a similar purpose. Difficult to control, difficult to duplicate in the experience of the student, too aberrant to make plausible a prediction of its exact recurrence, too disorganized and complicated to provide a complete and satisfactory study, it nevertheless should serve to illuminate the social process, to give the type of understanding which springs from the very characteristic which makes it in other respects so unsatisfactory—distortion.

For this research we selected a culture that presented an interesting unsolved technical ethnological problem: Why is it that accounts of visions do not appear in Antler myths and folk tales as they do among neighboring tribes? A Columbia University grant made it possible for my husband to undertake research on this question. In turn, his fieldwork made it possible for me to carry out my special research on women in my role as a helpful wife, without using the name under which I had already published and later would publish again. Why I realized from the beginning that I would want to protect the identity not only of the individuals (as I had done in my Samoan study) but also of the tribe, I am not sure. But this is a decision I have never regretted and to which I still adhere. Any ethnologist can, of course, place the "Antlers," and interested members of the tribe have known about the book for many years. But where pride in group identity enters into a picture that also includes disintegration, demoralization, and despair, the group as well as the individual must be shielded from casual reproach. The requirements of anonymity prevent me from referring specifically to earlier publications on the culture, on which I drew heavily, and to my husband's fieldwork, to which I am deeply indebted.

In recent years there has been considerable discussion of the role of the observer who is self-identified as a research worker as against the observer who appears in some other guise. In my introduction to the first edition, I described the position I took for the purposes of this research:

The Indians were not cognizant of the fact that any such investigation was being conducted, but believed that I was merely killing time in idle conversation or attendance at ceremonies. For the most part, no notes were taken in the informants' presence but conversations were written up immediately afterwards. The one exception to this was detailed reorganization of census material which the informant believed I was doing for another investigator. Such unawareness was essential to the successful prosecution of a study involving intimate details of contemporary life. I took into the house with me a young Indian girl from one of the more conservative families. As these Indians do not work habitually as servants, and as most contact between white and Indian on the reservation is superficial and extradomestic, this was a sufficiently aberrant situation to set up more intimate relations with all her kin than would otherwise have been possible. As I became responsible for her chaperonage, I gained a most vivid insight into the mother and daughter situation on the reservation. At the same time, as I accompanied her in a less official capacity to many festivities, I also became well acquainted with her age group. From among the many women with whom I became acquainted, I selected a few as capable spokeswomen of different general and special points of view. So I had one special informant from the first generation who went away to school, and one of that generation who did not go away; a wife who had clung hard to the older customs, and a wife who had married an Indian from another tribe and therefore had to make a different adjustment; a woman from another tribe who had married an Antler, a white woman who had married an Antler, a half-breed woman who had married a full-blood, etc. These special informants, with whom I grew more intimate than with the majority of the Antler women of my acquaintance, I used to illuminate the problems which were especially relevant to their position in the tribe. In the limited time at my disposal this was the only possible method to pursue. I spent a great deal of time acquiring, with apparent casualness, the personal histories of people whom I had not yet met—so that when I met them, I could divert the conversation along revealing lines. In this way, chance contacts at dances, in a store, at someone else's house, could be utilized. I was able to give less attention to the children than I have ever given before, partly through pressure of time and partly because of the scattered residence conditions. I knew well two small girls of nine and twelve, and knew enough of their friends so that I could use them in some measure as informants.

I also knew a few men, selected because they were typical of some group in the tribe. Work of this sort and participation in group activities such as dances and funeral ceremonies were supplemented by various types of tabular treatment of the original census lists. Conditions or tendencies revealed by such analysis were then reexamined with individual informants.

Carefully rereading this statement thirty-three years after it was written, I think I would now qualify it in several ways. I would now delineate more sharply the difference between material that is written down immediately from memory, even with highly practiced recall, and verbatim materials taken down by a shorthand device or on tape. I now would regard the loss of verbatim materials as a serious handicap in any situation in which it might otherwise seem preferable to disguise one's research interests. I am still uncertain as to whether the sacrifice of genuine authenticity that one must make whenever the fieldworker's actual role is altered by disguise is not the more important issue. Such a disguise may make it possible to publish safely material on an underworld or on shameful activities or activities about which the subjects of the research may feel shame. But the fact of loss cannot be gainsaid.

Contemporary studies of drug addiction, delinquency, and crime, as well as studies of the home conditions of culturally deprived children, involve parallel difficulties and raise the same issues. In this study the actual distortion was very minor. My husband's ethnological aims were openly and clearly stated. The disguise I adopted led to a diminution of my role from working wife to wife and the interest I took in everyday life took the form of gossipy curiosity rather than fieldwork that required the open use of paper and pencil. But the problem of the declared role of the investigator is becoming more, not less, important in contemporary research. For today we have available long-distance tools of observation that do not, in the same sense as immediate deceit, lead to distortions of the data. However, I am certain of one thing. Materials gathered without an open declaration of purpose must be presented in publication in such a way that the presentation protects the anonymity of the subjects, not only immediately but also many years later. In the contemporary world a people's values shift and change very rapidly, and ancient practice or belief may one day become shameful. So, for example, the term "animist," which has been used descriptively in discussions of local religions, is now bitterly resented when it is applied to the members of a proud nation-state. We cannot assume prescience about the aspects of a current situation that may be regarded as shameful later. We can at best assume that changes will take place. For this reason, in any new study that is undertaken, disguise of individual names would seem to be a minimal precaution.

The other problem raised in the original introduction concerns sampling and the extent to which small primitive societies can be expected to provide statistically valid data. I would claim now, as I did then, that data on primitive societies allow us to formulate invaluable hypotheses. These can later be explored experimentally in valuable but less limited contexts. In my discussion then I also elaborated on the idea of using the abnormal to illuminate the normal—an argument that scarcely needs elaboration today.

I also stated for the first time that delinquency might become a characteristic of a whole culture, in the sense that departure from approved conduct can be the mode and not a statistically unusual event. In later fieldwork among the Mundugumore of New Guinea, I found an example of a culture where this was, in fact, the case. But it is still a moot question whether the frequency of behavior that is morally condemned is a common feature in transitional cultures or whether it is closely bound up with the inclusion of a hitherto distinct cultural enclave within the wider society.

When I wrote this book, I would have subscribed to the belief that slow change is smoother than rapid change and I did not fully appreciate the significance of the contrast between the members of the grandparent generation who had received an American education and the parent generation who had received a less complete education. My later experience with culture contact, particularly my restudies of the Manus, in 1953[8] and 1964 suggest that the more rapid and complete the change, the better the chance is that a people will remain individually intact and the culture will be transformed rather than broken. It is slow, uneven and fragmented change that produces the kind of destruction of human personality described in this book.

The American Museum of Natural History
New York
July 1965

[8] Margaret Mead, *New Lives for Old, Cultural Transformation—Manus, 1928-1953* (New York: Morrow, 1956).

PART I

GENERAL BACKGROUND

Chapter I

RETROSPECTIVE SKETCH

The Antlers are a Mississippi Valley tribe, living at present on a reservation which corresponds to part of the territory which was the most recent of their aboriginal habitats. The additional complication, present in so many tribes, of a change, not only of economic base, but also to a completely strange locality, is therefore not present in their case. In this same region they have planted their maize and maintained their permanent villages. From here they set out each year, and from here, too, occasional war parties — for the Antlers were, on the whole, a peaceful people — set out to gain war honors and capture horses from the enemy tribes. During the winter, their diet of sweet corn, mush, and hominy, choke-cherry meal, beans, and squash, was supplemented by considerable hunting within range of a day or two from the village. The invasion of the white man was gradual, and unaccompanied by bloodshed. The earliest contact — about the middle of the seventeenth century — was with French traders, some of whom took native wives. These are still remembered in the names of some of the prominent families today. Contact with the French ceased at the end of the French and Indian War, and with the Louisiana Purchase the Antlers occupied United States territory. About the middle of the nineteenth century, the present reservation was marked off, and it was surveyed a quarter of a century later. About a decade later the Antlers became United States citizens, as allotments had been made to them earlier. A few years later the older allotment act was modified and the Antlers were given possession of their land in severalty.

There is no record of Roman Catholic contact; the first organized missionary effort which the Antlers encountered was that of the Presbyterians in the first half of the nineteenth century. The establishment of a local mission station some years later was followed by a peaceful nominal conversion of the tribe — who with a few recent exceptions, all consider themselves Presbyterians.

The abolition of war and the buffalo hunt tended to weaken the old political organization which had centered in a group of chiefs who validated their positions by a conspicuous series of property distributions and whose primary duty was to preserve peace and order. Traders and early government officials tended to select, from among the influential Indians, men friendly to their purpose who were then declared to be "chiefs." The Antler conservatism and the factional interests represented by the so-called "chiefs" had tended to detract from any authority which these might have had. A number of these leading men were half-breeds, the descendants of French traders. The old political organization gradually disappeared, formally resisting complete decay in the obstinate fashion characteristic of most Antler institutions — the body of chiefs was replaced by a body of "sons of chiefs."

The Antlers, when Europeans found them, lived a threefold seasonal existence. During the spring and autumn, they occupied earth lodges, houses constructed of a framework of rafters overlaid with earth. Many of these lodges were large enough to shelter a gathering of over one hundred people. The fireplace in the center oriented the interior of the lodge, which was usually occupied by two or more families. The village of earth lodges did not correspond to any aspect in the social organization; houses of relatives were, however, likely to be built near each other. The tribe which, during the buffalo hunt, camped in one circle in which gentile divisions were scrupulously observed, split up during the village-dwelling season into several villages. Social events took place upon the village green or in the earth lodge of an important man. The maize patches were situated near the village. Owners' titles in these scattered sites, which did not press upon one another, were vested, by custom, in certain families, but lapsed with discontinuance of cultivation. During the winter season, the villages broke up and the people went to live in tipis in small camp groups in the sheltered ravines to escape the ravages of the winds. This was the least popular season. The people were split up into small kin groups; there was little festivity; the men were away all day hunting; the women were busy from morning till night grinding corn and dressing skins; the grandmother sat in the far corner mending the moccasins, and the grandfather spent his time admonishing the children in long homilies and legends.

In the spring, life in the earth lodges again gave reason for ceremony and festivity. The gardens were planted and the tribe set out on its annual buffalo hunt, returning only when the flowering of a small prairie plant warned them that the maize was ripe for harvest.

The first disturbances in this cycle came with the fur trader and the increasing demand for furs. The introduction of guns and of steel traps reënforced the Indian's ability to obtain game — but his work was nevertheless augmented, and his wife's labor in dressing skins was enormously increased. The introduction of beads and the substitution of beadwork and ribbon appliqué for the more laborious decoration with porcupine quills did lessen the woman's work somewhat, as did also the introduction of iron kettles and broadcloth. The man's labors in making stone tools and bows and arrows were similarly reduced, but the drive to obtain furs with which to purchase cloth, beads, knives, and kettles served for a time to stimulate the tribe to a greater display of energy than before. Before this period the introduction of the horse had of course widened the field of activity and complicated intertribal relationships through organized horse-stealing and trading.

The first period of contact with the whites, the energetic trading period, drew to a close almost contemporaneously with the influx of white settlers, the establishment of an

agency and a Presbyterian mission, and the disappearance of
the buffalo. The Antlers were therefore called upon to make
a series of readjustments — to the disappearance of the
buffalo, to the curtailment of their trapping area, to the loss
of power by their own chiefs, to the intrusive influence of
Christianity, and to the government with its schemes for their
improvement. The reservation was surveyed and 160 acres
of land given to every adult. The government began erecting
frame houses and purchasing agricultural tools with the proceeds of extensive land sales which had been negotiated for
the tribe. Under double pressure — from government and
missionary on one hand, and from the forward-looking optimistic leaders on the other — the people abandoned earth
lodges, tipis, hunting, trapping, and fishing, and settled down
in the last quarter of the nineteenth century to an existence
which had a superficial resemblance to a rural American community. Their dwellings were on isolated farms — sometimes
ten minutes' walk from the nearest neighbors. They lived in
small frame houses of the style characteristic of that part of
the United States — cellarless, with a porch, a gabled roof,
sometimes a second story. Under government supervision,
caves, latrines, and small barns were built. The Indians were
encouraged to buy furniture and, especially through the influence of the Mission, the standard of household furnishing
was established which is still in operation.

Clothes made equal headway. Men abandoned the furs and
skins of the aboriginal days and learned to wear the conventional clothing of the white farmer. The large Stetson hat
became the stereotyped headgear. The Antler man still wore
a broadcloth robe or in lieu of that, a blanket, on all occasions of ceremony. The women clung to their moccasins and
their long hair arranged in two braids joined with a small
bead weight in the back. For their skin dresses and leggings,
however, they substituted voluminous petticoats, a calico two-
piece dress, and a shawl.

The purchasing power which had provided the people with

this white material culture came from two sources, the last years of trapping and hunting and government administration of individual shares of tribal land-sale funds. This procedure, by which the agency expended or authorized the expenditure of money regarded as the property of an individual unable to administer it wisely, had very definite effects. Houses, furniture, farm implements became, and have continued to be, the material setting for the "Antler as a government ward," — the "Antler in contact" — "What a good Indian should have." There is the added proviso that this being an external standard, it should be kept up by some means external to the Indian himself.

After the money from the tribal land sales had been expended and the Antler established in a setting considered appropriate to civilized Indians, some quite serious attempts were made at farming; there were Antlers who kept good-sized dairies and grew many acres of corn. Under Mission influence, new vegetables were introduced,[1] the women who had been away to school taught others how to use sewing machines, how to bake light bread, how to preserve fruits and vegetables.

These were the conditions in 1890-1900, to reconstruct them on the basis of informants' reports and of contemporary accounts. The few white settlers were traders and herders. To the cattle convention, the quick-shooting, hard-drinking, gambling, border convention, the Antlers took kindly, and they remember with pleasure the days before the country was fenced in. There was a good deal of land, more than enough for every one. Wild fruit, wild berries, were abundant. The Indian women had lost no old technique, except possibly porcupine quill work. They still dressed calfskin by the old methods, they dried meat and pounded it into meal, they braided and dried their own squash, they dried sweet corn, and made their own hominy. All of the domestic gardening fell to them. The even tenor of their ways had been but little

1 See list in Part III, p. 282.

disturbed, except that no longer did a woman help build and own her house as she formerly had her tipi.

With the men, however, it was different. All of their old techniques were abandoned. They had been encouraged to farm, but this new activity had no old base upon which it could be grafted. The settled routine of farm life conflicted with all their habits. Besides, it was woman's work. It presented no opportunity for adventure, for sudden display of skill, for personal distinction. In the old days, a man distinguished himself and rose to power by giving away many gifts and many feasts. These constituted his "count," more important among the Antlers than was the typical Plains custom of counting coup.[2] The gifts were mainly horses — "prairies" — riding horses in contradistinction to the work horses necessary to agriculture, and broadcloth and blankets — gained through trading furs. The "feasts" consisted primarily of meat. In other words, the materials by which these counts were obtained were based upon a hunting and war-raiding life. (The simplest way of obtaining the necessary number of horses to make a substantial count was always to go on a raid and steal them.) This system of prestige by which men attained rank and so could confer upon their daughters the distinctive marks of rank, was never properly incorporated into a rural agricultural way of life. It simply declined in importance and ceased to act as an incentive to effort as far as the men were concerned. Formerly, a young man worked hard at being a good hunter so that he might contract a matrimonial alliance with an important family. This incentive was also removed. The way of life inaugurated by the government was regarded as the government's business. A man had no harness, no plough, his barn leaked, his horse went lame. Let the office arrange it by selling a portion of his many and superfluous acres. Otherwise, the family went without, sup-

[2] War counts based upon the performance of an artificial grading of acts requiring bravery, e.g., touching a live enemy, stealing a horse from within the enemy lines, etc.

ported mainly by the women as gardeners, collectors and preservers of wild fruits, nuts, honey, beans, etc.

With white settlement and the beginning of the system by which Indian landowners — and at the beginning of the century, all were landowners — leased their land, keeping their houses for their own use and living on the rent money, another element entered into the situation. Never properly accustomed to farming, not yet sufficiently good farmers to make an income very superior, or half so reliable as the rent from a white tenant, two-thirds of the Indian men ceased to make any further economic struggle. Their wives' labors provided the necessary basis of food, the rent money purchased clothes, meat, kerosene, etc. There was no incentive to improving a standard of living already so alien to them. A period of lethargy set in, a sluggish reorientation of their interests to things Indian. Before this, the tribe had had the stimulus of those who refused to accept white ways and those who hoped to make all the white ways rapidly their own. Religiously, there were deacons of the church, and old medicine men. Both these differences dissolved, the first under the deadening, settling effect of the small, fixed income derived from leasing lands; the second, from the introduction of the Peyote cult which, by its inclusion of lost Christian and aboriginal Indian religious elements, reassembled the antagonistic elements in the tribe. The converted Indian could turn from the Presbyterianism which had made little fundamental appeal to him, without his conscience reproving him as apostate. The devotee of the old régime accepted with equal enthusiasm a religious service in his own language, cast in terms which he could understand. The result of both adjustments was the absence of choice which characterizes a stable culture as compared with a changing one. A few families stayed outside. A few "went white." These were the deviators who had married white people or members of other tribes. But, in the main, there ceased to be important issues. Government schools, formerly welcomed by the would-be "citizens," resisted by the conservatives, became accepted as a matter of course. The dates of the departure for and the return from school became incorporated into the social calendar, and people feasted the drummers — "because their children were going away to school." The isolation of the new life on farms had resulted in the building of large frame lodges in pleasant groves on different parts of the reservation where people could gather from miles around for moccasin games and dances. The costumes of the women had become stereotyped. The materials for a feast were set — light bread, soup, meat, and coffee (with sugar cooked in it and without milk). Equally set was the fact that instead of the old wooden spoon and bowl, each guest at the feast brought a porcelain plate, a small round bowl, and a spoon wrapped in a square of white cotton material.

Which traits of old customs were once and for all abandoned was by this time clear. The menstrual hut and menstrual taboos vanished when frame houses were built; the elaborate rituals connected with early childhood were gone. Individual attempts to gain religious experience through fasting in lonely places were gone. Chieftainship, both military and civil, was gone. The outward discriminatory marks of different classificatory descent groups were not observed.

Certain aspects of the old culture were kept in attenuated form, notably the accumulation of counts so that one's daughter might be tattooed, burial and mourning ceremonials including the "give away" of all the personal possessions of the deceased, the watch at the grave, the contribution to the mourners, and the mourner's subsequent distribution of gifts to "end mourning." The kinship system was kept, in terminology-exogamic rules and gentile taboos, but polygamy (formerly, principally in the sororate form) under strong government pressure was abandoned. Contact with white culture had considerably weakened, however, the feeling against gentile incest. The levirate formerly prevalent, was abandoned, possibly due to the decreasing institutionalization of marriage as a matter involving kin groups. Matrilineal residence during the early years of marriage continued to be the rule. Shamanism remained very much abbreviated, with whole vision societies disappearing and new recruits obtained but rarely. The curing powers of the shaman were largely eclipsed by the curative properties of Peyote. While fear and reverence for the medicine bundles of their ancestors were still entertained, the younger generation, on the whole, regarded them as *passé*, powerful but irrelevant to present-day concerns, involving a burden of responsibility and giving few rewards. Of the magic associated with these bundles, for war, hunting, love, and sorcery, only the last two remained.

Certain new institutions sprang up, features which were definite adjustments to the new conditions, but were nevertheless felt as completely Indian. The introduced Peyote cult was, of course, the most conspicuous of these. The erection of lodge buildings and the secularization of hand games, with the shift of emphasis from bets to forfeits and gifts only, were other new features. The elaborate Peyote funeral, with its four-night watch, deserves mention here. So also does the tribal summer camp which is now exploited as a means of collecting admission money from the white residents. The gambling games, always popular, become more firmly attached to special promoting individuals who fed the gamblers and took a percentage. Leasing land and contempt for those who worked their own land was also a definite cultural attitude.

The Antlers might be said to have made a second adjustment to white culture. They had done this without sacrificing their tribal individuality, without giving up their language, with the surrender of half of their institutions, their political autonomy, and their existence as a self-governing community, and by absorbing a fair number of traits of white material culture. But they had made for themselves a sort of existence, although it was only the shadow of the rich complexity of their former lives. It was, however, a coherent standard, which, had its economic base been left undisturbed, might have successfully defied further modification for a generation, or perhaps more. The idle men drank a good deal, gambled a good deal, fought among themselves considerably. But as long as the reservation was self-contained, this had few repercussions among white contact.

The events that follow should be considered then as impinging upon a culture which was deleted and attenuated, but not broken, and existing in a state of just attained and slender equilibrium. Chief of these events was the onrush of white settlement, coincident with the end of the "period of trust" when by act of Congress the Indians were to receive fee patents to their lands. The importance of this coincidence need not be emphasized, as it would probably have been induced had it not so occurred. The twenty-five years that had passed had not prepared the Antler to own land. He had not become a farmer; he had acquired, if anything, a less realistic idea of money than he had in his trapping and trading days. So ill-equipped, he had to meet a condition in which white settlers, anxious to acquire his land, used every method, fair and foul, to bring about the alienation of lands which he had never learned to value.

CHAPTER II

DESCRIPTION OF THE RESERVATION

The part of the reservation at present occupied by the Ant-lers extends from the town of "Bergen" on the west, nine miles eastward to a boundary river and about fifteen miles in a north and south direction. At the south end is the town of "Wilmot," the oldest white settlement near the present area occupied by Antlers. At the northern extremity is the section of the reservation which was sold to the United States government as a reservation for a transplanted tribe which will be called for purposes of this study the Black Faces. At the center of the north-south extent of the reservation, and about ten miles west of the river, is the Antler agency and mission and a small, unincorporated village which we will designate as "Radner." Bergen and Wilmot are incorporated towns, and Wilmot has usually no Indian residents, but some trade relations with the Antlers living in the southern sector of the reservation. The town of Bergen has, however, about fifteen resident Antler families, exclusive of a large number of mixed bloods. This nucleus of Indian residents provides a base for friends and relatives trading in town and there is considerable Indian trading in Bergen. On market nights — Wednesday and Saturday — the streets are thronged with Indians, and after midnight, when the white population has retired, there are still many Indians in the streets. Bergen is not primarily an Indian town; the Indian trade, however, accounts for the presence of a large number of cheap stores with complex and unsavory credit arrangements, and Indians are also very much in evidence on the streets, where benches have been installed outside the shops for their convenience.

Radner, however, is the center of reservation life. It is un-incorporated, with only a handful of white residents, all of whom are directly or indirectly dependent upon the Indian residents. There is one large general store owned by a trader who has spent his life in this region and built up a substantial fortune from the Indian trade, which he now pursues in a less elaborate manner. There is also another store with goods slightly cheaper than the main store. In both stores prices vary considerably and discounts are given to permanent white customers. The prices are also higher than at Bergen, which is on the railroad, and many Indians are beginning to use their own and their friends' automobiles to protect themselves from this fact. Radner also contains two restaurants, a post office, a shoe and harness repair shop, two filling stations, a garage and car wrecking establishment, a blacksmith, a Pentecostal church, a deserted white Presbyterian church, a pretentious school building for which the township went heavily into debt, the agency buildings, now partially disused, and the mission. There are also a few white families on small farms adjacent to the village. There are twenty-eight Indian households [1] in Radner. In addition there are some dozen unstable units of one or more adult persons who spend much of their time with friends and relatives in the village.

The white population divides rather sharply. There is the local aristocracy, consisting of the chief trader, his sons and their wives, the postmistress, two woman clerks in the trade store, the justice of the peace, the missionary and his wife, the principal of the school and the three teachers and, until the recent closing of the Agency, the resident "farmer." [2] These last three groups are transitory; the first group represents early settlers who own property on the reservation and have an extensive background of long contact with the Indians. The rest of the white population is a group of very poor,

[1] Throughout this study I shall use "household" as the unit rather than family. A household is for purposes of this study a group of persons habitually living together under one roof, sharing living expenses and eating common meals.

[2] A term used for a subordinate official in the Indian Service whose special duties were originally to supervise and encourage the agricultural activities of the Indians.

shiftless drifters who regard their Indian neighbors with a considerable degree of antagonism and who in turn are despised by them.

Outside of the two towns of Bergen on the edge of the Indian area and Radner at its center, the Indian population is scattered over an area of about 145 square miles, but is most unevenly distributed. There are 51 families southeast of Radner towards Wilmot, and 44 households lying in the general western direction of Bergen. The remaining 19 households lie to the northeast, consisting of the few outlying farms which have been left behind in the general movement of population towards the southeastern corner of the reservation. This concentration has been accomplished through exchange of plots of forty acres of land so that Indians finding themselves isolated among a group of farms which had been sold to white people will exchange, with an Indian who is only renting his land and is indifferent to its location, the isolated land for forty acres in a more populated district. There has also been a tendency among Indians with holding or fee patent rights to outlying sections of land to sell these and buy or build houses in Radner. The artificial dispersal of a sociable and gregarious people through the allotment and isolated house system is thus being progressively changed.

As a social center for strictly Indian affairs, the village is inadequate, as is also the partitioned frame residence. In fine weather the tribal camping ground — which is situated on the edge of Radner and fenced and provided with benches, water, latrines, etc. — serves as a gathering place for hand games, dances, gambling games, committee meetings and the weekly Sunday shinny game in which a hundred or more men and boys participate. These grounds are the center of tribal life during the annual ten days of camping. The agency building and its wide, shaded lawn also provide a meeting place for the tribal council and committees concerned with tribal business. Here the agent can meet the council, and here groups of the tribal politicians lounge, day after day, hatching schemes of intrigue. But the agency grounds are regarded as the point at which Indian life impinges upon the United States government. They are at once sanctuary, court and political battleground, and are not repaired to upon occasions of feasting and dancing.

For these purposes, in addition to the tribal camping ground, lodge grounds are used. There are four lodges: the Buffalo Lodge, which belongs to the small group of residents far north of Radner; a second, the Little Deer, an offshoot of this, which has built a lodge within walking distance north of Radner; a third, the Rainbow, within walking distance southwest of Radner; and a fourth, the Badger, some miles to the southeast, distant enough and situated in a sufficiently populated area to provide the meeting place of a local group which seldom goes to Radner and which feels itself to be in some respects separate from the rest of the reservation.

The south corner of the reservation likewise contains the largest proportion of independent Indian farmers. Analysis of lodge membership shows that it rests almost entirely upon a neighborhood, rather than a kinship basis. The members of the Little Deer Lodge are the sons and younger brothers of the old Buffalo Lodge which is now located on the periphery of settlement and is very little used. As the Little Deer Lodge and the Rainbow Lodge are so close together and both are near Radner, the territory from which membership is drawn overlaps. Lodge membership is informal, without initiation ceremony or formal dues, but depends entirely upon habitual attendance at festivities managed by a particular lodge. Around these four lodge buildings, small groups form, exist for a few months and dissolve again. Lodge buildings are used for hand games, feasts, and for the occasional marriage which follows the old usage of affinal exchanges.

The reservation is open in every respect. Land has been sold to white people in every section of it. Everywhere Indian land abuts on white-owned land. The addition of white renters, who either live in Indian or white-owned houses, and rent additional quarter sections or eighth sections from Indians, adds also to the distribution of white settlers among the Indians. Hardly a house or farm building on the reservation makes any claims to pretentiousness, so that often it is possible to tell an Indian occupied house from one occupied by whites only by the state of the yard. The lack of building materials on the reservation, the high cost of lumber, the absence of stone, results in a paucity of outbuildings.

On both white and Indian places it is a common occurrence to find a great number of rusty pieces of farm machinery lying about the barnyard. Indian homes are usually further characterized by old pieces of furniture standing on the porch or in the yard, piles of bedding on the porch and, in summer, by rugs and quilts spread on the grass, and cooking utensils grouped about an outdoor fireplace with a kettle suspended over it from a tripod or cross bar arrangement. A light frame which, when covered with blankets, constitutes a sweat house, stands in many Indian yards. Glass is very often missing from many of the window panes, some of which are stopped up with cardboard; a bedraggled lace curtain sags here and there. The houses are seldom screened and, when they are, the screen has usually rusted away at least in part and has been replaced by cardboard. Hand pumps are the rule. The prosperous white farmer has, on the other hand, a windmill, more adequate outbuildings, fewer pieces of rusty machinery and old wagon parts lying about; the house is screened, the porch contains only conventional pieces of furniture; there are flowers and a neat garden. On only one Indian place did I see any attempt to grow flowers, and this displayed the usual Indian appearance in other respects. Sometimes there are children. Usually there are dogs of every known breed — from mongrel Russian wolfhounds, slight emaciated shadows still preserving the familiar outline, to small white poodles — these latter making an odd picture in the arms of a husky Indian in a broad-brimmed hat. There is a saying on the reservation that "the poorer the Indian, the more dogs he has." Puppy meat is still appreciated in emergencies.

The fields adjoining an Antler house are, if cultivated by the Indian owner, almost invariably full of weeds. In the autumn the whole reservation is a glowing mass of sunflowers. A few miles west, in a region of large prosperous German-owned farms, hardly a sunflower is to be seen. The Indians say they can tell at a glance whether a fellow Indian is renting his land or farming it himself. This is almost invariably true.

The distribution of whites and Indians over the same territory does not make for much contact between the races. The two groups live separate lives, often curiously centered about the same event, as carnival or fair. At the mission, over the leases in the agency office, in the school, in court, in the shops, at a rodeo, or in the moving picture theater at Bergen, the two races mingle, do business together, talk together across a gap as deep as if they shouted to one another across a canyon. In the field of pleasure they never coöperate, although years ago they are said to have done so. Indians do not go to white dances, or white church socials, or quilting bees. Indian girls do not associate with white men, with a few rare exceptions. The whites do not go to Indian dances, although they pay admission to see the festivities of the annual camp, when the Indians make definite attempts to entertain the white visitors.

In dress, white man and Indian can hardly be distinguished. Both men and boys wear overalls the year round — the Indian's may be more patched and darned and faded than the white man's; often they are also cleaner. Both races wear broad-brimmed straw hats in summer and a wide variety of nondescript headgear in winter. The dress of the rich Indian tends towards the old Wild West convention — broad-brimmed Stetson hat and high boots; that of the more well-to-do white men, towards the conventional urban attire. But the majority of both races wear overalls, which are acceptable on almost every occasion except attendance at church.

The dress of Indian women is more individual and, especially during the vogue of short skirts, easy to distinguish from that of white women. The Indian woman wears a two-piece calico dress consisting of a very full skirt with an extra ruffle around the bottom and many rows of decorative machine stitching, and a short, loose blouse, kept in place by a shawl worn twisted around the waist. Her hair is always worn in two braids, or if she is a young girl and has only recently let it grow out after bobbing, it is confined in the back with a barrette. About half of the older women wear moccasins part of the time. Indian women never wear hats, and their everyday costume is only varied on festive occasions by donning a dress of finer material. The black silk shawl is substituted for the woolen one, and colored stockings are worn.

The Indian woman carries her baby on a cradle board. The arched headpiece and the long beaded band running parallel to the length of the board are no longer in use except upon costume occasions, but the baby is bound to a plain board, upholstered with a soft flat pillow, by means of two bands, usually brightly colored pieces of an old blanket or shawl.

Both whites and Indians go about in rickety wagons drawn by two horses if they are poor; in old Fords if they are a little richer, and in more imposing cars if they are rich. There are poor members of each race who walk.

The reservation and the reservation towns thus present this external picture of a mixed population, using the same roads, driving in the same kind of vehicles, trading at the same stores, watching the same side shows and the same movies, speaking the same language when they meet, buying and selling from one another, and cheating one another when they can, without any sense of community of interest. This continual contact in a familiar setting only seems to strengthen the popular white belief that the Indians are merely bad and inefficient editions of themselves, and encourages them to set down the deficiency of the Indian to his race, not to his culture.

CHAPTER III

THE ECONOMIC SITUATION

In analyzing the present economic condition and outlook of the Antlers, it is necessary to consider first their former attitudes toward such matters as personal property, land, prestige gained by economic means, and inheritance. In common with most American Indian tribes, their attitudes about land were loose and undefined. Large tracts of land were regarded as the proper hunting ground of the tribe; if other tribes, stronger and more warlike than themselves, drove them from these tracts they moved to new village sites and new hunting grounds. The village sites and tipi camping sites for winter were simply places where the tribe, or a division of it, habitually lived. With the formality of a stable society, the cultivated land about the village was more or less allotted among individual families. Such and such a family was in the habit of making a garden in this place; as long as it continued to use the plot, no one else would be so churlish as to intrude. When the mother died, if her daughter who was living on the opposite side of the village took up new and more convenient garden land, then, once the old plot had fallen into disuse, some other might cultivate it. There was plenty of land for all. This was the old attitude. Land was never formally owned, nor bought and sold. Its occupation was simply a matter of neighborhood usage, comparable to a habitual seat in a village church which has only free pews, but where one regular church goer would never think of intruding upon the customary pew of another, until that pew has been definitely vacated by protracted nonattendance, removal, or death.

All about the villages, wild fruits and berries — plums, gooseberries, chokecherries, and wild grapes — grew in profusion. In the fields, the field mice heaped up the wild bean in earth caches against the winter and the Indian woman tracked them to their stores and robbed them for her own use. Hazel nuts and walnuts and wild honey were also gathered in abundance. Many fish were taken from the rivers and small game was trapped and shot near at hand.

Personal property, except often a horse or two, was usually distributed at the death of the individual who owned it. The individual tipi, although made and owned by the woman, is said to have been given away at the death of either spouse. The most personal of the individual possessions, such as underclothing, pipe, or workbasket (for a woman), were buried with the corpse. All other property, aside from such ceremonial possessions as the important medicine bundles, ceremonial pipes, personal bundles, etc., for the disposal of which provision was usually made by the deceased before death, was given away to others. In practice, these were given to those relatives and connections by marriage who had made the most generous contribution to the funeral feast (today this includes the expenses of casket, embalming, hearse, etc.). But the Antlers maintain a rigid refusal to recognize the reciprocity involved in such matters. The contributions of the mourners are gifts "to a corpse" and the idea of return is abhorrent. Similarly, gifts are distributed ostensibly according to no rule, but because of an expressed belief that any article belonging to the deceased retained by the close kin would be fetched by the returning ghost. This extensive distribution of personal property is thus phrased as insurance against being haunted; the new owner is not regarded as under danger of such ghostly visitation. Some idea that retention of the property of the dead is grasping and shows a lack of respect for the deceased seems to be included in this theory. Of course where there is such strict refusal to face the fact of reciprocity, accurate and careful return is not always made for each relative's contribution.

The use of private property during an individual's life followed several distinct patterns. All ceremonial possessions, all

charms, formulas, fetishes, and all membership privileges
within societies, had to be paid for — in skins, in aboriginal
days, and in historical times, in horses, blankets and firearms.
This carried the necessary corollary that while all private
property, except sacred possessions, was dissipated at death,
individuals could and did inherit important sacred knowledge, possessions, and privileges, from their parents and other
male relatives and fathers-in-law, which were actually intan-
gible property upon which many economic returns could be
realized. Hereditary positions as owners of certain fetishes or
guardians of certain ceremonial paraphernalia made it possible
for an individual to command large payments as his due.
These he could then use to enhance his position in society,
either by purchasing more privileges of a sacred order, or by
distributing the property in the prescribed ways for attaining
chieftainship — to mourners, to visitors, to chiefs, to the relatives of a murdered man. Merit was acquired, not by hoard-
ing property, but by its distribution in certain specified ways.
Individuals recorded in bundles of sticks, or notches on a
stick, the prescribed distributions which they had made. The
accumulation of a certain number of counts gave a man the
right to have a female member of his household, a daughter,
a niece, or wife, as the case might be, tattooed. This entitled
the man himself, and the relative who had been thus tattooed to membership in the "Society of Those Blessed by the
Night"; within this organization, rank, both among the fi-
nanciers of the tattooing and among the tattooed women, was
carefully preserved. Further distributions, particularly presents to chiefs, entitled a man to minor chieftainship. The
important chiefly positions were hereditary. Within this pattern of conspicuous distribution various small patterns developed or were incorporated from the usage of neighboring and
cognate peoples. Most notable of these was the "pipe dance,"
a version of the Pawnee ceremony, a complex ceremonial by
which gifts were solicited from another tribe, or occasionally
from a member of one's own tribe. The gifts bestowed upon

the soliciting visitors could be included in the regular counts for chieftainship and membership in the tattooing society. An even slighter version of this solicitory visiting was the ceremony which is known, in Plains terminology, as "tying tobacco." Here a visitor, or again, but less usually, a member of one's own tribe, makes one a solicitory gift of a small pouch of tobacco. The public bestowal of a substantial gift is then obligatory upon the recipient.

Another form of public distribution occurs in the pattern of ending mourning, and is, in reality, a further device for making return for the contributions made to the mourners at a death. The distribution of the personal property of the deceased was not sufficient to cover the large number of gifts, often including many horses, showered upon the mourners. After the period of mourning, which varies at the preference of the bereaved from a few months to a year or more, the mourners formally end their mourning by making a series of public gifts, at a particular ceremony, to individuals, to societies and to groups of individuals such as the drummers. These gifts may range from two or three chickens to a horse. Here, as in the former case, the reciprocity involved will not be recognized. Throughout this public circulation of property, there is, on the whole, a certain amount of definite evening up. Unless this were so, it would not be possible for a man who habitually possessed only two or three horses to have given away and taken credit for the gifts of some hundred horses. Nevertheless, there are certain aspects of the economic institutions which encourage the rationalization that all is free giving. Chief of these are the gifts to visitors from distant tribes. These visitors "tie tobacco" on their hosts and are freely showered with gifts. Unless the individual donor happens to go to the same tribe, at some future time, when he can, of course "tie tobacco" on his hosts with equal freedom, this is a type of gift for which one receives no return. Some other Antler, visiting the tribe in question in future years will reap the return gifts instead of the original donor. Presenting property to the notoriously poor was also a way of attaining high distinction but, of course, could not have been practised with great lavishness without the overgenerous donor facing insolvency.

Besides mourning and the practice of "tying tobacco," the exercise of which coercive privilege an individual invited by calling upon some man to whom he was neither related nor with whom he was associated within the close bonds of society membership, there were numerous other small ways in which intertribal giving of public gifts could be practised between men of means for the public acquisition of merit. Such, for instance, were the gifts given when a boy child had caught his first fish or his first rabbit or a girl child first fetched water. The proud father was then permitted by custom to give away a horse or a valuable blanket in honor of the occasion. Or a woman might make a small tipi for her daughter, furnish it with a special set of dishes and bedding and give it away, with a horse, in the expressed hope that her daughter might grow up to be a married woman with a tipi of her own. As the Antlers phrase it, those gifts were always presented "to some old man"; in practice, if the attenuated versions of the economic customs of the past are to be trusted, these gifts would be made to someone of similar economic status to whom one was indebted through some payment connected with mourning or possibly through tying tobacco. Thus numbers of extra horses and valuable blankets and broadcloths circulated about the tribe, conferring counts in an elaborate prestige scheme upon all those through whose hands they passed. But the charming assumption that no returns were made, that all gave freely out of the kindness of their hearts and the nobility of their minds, removed all atmosphere of bicker and barter from the stately public proceedings and added greatly to their dignity. Private comments might be made; it might be whispered that such and such a family were so close that they never helped out their own kin and if they did give anything away you could be sure they would "give it away in the ring." Or an old woman might deplore her inability ever to repay the kindness which had been showered upon her at her son's death, name over the many horses which had been given her and which she had immediately presented to some visiting "Short Knives," and remark that until she died she must speak softly of half the tribe, cook for them when they were ill, and go and straighten the limbs of their dead, because she, being poor and without a husband, could never hope to repay them. The more realistic may even let slip the comment that "I gave the drummers five chickens to-day because when my husband died they gave me a sack of flour"; or "when my husband's brother's wife died, we gave a fine big hog and I got all the dishes which she had collected while she was a Peyote cook." But these are private remarks and the attitudes which give rise to them are permitted no sort of institutional expression. The ceremonial of public gift giving was set and dignified; in the form in which I witnessed it, certain songs were sung by the drummers which were known to be those connected with gift giving. Anyone wishing to make a gift entered the dancing ring with his wife and daughters and danced through the song, at the end of which he announced to the crier the nature of his gift, the reason for which he was making it, and the name of the recipient. The crier made the announcement and the recipient, or if he was absent, some close relative, stepped into the ring and received the gift. The commonest gift was a horse, saddled and bridled in the old days; now on the rare occasions when a horse is given, it is merely covered with a blanket.

In contrast to the pleasant and euphemistic canons of this public gift giving, are two institutions where the economic motive is frankly recognized in speech and in practice. These are marriage and doctoring. Marriage, in the old days, was validated by exchanges of property between the two kin groups, the groom's family making the first presents, which were ultimately returned by the bride's family. The presents were collected from the man's kin groups involved by calling

a feast to which each relative of the groom made a contribution. The parents of the bride, after receiving the presents,
called a feast of their kin, distributed such of the bridal gifts
as they did not wish to repay themselves, and, with the return
contribution, made the repayment, the parts of which were
in turn distributed to the groom's kin. These marriage exchanges were not an engrossing part of the social life; people
made payments in keeping with their general wealth and importance, but nevertheless they were recognized as exchanges
in which the other kin were definitely obligated to repay their
initial expenditure.

Payments of doctors' fees are also in even sharper contrast
to the prevailing disregard of the economic motive. The doctors were members of vision societies and their society membership and the personal religious experience claimed by them
made them specialists in certain types of cures. There were
also a number of ailments which were believed to have been
caused by a doctor's intentionally projecting some foreign
object into the body. A group of doctors would then be
called in to choose the physician who would, for a large fee,
"extract" magically, without breaking the skin, the intrusive
object — a pebble, a minute turtle, or a piece of leather, as
the case might be. Doctors' fees were always high, often a
horse or even two horses were demanded, and the rapacity of
the doctor was also illustrated by his custom of first bringing
his entire family to dine at the feast provided before the curing session, and finally by his gathering up the table cloth and
all the dishes, including the cooking utensils, and carrying
them off as his rightful fee. The Antlers believe that the doctors have the power to make individuals sick so as to collect
curing fees and they do not doubt that this power is frequently exercised. This frank recognition of the piratical
behavior of their "sacred men" stands out in curiously sharp
relief against the general unworldly and sentimental view of
gift exchange in other departments of social life. When we
come to a discussion of present-day economic life, we shall

find the same type of contrast, sentimental sharing of property with all comers juxtaposed to the most selfish and aggressive individualism.

To summarize, in ancient Antler economy, beyond the necessary personal property and equipment needed for every household, the chief functions of wealth were to validate privilege; in the case of secular privilege, by accumulating merit ratings through the public distribution of wealth. Two crises in the lives of individuals, marriage and death, were recognized, one explicitly and one implicitly, by exchange of property. Intertribal exchange went on mainly under the guise of the Pipe Dance. There was no inheritance of other than ceremonial property and privilege. Within the ceremonial groups the inheritance of rites and sacred objects entitling one to large economic receipts was the rule and, with the hereditary chieftainships, formed a type of hereditary aristocracy. Land formed no part of this complex, and even the concept of tribal lands was far vaguer than the early treaties assumed it to be. Tribal lands were only such territories as the Antlers had been able to hunt over for some years without successful interference or ejection by enemy tribes. The association of land with private property or inheritance was completely alien to them.

This then was the complex of economic ideas with which the Antler had to meet the economic demands of white civilization. These are actually the economic ideas which he retains today. For the situations which have resulted from white contact he has a separate ideology. His actual personal property is sometimes expended according to one set of ideas and sometimes according to the other.

During the early trading days, and especially owing to the great stimulation which resulted from the introduction of the horse, the economic concept of conspicuous distribution was given ever freer play. The people had more property, especially more foreign property. Horses could sometimes be obtained by raids upon the enemy camp and the young men acquired merit, by the recounting of horse thefts which was another guise under which property could be publicly given away. (That is, a man who wished to "count coup" would pick up a feather, accidentally or purposely dropped from the costume of some dancer, and holding the feather in his hand recount his war exploits. Afterwards he was obligated to give a feast to certain chosen individuals.) Although the women were kept busier, dressing skins for the fur trade, nevertheless they shared too in the general stimulation of economic life; as wives and daughters they shared in the public display, or received more honorable tattooing, and sometimes themselves entered into the gift exchange, even forming friendships, involving gifts, with women of other tribes.

In the early days of allotments, during the period when frame houses were being built for the Antlers and they were being definitely settled upon the land, it was still possible to keep up this old economic behavior. Poverty had not yet gripped the reservation. There was still hunting and trapping to some extent; the live stock which had been purchased for individual householders by the sale of tribal lands had not yet dwindled and died under persistent lack of interest; there were plenty of horses to circulate within the tribe; the supply of wild fruits and nuts was still almost unimpaired and substantially added to their food resources; the new furniture which had been purchased for them added a new element to the "give aways" at death. Bureaus, bedsteads, clocks, lamps, all were given away with a lavish hand, being after all not necessities but merely luxuries of living. With the mass granting of fee patents in the second decade of the twentieth century and the ensuing land sales, a great deal of money came into the tribe. Although the pattern of individual spending was already developing, a large amount of money was still available for conspicuous public displays. After the Oil Indians became rich from their oil lands, they formed the habit of attending Antler ceremonies and adding the final lavish touches to their "give aways." Since 1920, conditions have been getting steadily worse on the reservation. Those who received fee patents to their lands have, almost without exception, sold them — the usual purpose behind the obtaining of the fee patent — and spent all their money. Each such sale makes one or more persons pensioners on their relatives and doubly impoverishes the tribe as a group. Also much heirship land had been sold and the proceeds spent by the heirs, always adding temporarily to the supply of ready money on the reservation, but increasing the number of dependents upon an ever-lessening amount of land. The agricultural depression which has involved the Middle West has provided less opportunity for those who were willing to undertake work for the surrounding farmers, feeders, etc. The fairs, the rodeos, the powwows, have also suffered. The price of goods has increased although, owing to the old exorbitance of traders' prices, this has probably directly affected the Indian less than his white neighbor. The automobile, a drain upon wealth, has become the ideal of every Antler. Leasing has steadily increased with resulting diminution of family incomes. The country no longer offers rich resources in wild berries, fruits, and nuts. And there has been a relative increase in other desires, besides that for the automobile, which can be satisfied only by American goods. This is mainly the result of the dying off of the older Indians with conservative habits of dress. Their place as consumers is being taken by young people who demand more American clothing. With occasional startling exceptions, consisting of those who have just had a land sale and of the few prosperous farmers, there is no surplus on the reservation today which can be dissipated in the extravagant fashion of twenty years ago.

Nevertheless, the old economic patterns die hard and many of them survive in cheapened and attenuated fashion. The "give away" at death is now limited to a few of the articles of clothing. The gift to mourners is five chickens or a bag of flour, where formerly it would have been a horse or a hog. The payments to visitors who tie tobacco may be only fifty cents or at most a small broadcloth or a pair of moccasins. People no longer make occasions for public display beyond the mere necessity of discharging obligations incurred through mourning. The gifts for the boy's first catch, or the girl's first carrying water, have disappeared completely. Only one marriage in ten or fifteen is now validated by exchanges of property. Payments to doctors have dwindled in corresponding fashion, and no one attempts to collect enough property to buy the few ceremonial privileges which have not already become obsolete. At the hand games which were formerly supported by large wagers and gifts in memory of the dead, a contribution of five cents is accepted with thanks and the whole society will shake hands with the donor of a dollar. The last tattooer is dead, and only occasionally are heard the old insults from those who have been tattooed to those who have not. At the last powwow only one horse was given away, where once thirty horses, or even more, would have been brought into the ring. But the persistence of the old patterns in terms of bags of flour and nickel contributions has had one important effect: it has kept alive the old economic values, the ideal of spending rather than of saving, of carelessly, lavishly throwing away everything that one has, and of enshrining in a wealth of social ceremonial every contribution to the social welfare.

Before considering the new economic attitudes which have been introduced with the concept of ownership of land and of property inheritance, it is necessary to discuss one other trait which the Antlers share with most primitive peoples and which Morgan called the Law of Hospitality. This is the compulsion to provide freely for anyone who enters one's house, those who feel free to enter being for the most part relatives only. The peculiar formalities which so often surround ordinary intercourse between families in a primitive society is, of course, one protection against the overuse of this privilege. In a primitive state, although sometimes irksome to certain individuals, and usually providing for an idle life on the part of a few lazy people, this cultural compulsion does very little harm. There are no great differences in wealth; failure to play any part in the economic life is accompanied by a loss of standing in the community, and it is one of the characteristics of primitive society that such loss of prestige is usually a powerful deterrent from unsocial behavior. Among the Antlers, deviations from the customary code brought down mockery and obloquy upon an individual, and the old records are full of admonitions to the young woman such as: "If you have a house of your own, you will not have to have your hand always on the water kettle ready to go for water"; "if you have a house of your own, people will speak well of you." Failure to provide for one's own wife, or failure to contribute to the larger household of which a young man was often a part, produced a stream of derisive comment. Without any alternative standard to oppose to his critics, the delinquent individual was shamed and helpless. So that while no one went hungry, and the sick, the ill, the unfortunate, and occasionally the thriftless, could find shelter in the earth lodge of a relative, this privilege was not exercised to excess. Children were trained in the minutiæ of behavior, forbidden to ask for water even in the house of a grandparent, unless the water was in plain sight. The provision for tying tobacco upon someone who visited without reason also served to keep too much visiting in check. Behind this careful network of punctilious observance, there was the invariable custom that all those who sought one's hospitality must be accorded it.

There was just one check, aside from etiquette, upon the overuse of this privilege. The Antlers preserve a very elaborate sense of rank. Rank in the tattooing society, birth in certain chiefly or priestly families, conferred special prestige and importance upon an individual. These ranking individuals were usually, by virtue of the economic emoluments connected with the privileges which they enjoyed, richer than the majority of people. If poor relatives sought shelter within their lodges, they quite frankly phrased their continued residence as that of "servants." They became hewers of wood and drawers of water, visitors of traps, and chaperons for the carefully sheltered daughters of chiefs. The rich family had, therefore, this way of using the labor of its pensioners. They might also "give away" their daughters to young and successful hunters of less wealth and position, thus enlisting their services in the large household.

It is seldom, in the primitive societies of which we have careful records, that this obligatory hospitality, with its accompanying obligations to help relatives in making exchanges or meeting doctors' fees, really works a conspicuous hardship upon any appreciable number in the community. The society will be found to have arrived at a state of equilibrium in which the checks on such activity serve to prevent its transcending the reasonable limits of mutual aid. When, however, the equilibrium of the society is disturbed by outside forces, when opportunities for earning or acquiring wealth are open to some members of the society and not to others, this customary behavior may become a definite barrier to the social advancement of a people and an obstruction to their economic adjustment.

The new economy, introduced by the white man, was based upon the ownership of land. Although it was the original intention that it should be based upon farming. Antler farming is so undeveloped that it is hardly fair to say that a farming economy has ever been established. However, every individual was presented with an allotment of land, of some of the very finest farming land in the state, upon forty acres of which a man can make a living for himself and family. The government paid a bonus per acre for all land cleared and broken, as an incentive to the Indian to get his land under cultivation. Moneys from sales of tribal lands were available for machinery, buildings, and seed. The whole scheme looked sound to the eyes of officials of those days, reared in the psychology of American pioneer days. There was still so much free land in the West that they believed the Antler lands would be safe. The land-hungry feeling brought from the Old World and the eager labor of the white pioneer both served to reassure the government that the Antler would appreciate and earnestly till his lands.

But the arrangements were none the less shortsighted and quite inadequate. The American in the New World, intoxicated by the breadth of the lands open to settlement, forgot every lesson his ancestors had learned in Europe, where land was dear and cherished from generation to generation. He was providing the Antler with an agricultural base which was to support himself and his children, in that particular corner of the state, forever. He was giving this land to a people who had never owned land, who had no item of customary law or usage to govern their disposal of it. The Antlers had no sentiments for land beyond the vivid affection they felt for a familiar landscape and for the resting place of their dead. They witnessed with terror the eviction of the "Short Robes," their unhappy banishment to more barren lands and the pitiful return pilgrimage which a few of them attempted. But this was not the terror of the landowner, the man who had, for generations, regarded his own and his children's welfare as inalienably connected with certain plots of arable land; it was rather the fear of exile, of an unknown existence in an unfamiliar land. It was nevertheless sufficiently violent, so to impress those white people interested in the welfare of the Antlers that a bill was pushed through Congress changing the terms of original grants, which did not provide for individual ownership, to a new set of allotments giving individual trust ownership, to be eventually proved and converted into fee patent ownership.

Every adult now had eighty acres of land, and sometimes more, through the untimely death of an "allotted" parent. Yet the utilization of such a large amount of land by individual farmers was still in the distant future. The gardens tended by the women, supplemented by their collections of wild fruits and berries, still formed the basis of their livelihood. This took up a scant ten acres. An illusion of vast wealth, of unlimited lands, grew up, which still remains despite the sad curtailment of the acreage owned by Antlers.

No attempt was made to deal with the problems of inheritance. The laws of the state were simply declared to be in operation, laws which took no account of the need of preserving a farm intact if it were to continue to support a kin group. When an individual dies, the land is parceled out among his widow, his children, his grandchildren, his nephews and nieces. Sometimes fifteen or twenty heirs share in the estate, each receiving a fractional part of the original allotment. If his widow marries again, and dies, her share goes to her second husband and to his children, often passing quite beyond the bonds of the gentile group. Thus many Antlers have inherited claims against land on other reservations, while dividing their own claims with foreign claimants. The original allotments have been divided and subdivided in a fashion utterly incompatible with western farming. If any one individual inherits forty acres which is part of a larger section of land, the government partitions it off if he wishes to farm it, but smaller claims than this are usually impracticable to handle in this way. The office is then faced with two alternatives: the land may be leased, or it may be sold. Leasing is accompanied often with almost insurmountable difficulties to the office and also to the unfortunate white "renter." It is a rare case if many of the dozen or so heirs are not at odds with one another, so that if one party signs the lease, the other party refuses to do so. The renting official argues, pleads, threatens, in an attempt to get at least a majority to sign the lease. While such a proportion is regarded as legal, it means that the dissenting owners will air their contravened "rights" for months thereafter. Meanwhile the renter stops his work, makes a trip to the agency office, there to wait his turn with the groups of other renters and Indians with grievances which throng every office day. As often as not, he will be told to go away, a whole day wasted, and return in a few days, when the requisite number of names has been obtained. Meanwhile, the tendency to save time and trouble by offering interpreters fees of several dollars per signee, grows. The office has a special calculating machine to work out the proportions of the rent due each of the numerous heirs — a clumsy, intricate business.

The alternative is to sell the land. Once such a course is decided upon, the lands are put up for sale, and sold in long lists, in a market where the government is distinctly at a disadvantage. Each heir receives a division of the selling price. Such money is conserved for minors and for some restricted Indians. In the case of young Indians, speaking English, the money is usually put at their disposal and they are allowed to draw on it until it is gone. The land, given to their grandfathers as a perpetual economic basis for their existence is irretrievably lost and nothing remains in its place. Yet the disagreements, friction, bribery and corruption incident upon leasing land owned by a large number of heirs is so great as to bring continual pressure upon the government to permit the sale of "heirship" lands.

Meanwhile a contrary tendency has served to pile up the land in the hands of some few individuals. An only child, of parents who were only children, may occasionally inherit several hundred acres of land. Some old person, incensed at the treatment which he has received from his relatives, may take the unusual trouble of making a will and in revenge leave all to one grandchild. Land once subdivided, may pile up again, as in the case of a woman who receives forty acres from her husband's estate and subsequently inherits, by the premature death of her son, her son's forty acres also. But all of these different developments only reflect the inadequacy of the whole system, the crying need for some law of entail, some recognition of the essential incompatibility of recognizing a group of heirs and at the same time preserving the land in reasonable units. The white man, under the same law, meets the situation in different ways: by willing his farm to

one son; by charging his estate with other claims which, however, the inheriting son is quite able to meet; by sending some
of his sons into other occupations; or by buying more land,
so that his large estate, subdivided, may still provide ample
livelihood for his children. The white man has usually not
been married so often as the Indian, nor does he necessarily
recognize the claims of stepchildren. Collateral relatives are
more often than not ruled out altogether.

But with the Antler, all these conditions are changed. If
he does make a will, he disinherits only because of marked
ill will, of which no Antler likes to be accused. His strong
sense of relationship with his paternal collateral relatives is
extended by the law to include his maternal collateral relatives also. (The old provision that a man's brother provided
for his dead brother's wife and children has been abolished
together with polygamy and the breakdown of any reality in
the gentile organization.) The situation is sometimes met by
prevailing upon a dying man to "deed over" his land to his
children. A farsighted agent who, at the end of the first
decade of this century, was aghast at the possible results of the
wholesale granting of fee patents, originally had recourse to
this procedure. He attempted to prevent the loss of these
lands by this deeding-over system, but his intention was
balked by a state supreme court decision that lands once
given in fee patent could never be subsequently restricted
against sale for default of payment of taxes. The deeding-
over system remains, complicated by bribes offered by land-
rich mothers to unwilling sons-in-law whom they wish to lure
into marrying daughters already burdened with illegitimate
children, or land bribes offered by old men to younger wives.
But in most cases the practice came in too late to save the
wholesale parceling out of the land, although it may serve to
save a small portion of it. It is a final desperate adaptation
to a situation which has become steadily more hopeless. The
other solutions open to the white man, such as sending his sons
into some other occupation or buying more land for them,

are theoretically, but not practically, open to the Antler. The Antler does not value his land enough to hold on to it; his farming never brings him much above a bare subsistence and land sells for as much as two hundred dollars an acre. He occasionally trades in his land for a house in Bergen or Radner, or even invests the money resulting from the land sale in building a house in the village, but he does not buy more farming land. There are only three cases of Indians who are leasing land to cultivate today. As for going into other occupations, this is still not regarded as an acceptable way of life. Occasional Antlers leave the reservation to work for more than a few weeks of casual labor, but they always come drifting back. Some sort of subsistence from the land, either as a casual farmer or as a landlord, is the only sort of existence which is culturally recognized.

The alienation of lands by direct sale has also been steady and devastating. This has been of two types, sale of lands to which a fee patent has been granted, and sale, with official permission, of pieces of restricted land. The original individual allotment bill provided for the granting of fee patents after a probationary period of twenty-five years. Twenty-five years of landlordism and lack of interest in farming had done very little to prepare the Antlers for unrestricted rights to their lands. The government made the granting of fee patents individual rather than wholesale, but only partially prevented the foreseen disaster. The district patent clerk arrived and the Antlers presented themselves before him. They could read and write English, understood everything which was said to them, were obviously quite capable of owning land! In this way, fee patents were given to a large number of the best educated and more progressive men in the community, those who had been East to school and were inclined to view the white man and his ways with deference. Granting them fee patents exposed them to every type of attack by the land sharks who were assembling on all sides. The fee patent land was now taxable, as mentioned above, even when deeded to the descendants of the owner; it could be mortgaged or sold at the will of the Antler owner. He no longer needed to go to the office for advice; he could sell his land directly through a real estate broker. Nor need he submit to the ignominy of having his money doled out to him from the office. He could start a bank account. All this was fatal to a group of men, unversed in the ways of business, essentially unfamiliar with the value of money, ignorant of any method of saving. Every type of pressure was brought to bear upon the owner of a desirable tract of land. He was given unlimited credit at some store, or he was escorted to a near-by city and habits of expensive debauch were carefully cultivated in him; he was taken riding in motor cars, and subjected to endless sales talk. The Antler, who had never yet learned to enjoy or to respect agricultural labor, who had had long experience, either personally or vicariously, as a landlord, of the pleasures to be derived from ready money, who had been reared in an unreal and nevertheless curiously safe world where the office provided for all emergencies, succumbed completely. Some Antlers, who today own one pair of overalls, ran through from seventy-five to a hundred thousand dollars. Under expert guidance of the skillful land shark, definite habits of expenditure grew up which still provide dominating patterns. These patterns have also been reinforced in recent years by the example of the wealthy Oil Indians.

Perhaps the most striking aspect of this new spending pattern was its extreme selfishness. The easy give and take and mutual hospitality were gone completely. The wealthy Indian divorced his expenditures from a land sale from his expenditures as an ordinary landowner on the reservation. The Antler, so swift to criticize his neighbor or relative who was stingy about a bag of flour, learned to say of the concentrated expenditure of ten thousand dollars, "Well, its his own money. He has a right to do what he likes with it." A new set of values had been evolved to meet the unprecedented situation. The automobile helped greatly to establish this pattern of aggressive economic indulgence. A horse might be wheedled away from one; the earlier pattern of investing in handsome horses was abandoned in favor of a car which was too large to be so begged away, and in which, moreover, one could escape from the continual visits and exactions of friends and relatives. Cooking at home is frequently abandoned for the same reason. When a rich man is known to eat at restaurants, it is no use for guests to gather — for again there is no obligation to take one's relatives out to meals. When the land sale was large enough to justify it, the Antler took trips, to the South, to the West, traveling in large cars with some favored relative as chauffeur and an indigent kinswoman as maid. The sense of freedom in spending one's own money was enormously enhanced if the *nouveau riche* individual could leave the reservation entirely, dress himself and his wife in expensive American clothes which his kinsmen of humbler circumstances would be ashamed to borrow — for there is a hearty ridicule for anyone who, while living on the reservation, dresses like an "imitation Oil Indian." He could stay away from the reservation, "living in hotels like white people" (an ideal which was held up to them years ago by a well-intentioned lady of missionary leanings) until the money was gone. Then, one by one, the alien clothes and possessions would be sold for food, and the wanderers return to the reservation, as poor as they had been before the land sale.[1]

But this whole pattern of absentee consumption of capital militated against any contribution to the economic resources of the tribe through purchases from land money. Sometimes not one tenth of the money went into clothes, furniture, or utensils which would be of any permanent use to the Antler after he had resumed his normal existence on the reservation.

[1] There is a tale told of a Black Face who inherited twelve thousand dollars and went on a long debauch, never pausing until every cent was spent. He then returned soberly to the reservation and went back to farming. A year later he inherited fifteen thousand more, and greeted the announcement with a despairing, "Oh, do I have to go through all that again?" While despair is not at all the typical attitude towards wealth, the sense of a compulsion to dissipate it as quickly as possible is typical.

The American clothes of the women could not be worn, the good clothes of the men had to be sold piece by piece for pocket money or gasoline to keep the car running. The car itself was usually lost through a mortgage, in which the Antler got only a bare fraction of its value.

This type of behavior had one other very bad effect, in being distinctly unsettling to the rest of the population. The contrasts are too sharp between an Antler in overalls and without ten cents in his pocket, on foot or driving two broken-down horses to an old wagon, and an Antler in a handsome car, his wife and child well dressed, himself resplendent in a twenty-five dollar Stetson hat and a shirt of delicate green with tie to match. The gap between the meal which the first will make from cornmeal mush with a slight seasoning of suet and dried squash, and the large beefsteak which the second is on his way to order in a near-by city, is too great to be bridged by any sort of hard labor or careful savings. It is completely discouraging to any kind of effort. If the white renter, coming in with two skinny horses and a wagonload of children had any standard to offer the Antler which could match in romance and colorfulness the standard set by the Oil Indians and the temporarily rich Antlers, a different picture might be found. But the drab workaday life of a people who scrimp and save and buy more land, and scrimp and save to meet the increased mortgage, cannot possibly compete in the Antler's estimation with the appeal of even a few weeks of absolute opulence. All his old premiums on spending rather than saving, on conspicuous parade of wealth, coöperate with his new aggressive individualism, his determination to enjoy *his* particular windfall while he can.

On the reservation this summer there were only three such conspicuous consumers, two men and one woman who had shared equally in a large land sale. All three had large cars, ate in restaurants, lived a gay, idle life, out of which they contributed hardly a cent to the relatives who had supported them in the lean years which had gone before. There were also, however, several other individuals or households living at a fairly fast pace, with a car and extra clothes for the children, from smaller land sales; there were the young men who had married women who had been only children and who were therefore in possession of fat rents. There were several sets of parents who were living on the rent money of their wealthy children. These few wealthy people were in the most striking minority, but nevertheless they served subtlely to set the pace of the economic life, to discourage all effort which could not lead to an equally brilliant goal, to make young men born landless (in the Antler phrase "born too late") simply fold their hands and growl at their cursed luck, to make all good counsel of thrift, hard work, and conservation of lands so much purposeless preaching to empty ears. There are no rewards which the Antler feels makes ordinary labor worth doing. If he has a farm of his own, *i. e.*, a farm which is restricted against tax assessment or debt levies, he will work on it enough to grow corn which will yield him a few hundred dollars cash in the fall. But if his farm is leased, he will merely subsist on the rent money.

Thorough as he has been in taking over the white man's economic individualism in everything relating to actual sums of money derived from land sales, the Antler remains conservative and bound to the hospitality rule in every other respect. Every small source of income, a small corn crop, a pension, a veteran's compensation, rent money, and the smaller windfalls from the sale of wild grapes, hazel nuts, giving evidence in prohibition cases, playing a part in a fair or a rodeo, is regarded as inevitably subject to the demands of relatives. There are only two ways of escaping the continual exactions for small loans, a meal, a week's lodging, or even a month or a year's lodging; one is to be rich enough to be accorded the right to spend one's own money as one wishes, the other is to "go white." [2] Although there are other criteria of "going white," such as matters of dress and house furnish-

2 See Part III, pp. 286-87.

ings, church membership and social association with whites, the most important point is one's economic attitude. The Antler who has a roof over his head and any possible way of obtaining food and yet refuses to share roof and food with any relative, no matter how distant, because he wishes to provide properly for his family, or to avoid further borrowing upon his corn crop, is branded as having "gone white." This is an accusation which carries with it an amount of social scorn and near ostracism which is exceedingly difficult to stand with equanimity, especially as the thrifty Indian may imitate the white man's economic standards and even his standard of material comfort without being accepted by the white man as an equal. The sober, thrifty Antler has to bear the social consequences of being a member of a large community of unthrifty anti-white Indians, which earns him an amount of undeserved odium which he cannot live down. It is therefore not surprising that only about eight families can be said to have "gone white" in this way. The rest of the community live in a state of grudging hospitality which is nevertheless accorded so freely that those without property are seen gambling almost as frequently as those with property. Owing to the shifting and uncertain nature of wealth based upon inherited shares in property, the same individual is one year parasite, the next, host, and possibly the third year the rich spender. But this alternation is not sufficiently the rule to bring about anything like an equalization of the economic burden borne by different members of the society. Furthermore, with the habit of conspicuous consumption off the reservation for those with money, the returns from land sales are never poured back into the communal purse.

Chapter IV

POLITICAL LIFE

The old political organization of the Antlers was firmer than was customary among many American Indians. It was based upon two principles — rank and wealth. Sacerdotal and ceremonial privileges were inherited in certain families, in certain gentes, which in turn were grouped in a dual division and the members of each moiety pitched their tents upon opposite sides of the camp circle. These privileges, and prowess in hunting and horse stealing, made it possible for a man to accumulate wealth. By distributing this wealth in certain specified ways — to strangers, to mourners, to the holders of special offices — a man acquired merit and, if he persisted in so disposing of the requisite amount of wealth, he ultimately became a minor chief. Above the group of minor chiefs was a council of seven chiefs; rank was strictly preserved even among them. Their function was to maintain order, keep the peace, and by precept and example preserve decorum within the tribe. Bulwarked by prestige and wealth, the moral pressure exercised by the chiefs was sustained by tribal police composed of young men with the requisite number of war counts. There were also numbers of hereditary officials with special functions to perform in regard to the buffalo hunt, etc.

Besides possessing a coherent and well integrated political system, the Antlers added the supplemental elements of a carefully rationalized mythology which depicted each bit of practical tribal organization as a carefully thought-out plan on the part of their ancestors. "The people took thought," "when the people saw that it would be necessary," etc. These phrases occur and recur, giving the sanction of wise solicitude on the part of their elders to the political expedients of every-day life.

There were organized methods of administering justice. It was the function of the peace chiefs to intercede with the relatives of a murdered man, attempt to make them accept gifts and refrain from vendetta. Brutal and wanton murderers are said to have been killed, not merely condemned to several years' exile, as in many Plains tribes. A man who seduced another man's wife was liable to have all of his property destroyed or appropriated by the wronged husband and his kin. A similar punishment awaited the seducer of an unmarried girl; in such an event it was administered by the girl's kin. A girl or married woman could also be roundly beaten for unchastity.

The political history and political measures of the tribe show a perpetual fear of disruption, the fear of the loss of individual bonds, of the breaking of the bonds which held the many gentes in one camp circle, owing allegiance to one set of tribal fetishes. Numberless intergentile arrangements were made — one gens kept the pipes for a ceremony, another gens lit them. A hereditary tribal official controlled the impatience of the kin groups in the buffalo hunt so that all might advance together upon the buffalo herd. The hereditary medicine societies also crossed gentile lines, but had a tendency to be endogamous, so that firm interlocking groups were formed which served to check the ever-present tendencies towards disruption. In historical legend, it is always the gens, or in current Indo-American, the "band," from which secession was feared. Gentes were said to have very definite personality traits, and the people thought of a gentile group as "difficult" or "tractable." The fact that matrilocal residence was very common, and exogamy the rule, makes it doubtful whether this gentile personality existed in reality; there is no trace of it now.

We must, however, conceive of the Antlers as having a well organized tribal government which controlled peace and war, migration, communal hunts, etc.; a number of intergentile sacerdotal corporations which served to bulwark a formal unity; a group of tribal fetishes relating to the hunt and to war which served to integrate the feeling of every member of the tribe about these symbols of common purpose. In addition to these formal and conceptual points of organization, there were the usual strong bonds of customary behavior, the infringement of which brought ridicule and censorship from other members of the tribe.

The transition from this well articulated tribal life to the present day has been indicated in the historical sketch, Chapter I (p. 21). In sharp contrast to its earlier conditions is the Antler community today.

Every Antler is a citizen of the United States, and of the state in which the reservation is situated. He is subject to the criminal and civil laws of the state and, with white citizens, possesses an equal legal claim upon the public law enforcing educational and medical services of the state. If this routine citizenship were the only political status, the Antler relationship to his white neighbors would not be nearly so complicated as it is. But every Antler on the tribal roll is, additionally, not only a United States citizen, but a ward of the Federal Government. This ward status places him in a peculiar legal position. It gives him a claim upon all types of United States service to Indians. The services of the reservation doctor and field nurse and of the hospital are free. He has a right to send his children to the government boarding school, where they will be maintained free of charge. All of his property, to which he has not received fee patent and which is part of the original allotments of land granted to the Antlers, and such things as have been purchased from the sale of such property, while still held in trust by the government, as houses, buildings, horses, furniture, farm equipment, is classified as "restricted." The implication of this term is wide. "Restricted" property is not taxable unless leased, and it cannot be sold, purchased, mortgaged or levied against for any debt, without the consent of the government. The Indian who "owns" only restricted land, and whose house, furniture, horses, etc., were purchased from the sale of other restricted land is in a peculiarly strategic position. If he leases his land, the leasing is arranged through the office, and the taxes (land which has been improved over twenty-five years, if leased, is taxable) are automatically subtracted from his rent. If the Indian in question is old, sick, or a minor, the office assumes not only the burden of collecting his rents, but of holding them for him and distributing the payments weekly or monthly according to his needs. Until recently the office would also issue "orders" against future rents, but this practice has been discontinued except in most unusual cases. If an Indian needs farm equipment, or money to mend the roof of his barn, and has a large amount of land, the office will sell the land for him and authorize the purchase of the needed equipment, lumber, etc. Any money lender who takes a mortgage upon restricted property is liable to prosecution and imprisonment. The office, furthermore, uses its position of financial trustee to enforce certain rules of behavior: this position was used in the past to stop the practice of polygamy, and is used now in an attempt to discourage common law marriages. The state of X about 1912 passed a law prohibiting marriage "by Indian custom" — cohabitation validated by affinal exchanges — and insisting upon regular civil marriage.

The Antler Indian, citizen of the United States, citizen of his state, ward of the United States government, is in a curious and anomalous position. He can vote, he can serve in the Army or Navy, he can come and go as he likes, he is subject to no miscegenation laws, he can contract debts but he is not under the same compulsion to pay them as his white neighbor. When a member of his family dies, he can call upon the county or upon the agency, if he lacks the funds to bury his dead. He can call in the agency doctor for nothing, as he can consult an outside doctor, if one can be found willing to work for a most uncertain fee. His children have rights in two kinds of schools, sometimes he pays nothing for either. They are, moreover, subject to the truancy laws of the state and the educational programs of the Federal Government, which maintains a special educational agent also. He uses the same roads, the same bridges as his white neighbors, and unless his land is leased, he pays nothing towards their upkeep. In other words, nominal citizen though he is, his position, with the exception of the right to vote and to serve in the Army or Navy, is that of a child; he has privileges, special and often irksome supervision, and no obligations of any sort.

If the reservation had not been thrown open to white settlement, but instead the Indian community had remained intact, the confusion of the Antler's political position might have been in some degree obviated. Roads, schools, medical work, local officials, would then have been definitely Indian in character. He might possibly have been led to have some pride in his local community with which to match the vociferous localism of a small town like Bergen, with its chamber of commerce and its town band. If Antler children had been continuously in the majority in any one of the public schools, that school might have developed a competitive pride. I say *might* most advisedly.

As it is, however, the Indian's political status lacks the realities of obligation, participation, strong locality feeling, which serve to make concrete the status of his white neighbor. The chief political fact in the Antler's mind remains that he is an Indian, an Antler Indian. And this fact of membership in his tribe has almost no real political significance. Twice in the last ten years there have been annuity payments made to every man, woman and child on the Antler roll. These payments were for interest on computed losses due to faulty surveying, etc., on tribal lands in the past. At such times and only at such times membership in the tribe counts, economically.

For the rest, the Antlers have no local autonomy. They can neither make laws, nor enforce any laws contrary to those of the state, nor have they the right, possessed by the borough councils of small incorporated white communities, to pass local ordinances, because they are not a geographical unit in the state. If they passed the slightest sumptuary ordinance, the state laws would uphold the freedom of any Antler who violated it. They no longer possess even the right to adopt outsiders as members of the tribe — although individuals can of course adopt minors if they wish.

Their largely fictitious political existence is expressed by an elected council of some twenty members. These men, as accredited representatives of the tribe, can legislate concerning the tribal land, which is held in common very much as some fraternal order might hold property, except that it is not taxable nor subject to attachment for debt. They also, in coöperation with a special committee, elected from among themselves, plan for and arrange the annual camp ceremony. Funds derived from admission to the ceremony and from contributions levied against white candidates for office, are under the control of this council. Such funds are usually expended in payment of all participants, paying of the debts initially incurred, advertising, purchase of tents, lighting, etc., and if there is any surplus, it is used to send a representative of the tribe to Washington.[1]

A large number of the Antlers remain aloof from these rather modern political concerns, which are in the hands of a small group.

If, then, the Antler makes so little — except in phraseology and sentiment — of his political status, which disregards the fact of his Indian blood, and of his tribal membership in an emasculated and meaningless tribal organization, what politi-

[1] There is one Antler who makes his entire living by interpreting and by collecting a percentage of any moneys involved in the transaction and by representing the tribe in Washington. He claims the credit for having persuaded business men in near-by cities to advocate the payments of the back interest — a payment which amounted to over half a million dollars — on the ground that all this money would go back to the shopkeepers' pockets. Whether he was really responsible for this argument or not, it was certainly used in the interested local campaign for righting the financial wrongs done to the Antlers a generation before.

cal status has reality to him? There is just one — and that is race, all the feeling usually involved in citizenship and nationality is centered about the magic words "American Indian." [2]

About his Antler nationality is centered his sense of home, of kinship, of security, of familiar phrasing of experience, but his status in the world is simply "an American Indian." This attitude is fostered by many things, by the government schools where children from a dozen tribes are educated together and every effort is made to discourage tribal cliques, by intertribal marriages resulting directly and indirectly from contacts formed in the coeducational schools, by friendships formed between Indians from different tribes — in Oklahoma, in Texas, in Arizona, on expeditions after peyote, in the Army during the War, at rodeos and fairs. The great similarity of reservation conditions gives two chance-met Indians from widely separated tribes a common background, in addition to the claims of a common race. But perhaps more important than these internal conditions are the attitudes, spoken and written, of the white people. The Antlers have seen "the American Indian" in the pictures, in the newspapers, in the magazines. They are constantly being employed, singly and in groups, to represent the American Indian at rodeos, in traveling shows, in carnivals, pageants, floats, tableaus, etc. Promoters of fairs send trucks to convey several Indian families, complete with costumes, tipis, etc., to a fairground a hundred miles away, where the spectators are quite ignorant of their tribal affiliation and may never in fact have heard of this particular tribe. Secondly, in the speeches of politicians, a mass of sentimental attitudes toward the "American Indian" are expressed. The Indian's vote is solicited with stirring comment: "You are the original owners of this land, the first Americans, the true Americans, the real

[2] At a ceremony last summer at which Indians from other tribes were present a small half-breed girl seated by my side suddenly asked, "What tribe do you belong to?" "I'm afraid I don't belong to any." "Oh," there was scorn and indifference in her tone and averted shoulder, "Well, I'm an American Indian."

Americans. When I was in France I fought side by side with your Indian boys — we were all fighting together, side by side, for the same cause — the red man and the white man for the same cause." Under the influence of this stirring oratory, the Antler forgets the exorbitant taxes on his leased lands, or the greater willingness on the sheriff's part to jail an Indian than a white man — matters which are current causes for complaint on the reservation.[3]

A practicing lawyer who is a candidate for office will undertake an Indian's defense free, out of his love for the Indians, his interest in justice and human rights. In the course of the trial he makes many rhetorical references to his affection for the Indians, his desire to see protection and justice for every man, woman and child on the reservation.[4]

Day in and day out, those who wish to get votes, concessions, benefits, from the Indian utter this string of platitudes, of stock phrases and stock jokes.[5] The individuality, the dignity, of his political position as a member of a tribe whose elders had "taken thought," has been replaced by this empty mock-heroic rôle thrust upon him by the politician who is only too ready to cheat and exploit him the minute that he gets into office.

[3] Complaints run: "Yes, when a group of white women get together and play bridge all afternoon for a prize, the law doesn't say anything, but when a few poor Indian women play a game of cards for a pair of moccasins, they call it gambling." Or "The other day, a white girl was walking along the Bergen road, and a white man picked her up and carried her off to his house and ten men had her. And not one of them is in jail. They took the girl off to a Y — city doctor and hushed the matter up. Now, if it had been our Indian boys —." As violent defense is made for the political candidates, criticized in terms of local happening. "Ah, well, I like C —. He always speaks nicely to me. He's never cross."

[4] In amusing contrast is the tale of one mixed-blood lawyer who is said to have charged an old Antler, who could not speak English, six thousand dollars for making her will. The Indian office is said to have allowed a claim of only four thousand.

[5] A sample joke is the old story about the white man and the native, the former commenting jocularly upon the food which the native placed on a new grave. "Do you expect the dead man to come up and eat that food?" and then the reply of the shrewd, wise native, who mocks the rude and stupid white man by answering, "as soon as your dead come up to smell the flowers you place on their graves."

When I say that his most real political status is that of "the American Indian" *in vacuo*, this should not be interpreted to mean that the Antler feels such a strong sense of solidarity with other Indian tribes that it blots out old-time animosities and intertribal jealousies. Towards their ancient military enemies the Short Knives they still have mixed feelings, and for the Black Faces, who live at the other end of the reservation and speak an unintelligible dialect of the same language and share a great number of their customs, they have the most overwhelming contempt.[6] Of all the intertribal marriages, an Antler marriage with a Black Face has the worst chance of continuance.[7] The presence of all these small but bitter animosities makes the fictitious political rôle of the "American Indian" just that much more narrow and lifeless, as the national and religious animosities in the ranks of labor often make the Communist or Socialist ideology only a series of unreal phrases.

One other aspect of the Antlers' political attitude deserves mention, that is, his attitude towards the Federal government.

[6] The two worst insults are "Negro" and "Black Face." Jesting will run in this wise. "Oh, here's my little granddaughter. I didn't recognize her because her face has gotten so black, I thought she was a little Negro girl," and this retort: "Oh, I looked and saw an old woman with beads hung in a strange fashion around her neck. I thought it was a Black Face woman, and now I see it is only my grandmother." A candidate for government office, speaking at an Antler festival, innocently lowered his political stock by a speech in which he referred to his pride in having been adopted as a member of the Short Knife tribe, and his past pleasure in having appointed as a nurse a member of the Black Face tribe. He requested that this appointee, who was present, should stand up, which she wisely refrained from doing. The candidate somewhat retrieved his lost prestige by concluding his address with the following remarks: "If I am elected governor, there will be an inaugural ball at the State Capital, and I should like nothing better than to see a group of Antler Indians, of the first citizens of this great country, of the real Americans, come down to the capital and lead this ball."

[7] One boy, who had led a truant group of five small Antler boys home from the Indian boarding school some years ago, told me that "The big Antler boys got into a fight with the night watchman. That made the superintendent down on all Antlers. We weren't going to be treated right, so we left." Strong personal characteristics will make members of one tribe more popular than others with superintendent, matron, and other employees, and this is seized upon by the students, as shown in remarks such as "when Jennie Prince was at the school, the matron liked all Antlers, now she don't like them no more."

We have seen that his attitude towards local government is one based upon sentimentality, small sense of grievance, and lack of any real participation.[8] He grumbles about roads for which he does not pay taxes, or grumbles about the taxes which are subtracted from his rents, he criticizes the public schools, he levies continuous assessments of hogs, beeves, cases of pop, ten dollar bills, against politicians who are in office or seeking election.[9] He never has any opportunity to vote on matters which affect his community, because he rejects the hybrid Indian-white locality groups in favor of the politically unrecognized tribe.

Towards the Federal government the Antlers' attitude is one of hope, resentment and criticism. The Federal government, through Congress, and more immediately through the Indian Bureau, is felt to be ultimately responsible for their condition, social, political, economic. The colonizing white man is the villain in the piece, come from across the sea to steal their hunting grounds; the poor white in their midst, especially if he does not speak English, is the local villain. The government is the thankless knight-errant who undertakes to right the wrongs of the Indian race. This version of the Federal government's rôle leads to two or three other attitudes. All government officers, not always with the exception of the superintendent, are referred to as "employees." This phraseology, originally only a technical description under the Civil Service, nevertheless sums up the Antlers' attitude. The white officials who are given such great power over them, who can control their domestic affairs, withhold or give a recommendation to grant them a patent in fee to their land, order their children off to school or refuse to let

[8] This fall a woman whose mother was half Antler — she herself was the wife of a prosperous farmer — ran for sheriff. Although she attempted to make some appeal for support from the Antlers on the strength of her Indian blood, she got none, as the idea of a woman sheriff appeared, under the expert guidance of white male politicians, intrinsically ridiculous. The Antler women decried the idea with more violence than did the Antler men.

[9] One office holder, eager for reëlection, even contributed three dollars towards the refreshments of the school girls' dancing society, the "Honey Bunches."

them go, arrange a lease to their advantage or permit them to be fleeced — are not regarded with either the voluntary submission accorded elected holders of high offices, the awe and respect with which native peoples regard the appointed officials of the British or Dutch government, nor even with the scanty pride and interest with which a local school board views its own appointee to the village school. The Antler attitude is rather that of a rich man in a hotel or restaurant, who is served or neglected by the servants of the institution. The Antlers consider the government employees there for their benefit, to serve them, to be bullied, insulted, or wheedled as the case may be.[10] The assumption on the part of the Antlers is that every employee seeks to evade his duties, betray his responsibilities, grow rich upon the possibilities of graft which are open to him. They know the salary of every official, and count over the personal property which he possessed when he came and the amount which he accumulates while he is on the reservation.[11] The presence of Indian clerks, Indian policemen, Indian interpreters in and about the agency institutions make for a continual leakage of semiofficial gossip, tales of favoritism, small graft. There are numberless Indians who make it their business to keep a sharp eye upon all the employees, and if necessary to take it up with the Indian Bureau or with their congressman. Every employee lives in perpetual anxiety that, whether he has or has not violated some of the endless detailed regulations surrounding a government servant, some malcontent will succeed in making him lose his job. Salaries in the Indian service are so meager that this is a real threat. I once had a conversation with a government official who was retired from the Indian service and had nothing more to fear. Yet when I remarked,

10 One building on the reservation is equipped with a waiting room which has no door into the office, but only a small window with a falling shutter. When an Antler becomes too abusive, the white official can then slam this shutter down and cut short the Indian's profane loquacity.

11 This attitude is summed up in the current saying, "there's not one of them but comes in here with a suitcase in each hand and goes out in a limousine."

"Do you know the latest Antler gossip? A certain Indian politician is collecting ten dollar 'tips' which he claims have been demanded by his congressman in return for help at Washington," the official laughed uneasily at the characteristic tale, and added: "That is the kind of thing which we would expect from this person in question. I know who he is, you know who he is — *we need not name him.*"

Setting aside for a moment the question of actual abuse of power by government employees for personal advantage or because of personal prejudice, let us consider only the implications of the Indian attitude. It means that all government employees, no matter how honest, how tireless, how enthusiastic, would be voted as merely "doing their duty" and given neither laurels nor thanks by the Antlers. And meanwhile the constant anxieties, the constant fear of political pressure being brought to bear against them, the bad manners of the younger Indians who always command except when they are constrained to beg — all this is not an atmosphere in which mutual respect or ordered administration flourishes. Add to it the heartless, automatic character of bureaucratic, centrally administered, rulings [12] and the Indian is given ample incident to support his sense of being badly served.

The political game falls, then, as far as the Federal government is concerned, into two parts — first, getting your rights in spite of the determination of the employees to keep you from doing so; and second, both getting a lion's share of any benefits which the national government proposes to shower on Indians as a whole, and putting across for the Antlers special claims which will be financially recognized by the government.

The "rights" which the employees are believed to be withholding from the Indians are many and various. New rulings from Washington are not accepted until after many months of suspicion that they are local affairs. Such points are for

[12] There is a familiar saying on the reservation, "the Indian is wrapped in red tape; he can't get free."

example: (1) the Federal prohibition against giving orders against rent moneys owing to the Indian; (2) the five-year lease; (3) the ruling that Antlers living near a public day school, and possessed of sufficient means, should send their children there instead of to the government school.[13] This situation is sharpened by the frequent changes in national policy, for the Antler tends to regard any privileges he has once had as a right of which he is deprived, and any regulation at present in force as an irksome restriction.

The second attitude — a vigilant hope for substantial benefits to come — is explicable in terms of general native attitudes in other parts of the world. When I first went to the Admiralty Islands I was puzzled and annoyed by an invariable sequence which occurred in dealing with natives. If I gave them the most trifling gift, they would immediately ask for something else, and when that was refused, continued for half an hour to request different objects of varying value. This seemed particularly graceless behavior, especially when contrasted with the behavior of the Polynesian who, after elaborate thanks for the smallest gift, hurries away to prepare a return present. But in time I came to understand this apparent thanklessness of the Melanesian native, who is not accustomed to making gifts except along definite trade routes where return is assured. He did not understand why he was given anything. He was left with only two theories — either I owed him for some service which he had forgotten, in which case I was probably only paying him a part of what I owed him and he had better ask for the rest — amount unknown — or according to his categories I was mad, as mad as someone who distributed bank notes to a crowd. I had given him a fishhook — I might be insane enough to give him the lamp or the gun — there was no harm in trying it out. Hence his

13 When I arrived at Radner, there was general murmuring and discontent because many families had been denied the right to send their children away to school. This autumn there was a reversal in Federal policy, and a large proportion of the children on the reservation were sent away to school. Reservation grumbling immediately shifted to the "right" to keep their children at home.

ingenuous requests for everything in sight. The present-day Indian dealing with the national government has much the same attitude. He does not understand the premises upon which the government acts and so he believes anything to be possible.

There is no reason, in his own view of the universe, why the highest political authority of his sworn enemy, the invading white man, should take up arms in defense of the Indian. Yet, because of the phrasing of the treaties and government announcements, because of all the ideology centering about the old talk of the "great white father," the Antler, despite all the hardships which he has suffered from maladministration, graft and political exploitation, still conceives the local employees of the Indian Bureau as responsible for all his wrongs, and the government as the shining exponent of his rights. Although astute politicians, like the Antler representative in Washington, may realize quite clearly what type of local political pressure convinces Congress that some assessment, some land sale, some surveying of half a century ago, is a great wrong which should be righted by making payments to every member of the tribe, the average adult Antler does not. From time to time in history, the national government has simply handed money out to the Antlers and, they have heard, to other Indian tribes as well. Was there not an Iroquois agent on the reservation getting the Iroquois to sign a petition demanding payment to the Iroquois tribe for the land value of a large city in New York? Everywhere, on reservations all over the country, inexplicable large payments are made to different tribes from time to time, simply because they are wronged Indians. Are not their relatives, the Long Robes, going to receive something like a fifteen-hundred dollar payment each, next autumn? Where the reasons for government action are not understood, the Antlers are in no position to gauge the incredibility of their own hopes. Their tribal representative hears that a fund has been set aside from which Indians in need of funds for agricultural purposes may borrow. He promptly writes down to Washington, stating that fifty Antlers would like to borrow two hundred dollars apiece at once. They hear that Congress is said to be about to appropriate a million dollars to be apportioned among different tribes for the relief and care of aged and indigent Indians. Their representative writes to Washington, stating that the Antlers would like five hundred thousand of this million. All the excitement, the hazards of hunting buffalo, are now found in the amusing game of hunting the government, stalking its incomprehensible plans, getting a share of the kill for oneself. There are many Antlers who have no leased land, no heirship land which is in the process of being sold and from which periodic payments may be expected — no reason of any sort for expecting money from the office. Yet every month, on office days when checks are given out, they present themselves faithfully at the window, hoping that this time they will receive a check. Such behavior is of course used by employees to illustrate the stupidity of the Antler; really, it merely illuminates the huge gap between Antler and American psychology, a gap which is so wide that the Antler does not grasp the reasons which lie back of white behavior.

This game of hopefully gunning for the government is the most engrossing occupation of many of the men, who, having leased their lands, are left without other occupation. Although it results in some sort of interaction between the government and the Antlers, it can hardly be described as coherent political behavior. Rather, the Antler believes that he has been born with an inalienable heritage of wrongs to be righted by largess, if only he can track down the strange givers of this largess.

There are primitive peoples in the world who could possibly stand the loss of the political autonomy which had been the Antlers' without such serious hurt to their personal dignity and conceptions of status. The Melanesian, inhabitant of an anarchical little tribe, at odds with all its neighbors and having no important political institutions beyond the inter-relations of kin groups, has his dignity enhanced by being made a member of a larger political unit, by having ideas of loyalty and allegiance to a state superimposed upon a village government which is aptly described in pidgin English as "altogether boy he talk." Where, as in Africa, the native population is dense and the white man invades only to trade or teach or govern, holding himself aloof from strictly local concerns, local governments in which the native has a full sense of participation, through which he can govern himself in small matters and preserve at least the forms of independent political action and local autonomy, can be accomplished. Even the American Negro, disenfranchised, and politically discriminated against as he has been, sometimes, especially in the North, is concentrated in such numbers that he has control of ward politics, of such matters as school boards and other strictly local officials. But the Antler has had none of these advantages; his political conceptions were too rich for him to find anything but loss when they were wrested from him and an empty comic opera rôle substituted for his former dignity as a member of the tribe. And the persistent invasion of white settlers and white renters into every corner of the reservation, until there is no square mile of land exclusively Indian, has robbed him of any local political existence. From a member of a self-governing, politically self-conscious unit, he has been degraded to a member of a miscellaneous group of people who have hereditary claims to receive special treatment and to give nothing in return.

CHAPTER V

SOCIAL ORGANIZATION

Within the tribal unit which has already been discussed were two subdivisions, different in character; one was the gens, or as it is popularly known among the Antlers themselves, the "band," the other was the village. The grouping of the exogamic gentes into two moieties had political and ceremonial significance and was bodied forth in the arrangements of the camp circle, but is remembered today only in the traditions known to a few members of the tribe. The tribe dwelt historically in three villages, to the north of the present residence area, but the attempt of an earlier investigator to establish a census of these villages and to correlate village residence with gens and sub-gens membership proved fruitless. It is, of course, impossible to make any such investigation today. Gentile membership and residence were interrelated in several ways. In the camp circle, each gens camped by itself and the division of gens from gens was most formal. During the winter, when small groups camped in tipis in sheltered ravines, they tended to come from only one gens or even one sub-gens. But in the arrangement of the permanent earth-lodge villages, gentile membership was habitually disregarded. This disregard seems to have been partly due to the tendency of women relatives to build houses close together. Matrilocal residence and house ownership by women both militated against any strict observance of gentile affiliation in an otherwise patrilineal society.

Within each gens were certain families which possessed hereditary privileges, chiefly of a sacerdotal nature. In Antler political mythology, any function held in this hereditary fashion, by a family within a gens, was regarded as a gentile function, although exercise by any other than the lineal descendant of the particular holder would occur only if the line died out. Gentes were thought of, however, in terms of these privileges, in terms of their taboos, their distinctive marks in ornaments and their gentile names. So strict was the adherence to the use of gentile-owned names, in large proportion names referring specifically or metaphorically to the special taboo animal of the gens, that it is still possible to place a male in his proper gentile affiliation by his personal name. The subgentes had subsidiary taboos and were also effective in widening the marriage range, for although marriage was forbidden into the entire gens of one's mother, it was only prohibited to marry into the sub-gens of the maternal and paternal grandparents. With the breakdown of the gentile organization and the loss of traditional knowledge, many people now refer to their membership in a sub-gens rather than to the larger gentile membership; the sub-gentile taboo was also observed in these cases.

The kinship system was of the type which Dr. Lowie has called bifurcate merging. The children of a brother and sister called each other son and father, respectively. This disregard of generation was perpetuated and elaborated upon in the succeeding generations, so that it often happened that individuals two generations apart called each other brother, or conversely, that members of the same generation called each other by grandparent terms. As this terminology was primarily dependent upon actual kinship, although it was theoretically gens-wide, it was able to survive the collapse of the gentile system. The gentile system has suffered most severely from the break-up of the camp circle, the abandonment of the distinctive styles of ornament, the desuetude of the functions of the sacerdotal families, and the generally scattered nature of Antler life today. The kinship system has suffered from a similar set of causes. Chief of these are the scattered residence, the boarding school, and the breakdown of the gentes.

But the kinship system is disintegrating in a peculiar fashion. The white system of reckoning relationships has neither

affected it nor been combined with it in any way. The young
Antler can give the white relationships perfectly, remarking
meticulously, "I call him uncle, Indian fashion, but he is
really my cousin." Or, "I call her mother, Indian fashion,
but she is my aunt, that is, my mother's sister." The Antler
trait of learning the white values, as a separate set of ideas,
but failing to incorporate them into the stuff of the culture,
is particularly well illustrated here. The kinship system which
was carefully recorded forty years ago is still in use, not
changed in any detail. The loss is of a subtler variety.

It was not customary for children to be taught principles
by which kinship was reckoned. Instead they were taught
each relationship as it was encountered. "Call this man,
grandfather." "Don't talk with that man, he is your brother"
(to a young girl who might have been suspected of flirting).
It is presumable that in the earlier days of the camp circle,
young people would have learned to generalize these special
teachings to the extent, at least, of calling by the correct term
all the members of the father's gens. Furthermore, when the
people lived close together, every individual relative could be
brought to the child's attention by the grandfather or grandmother, charged with its instruction in the use of the kinship
terminology. But now the tribe is scattered and children go
away to school so young and for such long periods that the
anxious grandmother may have no opportunity to teach the
special relationship. Moreover the use of English names has
cut across any recognition of gentile lines. English names
were assigned to the Antlers by several interested white people
working among them, and there was no attempt to give one
gens the same name, but instead each adult male was arbi-
trarily assigned a different name. Adoption and illegitimacy
extended the range of the English names, but neither affected
the continued scrupulousness with which the older affiliations
were insisted upon in the giving of Indian names. Young
people may know that "All the Greens are related to my
grandmother," or "the Fallons are some relation to me, on

my mother's side," but this does not always prove a safe guide. Meanwhile other people's gentile membership is not known at all to the young people who are marrying today. With their remembered admonitions concerning special relatives and vague knowledge attached to certain English names, they attempt to thread their way among the pitfalls of exogamy. Meanwhile the old people, depending entirely upon the Indian names and cognizant of each individual genealogy, are still on the alert for incest which the young people are not properly equipped to avoid. This results in frequent runaway marriages which are subsequently branded as incestuous and broken up by the parents. There are as yet only a few young people with sufficient stubbornness to contest such objections and insist that they are going "to marry like white people." The younger generation is able to name so few relatives correctly, that the kinship system may be said to have preserved its form, but to have shrunk in usefulness.

Two conspicuous aspects of the kinship system, in addition to the regulation of marriage, are the joking and avoidance relationships. Avoidance applies to the parent-in-law of opposite sex and also to father-in-law and son-in-law, although this last is observed with most varying degrees of nicety depending upon temperament. The avoidance between parent-in-law and child-in-law of opposite sex is of a minor character, carrying a prohibition against sitting next to each other, direct conversation, except in emergencies, and contact of any sort. In the tipi, it was conventionalized by placing the mother-in-law on that side which was farthest away from the son-in-law; today, if a man is driving his mother-in-law to town she will always sit in the back seat of the wagon or of the automobile. At feasts, men sit in long rows and women in opposite rows. This order is observed even at small family parties "because there is then no danger of placing a son-in-law and a mother-in-law next to each other." This taboo does not prevent the two from communicating through the formal medium of a small baby, however, and the mother-in-law does not hesitate to abuse her son-in-law roundly as a slacker and loafer, by remarking to the three-months' old baby in her arms, "Your father is no good. I am surprised at the way he goes on. Here he has cut no wood for a whole week. He does nothing but gamble all day long." And the man replies, again apostrophizing the unconscious baby, "Your grandmother is a mean, scolding, stingy old woman," etc. Such conversations are unfriendly and critical and lack any element of jesting. The father-in-law taboo is less stringent and mainly involves an avoidance of unnecessary conversation and all appearances of jesting. These avoidances are still in force. Occasionally, the marriage of a full-blood girl to a mixed-blood will cause her mother's behavior to be questioned by the son-in-law, but these slight changes do not affect the fundamental conservatism of the custom. One loud-mouthed and boastful youth remarked, in my presence, that if he had a mother-in-law, he would hug and kiss her. But as his wife comes from another tribe and his mother-in-law is safely dead, his boasting was greeted by half-pitying, half-derisive smiles from his auditors.

The joking relationship between brothers-in-law and sisters-in-law and between girls and their mother's brothers (and men and their sisters' sons) classificatory rather than blood, is still in full force, although the more formal usages of English tend to tone down the jokes when spoken in English rather than in Antler. There is some difference between these two types of joking relationships. With a mother's classificatory brother, a girl or a woman can act easily, she can go up to him and talk to him lightly before all the people, steal a feather from his costume, or nowadays purloin the nosegay from his buttonhole. She can tease him and during one phase of the war dance, the girls who are dancing who have "mother's brothers" among the seated war dancers may approach them and ask them to dance. This behavior comes under the category of jesting because of the very strict prohibition of any social give and take between members of the

opposite sex. With a sister-in-law, however, a man may take
almost any sort of conversational liberty. Under the sororate-
levirate system which formerly prevailed, they were potentially husband and wife — a man called his wife's paternal
aunt and his wife's brother's daughter "sister-in-law" also,
as they were also his potential wives, and a great deal of joking
follows very broad sex lines. It also takes the form of mock-
ing and ridiculing the joking relative in public, especially
when engaged in some solemn public function.[1] This is the
type of intimate kinship behavior which defies white influence largely because it is so incomprehensible to the white
residents that they usually do not know it exists.

The informalized, but very important rôle, of the grandparents has survived to some extent. In the old days, the
grandmother took much of the manual care of the children
and constituted herself instructress and chaperon of the girl
grandchildren. To the grandfather was reserved the duty of
telling the children myths with appropriate morals attached
and generally training them in manners and morals. The performance of these functions by grandparents is partly ex-

[1] The following are samples of such jesting:

Old woman at a ceremony calls out as her brother-in-law walks away after
accepting a gift: "Now why is he carrying those things in that white shirt.
Here I do my best to keep him clean and he goes and gets himself all dirty."

Old man to old woman: "Now I am going off in the car with my sweetheart.
Perhaps I will not have time to kiss my sweetheart." And in farewell, "Goodbye,
but I had no time to lie with thee."

Man to his sister's son: "I know why you're going to stay single. So you can
sleep with all the girls at powwow."

Woman to the brother of her brother's daughter's husband (i.e., he is the
potential husband of her niece and indirectly, her potential husband also.) "Why
don't you throw away that girl you have married? She is an old black thing with
Negro blood. I can find you a much nicer girl to sleep with."

Old woman at a hand game when her brother-in-law loses: "I am glad of that.
Let him sit down. I don't like to have him stand up in front of all those people."

Man to his wife's younger sister who is pregnant: "Children, come away from
her. Her belly is all swollen up."

Same woman to same man: "Here comes big mouth. Now we'll hear a big
story." Note how much freer the men are than the women.

Man to his wife's classificatory brother's daughter: "What do you mean riding
about with that white man?" (Her employer) "I don't like it at all. I'm jealous."

plained by the customs of hunting life. The father was away for days at a time during the winter season, and on the buffalo hunt he was too busy to give much time to his children. Similarly, the mother was kept very busy grinding, cooking, and dressing skins. The residence custom through which a daughter usually remained with her mother during the early years of her marriage and went home to her mother for the births of her children also served to make the grandmother, even though the grandfather was living, an important element in the children's life. The premature death of the men from war, hunting, or exposure left many widows in the prime of life who devoted much of their abundant knowledge and energy to the care of their grandchildren. As long as the daughter lived in her mother's tipi or earth lodge, it was the mother who kept the reins of the household management in her hands and also, to a large extent, the care of the grandchildren. The attitudes towards chaperonage also conventionalized the relationship between grandmother and granddaughter, because the chaperon was supposed to be the actual grandmother, or at least a woman of the grandmother's generation resident in the girl's family. Chaperonage by any older woman is not deemed sufficient. The old woman has to be, through a very close blood relationship or residence, involved in the preservation of the girl's virginity.

The grandfather's part in the grandchildren's lives is very unimportant today. Children go away to school and pass out of his hands just at the age when they would begin to understand the myths. There is no longer any need to train their minds to a proper receptivity towards supernatural experience. The sense that the past is gone, never to return, has fallen upon the old men and paralyzed their interest in educating the children. It is possible that when the present middle-aged leaders of Peyote become grandfathers the old pattern will be revived, for it is still vivid in the memory of the parent generation. Only now it is completely tied up with knowledge of the old times. A man will say, "I know much, for I had a grandfather"; or, "I had no grandfather, therefore I know nothing."

In aboriginal times there were two types of marriage, dependent upon the status of the contracting parties: marriage by formal agreement between the two kin groups, and marriage by elopement, which was subsequently ratified by an exchange of property between the kin groups. The wealthier or more privileged the kin groups concerned, the greater the likelihood of arranged marriage.

Arranged marriage took three principal forms: marriage in which the bridegroom or the bridegroom's father took the initiative, marriage in which the kin of the bride took the initiative, and marriages arranged on either the sororate or levirate principle where the husband or brother took the inheritance. The first form, i. e., where the initiative lay with the bridegroom's kin, took place between people of approximately the same social status. Through an ambassador, who was often one of the peace chiefs, formal solicitory gifts, of which the principal gift was a horse, were presented to the girl's kin. If the gifts were accepted, it was a sign of the favorable reception of the proposals of marriage; if, after deliberation, they were refused, negotiations were automatically ended. This formal request could be made without any courtship, or the youth who fancied a certain girl, whom his parents approved, might spend many months in an indirect courtship, before the final proposal was made. Strong objections on the part of the daughter were usually sufficient to make the father refuse an offer of marriage, and it was therefore prudent for a young man to do what he could to advance his cause. He was not permitted to call upon the girl, but he might visit her father or brother and sit beside the tipi fire, permitting his constant presence and his eyes to plead for him. There were also small stated ways in which a girl might betray favoritism, as at corn husking. Here a youth, if he found a red ear of corn, might carry it cradled in his arms, past the group in which the girl was working with her parents. If she favored him, custom permitted her to say, "What have you there?" Flute serenades were also customary. In the close village life, at dances, or ceremonies, there was sometimes time for a stolen word, a whispered promise, but this was all the courtship allowed. A boy and a girl might not stand together, or be seen talking together. Girls were brought up to be exceedingly fearful of men and were rigorously chaperoned in all situations where men might have approached them. Marriages arranged through an intermediary between the two kin groups were subsequently ratified by an exchange of property which was similar for all forms of marriage except the sororate and levirate type.

Where the initiative was taken by the girl's relatives they often had either higher rank or greater wealth than the youth to whom they proposed to give a bride. In the early days, this method of giving away a girl was used frequently to attract into the household young men of proved hunting prowess who, under the system of matrilocal residence, would be a real addition to the economic organization of the household. The supposition was that the girl's family had something to bestow upon the young man concordant with the abandonment of the usual procedure. Coupled with this assumption was a general obligation for the youth to accept the girl, but this was not always done. There is one case remembered in which a young man was told by his grandfather that one of his grandfather's friends wished to see him. He went to the lodge of the old man and was told that he wished to give him his daughter. The young man looked long and hard at the girl and perceiving that she was pregnant, refused. Soon afterwards the girl gave birth to a child; the old man was so outraged that the midwives had permitted the illegitimate child to live that he stamped about the lodge, finally stamping the newborn infant to death.

In the sororate type of marriage, the customary affinal exchange was abandoned, in tacit recognition of the loss of balance implied in polygamy. The reciprocal relationship between the contracting parties was symbolized for ordinary marriage in an exact return of gifts made, but when a man wished to marry a female relative of his wife, he merely presented her parents or guardians with a horse or other valuables, and they were obligated to no return. The acquisition of plural wives, although carefully regulated by the convention of the sororate, amounted to nothing more than marriage by purchase. There are cases reported where the husband first took unto himself the young relative of his wife and *afterwards* paid her father a horse, which suggests that this apparent purchase may possibly be more of an indemnity, after exercising a permitted license, than actual wife purchase. It is not possible to obtain any statistical statement of the frequency of plural marriage, but the genealogies and records suggest that it was infrequent, as much the result of accidental circumstances as of design, and not a definite way in which the rich and powerful showed their prestige. It has been suggested that the increase in wifely duties incident to the fur trade gave a great impetus to polygamy, but it is difficult to understand how this could occur without some corresponding depletion in the ranks of males, or some fundamental disturbance of the usual marriage age.

The levirate was less formalized than the sororate and no payment was involved when a man inherited the widow and children of a male relative. In contradistinction to the sororate, it was here felt that the inheriting male was rendering a service to the woman, and therefore to her kin, in assuming the responsibility of her care, and no payment was required.

Marriage by elopement was the common resource of unimportant young people, of young girls who feared that they might be bespoken by their sisters' husbands, and of young girls whose parents either favored a match to which they refused assent or else refused to countenance a suitor favored by the girl. The young couple ran away to the man's kin. It was the duty of the latter, if they approved of the marriage and if the parents of the girl offered no resistance, to provide a large marriage payment with which they accompanied the girl back to her father's house.

If the girl's parents refused to sanction the marriage, they forcibly retrieved her from the boy's home and, in some cases, direct punitive measures were undertaken by the male members of the girl's kin upon the property and even upon the persons of the bridegroom and his male kin. The likelihood of such occurrences served to deter young people from elopements which were not connived at by at least some of their kindred.

The genealogies suggest that marriage was brittle even in the early days. A high death rate in the middle years and the tendency to remarry, no matter how advanced in years one was, also serve to accentuate unduly the picture of many spouses. But it was distinctly felt that quarreling spouses should not remain together, lest they become habitual quarrelers, and earn for themselves a reputation which would prevent remarriage. Another potent cause for divorce in the old days was the attitude towards children. The death of a child was attributed to the mother's neglect, and the men felt the desire, the right, to have children, which is found so frequently associated with patriliny. The death of a first child was likely to disrupt a marriage unless the wife became pregnant soon after. Marriages were dissolved without legal formality and cohabitation with a new spouse constituted remarriage. The Antlers did and still do regard willing cohabitation which, through common residence or explicit statement, is made known to the public, as marriage. The absence, however, of the proper affinal exchanges, customary in the ratification of a marriage, was a matter for reproach and shame, especially among women. It was this custom of recognizing cohabitation which became known as "marriages according to Indian custom" and was declared illegal by the state of X.

Although dissolution of the marriage bond was simple, if

it was coincident with either spouse taking a new mate, much hard feeling, sometimes ending in blows, resulted. Adultery which was secret and which did not result in the desertion of the recognized spouse, was treated most severely. The outraged husband was permitted to gather his kin and go to the tipi of his wife's seducer, to rifle its contents and take all of the rival's horses. There is a moral tale told to young girls which well illustrates the ancient attitudes towards adultery.

"Once long ago, the tribe lived in a wide circle of earth huts near a creek. [I always think of it as having been down near that creek there below Macy]. There was a young girl who was given away in marriage although she loved another man. But she was obedient and she was faithful to her husband. But one day she met her sweetheart accidentally at the Spring. Someone told her husband and he beat her publicly with a bundle of raspberry thongs. Her brother was sitting on the roof of his mud hut quite a distance away and she cried out to him, "Brother." As he ran towards her he said to himself "I wonder who is going to hold me." When he reached them he struck his brother-in-law with the arrow which he carried and said "No one held you when you beat my sister. Now we'll see how you feel when nobody holds me." He killed the husband and left the tribe and part of the tribe went with him and part of the tribe, the relations of the husband, stayed behind. Those who went with him wandered far away and we believe they are the A—— tribe, for they speak a language like ours.

"We tell that to young girls and say, 'If she had not been faithful to her husband, if she had been meeting her lover she would not have cried out. She would have taken the beating silently and no one would have gone to help her if she had been guilty.' "

Besides the exogamic rules governing marriage as between gentes, there was an endogamic tendency controlled by the hereditary medicine societies. Because of the great secrecy with which it was necessary to envelop the paraphernalia of the societies and because of the sorcery and other malpractices involved, a spouse who was not a member of the society became a threat to the continued secrecy. The society teaching contains injunctions to marry within the initiated group if possible. There is also a strict rule that a husband and wife must never question each other about, or discuss in any way, society membership in which they do not both share.

Antler society is organized in a way which relies upon marriage not only to provide economically for the women and children, but also as an institution integrally related to the proper conduct of social ceremonials. The unit for a ceremony was a man and his wife, not a man and his sister, which is found so commonly in unilateral societies. In informal affairs where a wife was lacking, a woman who stood in the "sister-in-law" and consequently "potential-wife" relationship could discharge the social obligations incumbent upon the wife of the master of ceremonies. The only point at which husband and wife did not function socially together was in the medicine societies and the attempt to attain society endogamy sought to overcome even that.

As I propose to discuss present-day marriage in greater detail below, I shall merely indicate here the formal changes which have occurred in recent times. Matrilocal residence still obtains in a majority of cases, although today it is often interpreted as a search for a roof rather than a desire of the girl to remain with her mother. The stress placed upon the daughter remaining with her parents has shifted to an emphasis upon the wife's invoking aid for herself and her children and also, but less importantly, for her husband, from some one of her kinsfolk. The custom of giving a daughter away to a desirable son-in-law still exists, although now the bait is a dowry in the form of land rather than a difference in rank. With the decay of the societies, the old emphasis upon society endogamy has disappeared almost completely. The controlling social motive behind the regulation of marriage at the present time is economic. The old people still

insist upon exogamy, but they conveniently contrive to for-
get its dictates if a very advantageous marriage has been
contracted, and insist with great violence where they disapprove of the marriage for economic reasons. Each new marriage is viewed from two economic angles by each kin group:
will it withdraw income from the household by diverting it
to the spouse, the subsequent offspring, or the household of
the spouse, or will it add more dependent members to the
present household? These are the negative considerations;
actual addition of income or earning power is, of course,
regarded as a strong argument in favor of a given marriage.
The question of the withdrawal of income operates to prevent the marriage of minor children whose parents are living
upon the children's rent money. The state recognizes the right
of parents to permit or prescribe the marriage of minor
children and thus puts into the hands of the parents a powerful weapon for manipulating the children's affairs. A mother
who wishes to marry her fourteen year old daughter to a rich
fifteen year old boy can have this marriage legalized. But a
mother who has spent all of her own inheritance from a previous husband and who is supporting herself and her second
husband on the children's share of her first husband's estate,
will be upheld by the law when she time and again brings a
runaway daughter home.

The second consideration, the addition of dependents to
the family income, operates among the rich as much as, or
more than, among the poor. Wealthy families will try to keep
their daughters from marrying poor men; poor families,
where half a dozen people are trying to live on the income of
the rent from forty acres, will do everything they can to
postpone the acquisition of dependent sons-in-law. If the
daughters are minors, the law will be invoked, if they are not
minors, they will resort to subtler forms of pressure, the old
rules of exogamy, or to scenes, broken windows, forcibly
dragging the daughters home again, etc. The Antlers are still
at the stage of household organization when every individual

has important stakes in the marriage of a close relative. At the same time the controls, such as respect for parental choice, dependence upon parental ratification of marriage contracts, exogamic regulations, society endogamy, considerations of rank, are all breaking down and, except in the legal control over minors vested in parents by the state authority, these adults, who have so much at stake, are becoming more and more powerless to enforce their choices.

The two most potent influences which have undermined the elder's authority in marriage choices are coeducational schools and the state legislation against marriages by "Indian custom." The Indian mother relied upon cultivating such an extreme state of bashfulness, fearfulness, inhibition, in the growing girl, that there was very little danger that she would make any positive moves towards the other sex. Girls who were still virgins were so impressed with the evils which awaited them at the hands of men, that they could be counted upon to run away whenever running away was possible. The parents were able, in the compact life of the village or camp, to protect them against being surprised in lonely places where their very fearfulness would have put them immediately at the mercy of an attacker. So complete was this subjection by fear that the society did not have to make any corresponding educational points with its young men. A good girl blushed, giggled, fled. A bad woman was fair game for any man. No discipline, no set of standards were enjoined upon the young men who, like male members of many puritan societies, regarded rape as a great adventure. An observance of the rules of exogamy, caution where an avenging father or brother was feared, that was all. In this earlier condition of Antler society, loose women were of very infrequent occurrence and were almost invariably divorced women. Divorced, unchaperoned, without any decreed defender, and no longer wrapped in a mantle of modesty, the divorced woman was the legitimate prey of the young men, and usually passed from hand to hand, until she finally remarried and settled down again. Such women, always regarded as potential victims, were likely to incur the rage of the younger and more unruly elements in the society if they resisted their pursuers, especially if they were quarrelsome and vituperative. For such as these, the society had a cruel punishment, known today as "ganging up on" someone. A woman would be taken out by a gang of men, and after long and brutal abuse, turned loose naked, to find shelter as best she could.

With the growth of coeducational schools for mature young people, the Antler system of control broke down badly. The elders still acted as though the young girls were timid, frightened, afraid for their lives, ready to hide behind their mothers if a boy so much as whistled at them. But the girls trained in the Indian schools where the classes are coeducational, where the young people of both sexes are encouraged to meet at "socials," knew that boys were not strange creatures from whom one must run trembling, one knew not why. A whole code of love letters, joking, signals, was developed at school which could then be taken back to the reservation. Meanwhile the boys still grew up in the theory that any women who yielded to their advances to the extent of a whispered endearment or a hand clasp were potentially "bad women." No deterring influence, no new code, came to soften their attitudes during the generation when the protecting bashfulness of the girls was being worn off by the schools. As a result, young people arrange their own elopements, which sometimes do and sometimes do not become marriages, with a complete diregard of their parents' wishes, and the parents, who are still laboring under the delusion that the old code is in force, are baffled and uncertain.

But even with a breakdown in bashfulness and a resulting number of love affairs among the young people, the older people might have retained control through the need of ratification of the marriage. If no woman was recognized as legally married unless her husband's people had sent her home with elaborate gifts to her people, no amount of promiscuity before marriage need have threatened the system. But the passage of the state law declaring such marriages illegal crippled this type of control. Economic difficulties and confusion between the two sets of economic standards were already making these affinal exchanges hard to manage. A man would invite a youth to ride home with him, and on the way offer him his daughter, whom the young man would accept. He would then go to the girl's home. His mother, informed of the ceremony, would kill a pig and prepare a feast, summoning the relatives to make their contributions for the exchange. She would then set off for the home of her son's parents-in-law to fetch her daughter-in-law, and they, in pique, would refuse, saying they would bring the girl home with gifts instead. This they would do, but the bridegroom's mother, annoyed at not having her own way, would never return the presents. There was no law which could compel her to make the return gifts. Or a boy from a modern household would bring home a bride from a most conservative household. His father, believing the conservative family expected it, would take his best horses, his finest hogs, and take the girl home, only to discover that the conservative family had decided to class the return of such exchanges under the heads of old customs which they were *not* obeying.[2] This tendency to default, which was by no means the rule, but which occurred frequently enough to make everyone anxious about making the necessary outlay, played right into the hands of the new law. Furthermore, the Office refused to recognize these marriages as legal and, wherever there was property which could be used as a lever, insisted upon legal marriage. If there were enough property, the Office would also insist upon legal divorce, if there had been a break up of marriage. Nevertheless, in spite of the supervisory policy of the Office, there were many runaway marriages, there were many marriages with neither license nor ratifying affinal exchange, and a new dis-

[2] This reads as a confusion in writing perhaps; actually, the confusion is in the society described.

tinction was set up to which some of the more Pecksniffian
of the Antlers attended — between people legally married,
and those merely "living together." Meanwhile, some few
oldfashioned people continue to adhere to the custom of reciprocal gift giving, but this is becoming increasingly rare.
No young Antler need feel ashamed if his or her marriage
lacks such traditional sanction; with the increasing landless-
ness and resulting slackening of Office control, no young Antler need worry very badly over lack of legal sanction. There
remain no methods of coercing the young which are con-
sistently available to the uses of the old.

CHAPTER VI

RELIGIOUS INSTITUTIONS AND ATTITUDES

The present religious status of the Antlers, reveals, as does every other aspect of their culture, the result of loss, deterioration of the old, and inadequate understanding and assimilation of the new. A discussion of religious conditions falls under three heads: the aboriginal religious ideas which survive; the Christianity which they received some seventy-five years ago; and the Peyote cult which represents most closely the present-day religious faith of the majority of the people.

The aboriginal religion has been discussed in some detail elsewhere and I shall give only the barest outline here.[1] Orderly tribal relations with the supernatural were in the hands of a hereditary priesthood; the specific religious gifts which they conserved were embodied in fetishes of tribal, or at least supergentile, importance. These fetishes were intimately knit up with the political existence of the tribe; they were also conspicuous and therefore good targets for missionary endeavor; and furthermore, they bore most closely upon aspects of the tribal life which were abandoned — hunting and war, so that they were among the first parts of the Antler religious complex to be abandoned. Most of them were obtained by collectors, a few are still retained, without a knowledge of their ritual, often with but a slight appreciation of their significance, by descendants of the family lines which originally owned them. To the extent that these fetishes embodied the formal religious life of the Antlers, that life may be said to have vanished.

Less general in their significance were the fetishes which belonged to societies or to individuals by inheritance. These were of the type which are usually referred to as medicine

[1] For the material of this chapter I am almost entirely indebted to a recent account of shamanism among the Antlers.

bundles, composite sets of objects each one of which was either a memento of supernatural experience or concerned in the correct discharge of ritual obligations towards these mementos. To the latter class belonged pipes, paint, feather fans, tobacco boards, tobacco pouches, etc. To all of these sacred objects, as well as to the rituals which were associated with them, rituals composed theoretically of an account of the empowering vision or visions, and the songs obtained in the vision, the Antlers had a peculiar attitude which can be best characterized by the name for it used by a cognate tribe, *nonka*. This was the belief that any disrespect or neglect towards the fetish objects, any careless handling or idle repetition of the ritual material, any casual comment about sacred things, and especially, any untruth uttered about sacred matters, carried with it its own automatic penalty of disaster and death. In many cases there are specific provisions, the infringement of which result in punishment, and in these instances *nonka* may be likened to the familiar concept of taboo. Of such character are the rules concerning the proper conduct of the inhabitants of a house or tipi which contains an important sacred object; shouting, quarreling, the frolicking of children, are all forbidden here. But this concept is extended to account for the illness or death of anyone who has been talking about sacred matters, of anyone who treated the seven chiefs rudely, and even for less formal matters. For example, a daughter-in-law who has shamed her mother-in-law before all the people by giving her a poor serving of food, and who subsequently cuts her finger, will be said to have done so as an automatic punishment for her lack of respect. The Antlers have evolved no system of confession, propitiation, or atonement, by which the relentless working of the supernatural punishments for *nonka* can be diverted or prevented. As a result, the respect in which all sacred things are held is a vise in which the people are held fast, their tongues, their very thoughts, held captive lest disaster follow the slightest incautious move.

Of less general scope, but of considerably more vigor and actual influence, were the shamanistic societies which held in their possession the power to cause and cure disease. Membership in these societies was obtained by payment, usually combined with blood relationship, affinal relationship, or, less frequently, by sacrificing a sick relative into the hands of death. The uninitiated believe that membership in the societies came through a vision in which a supernatural appeared to the petitioning mortal and taught him the type of shamanistic trick peculiar to the particular cult. Young men were sent out to obtain visions, but only those who had the proper connection and requisite entrance fees joined the societies. The two most important of these societies were the versions of the Midewiwin: one, which contained the sacred chiefs, did no doctoring and used its supernatural power only to kill; the other, was a society of sorcerers who were believed to cause the diseases which they were called in to cure. Members of the societies were very much feared; an ordinary man would avoid getting down wind from them. They were rapacious; it was believed that they made people ill, not only out of vengefulness, hatred, envy, and malice, but also as a systematic extortionist scheme for obtaining wealth. The societies held semipublic performances in which their respective shamanistic tricks were enacted dramatically, and the uninitiated were thus periodically reimpressed with their supernatural powers.

There were also a large number of more or less unorganized free-floating attitudes towards the dead. Dreams of the dead were believed to be threats of death and the Ghost Society, one of the shamanistic societies, was called in to cure a person so afflicted. The ghosts of the recently dead were believed to exercise sharp supervision over the distribution of their personal property after death. Food and tobacco offerings were ceremonially presented to them at their own funerals and at ceremonies. Food was placed on the new grave and a fire maintained there for four nights by the mourners. Sometimes

the voices of new ghosts were heard crying at night and offerings of food were taken out to them. Ghosts were feared, but
mildly, except as they appeared in dreams to draw the living
towards death.

With this brief summary of the old religious ideas, let us
examine what has survived of the aboriginal religious attitudes and practices. The priesthoods have vanished completely; no tribal cult exists today. Most of the shamanistic
societies have disappeared. Four of these societies are represented by only one or two members each and never meet.
The chief's branch of the Midewiwin, although still boasting
a half dozen members, no longer meets or functions. But the
shamanistic branch of the Midewiwin, the sorcerers' society
which had as its distinction the ability to project missiles into
the body of a living person and magically extract these missiles, is still functioning. It has, however, no members under
forty, and shows every sign of dying out with its present
membership. In its decadent stage, two or three individuals
whose curing prowess is in grave doubt have joined it. There
survives, however, another type of doctors, the root doctors,
who were not organized into societies; each one of these possessed one or more magical roots, believed to have been originally given to someone in a vision, but which was obtained by
its present owner through purchase, usually from a relative.
Accompanying the root or roots, is the record of the vision,
in most cases, and in any case a recitation of the uses to which
it may be put. Less official than the root doctors was a type
of crude folk surgery by which the forehead of a patient
with a high fever was pricked lightly to let out the blood.
This was believed to relieve the headache. Individuals who
knew how to do this were, and still are, paid for their services. There is also another type of individual practitioner,
the baby doctor. These men were believed to be able to
understand the talk of infants a few days old and when
a child cried too much, they were called in to interpret
its meaning. They would declare that the child disliked its

name, or disliked comments which its parents had made upon its personal appearance, etc. The parents were ordered by the baby doctor to correct these difficulties. Only one such doctor is functioning today, a man who is a leader in many of the other religious activities.

There is also a sort of free floating black magic, which was formerly highly institutionalized and now survives only in the knowledge of a few members of the chiefs' branch of the Midewiwin and of the shamanistic societies. This is the black magic of the familiar Old World type, the powers possessed by any individual over another if he can obtain his hair cuttings, nail parings, urine, faeces, or earth from his footprints. In aboriginal days, this was formalized by giving the chief war priest a lock of every child's hair, which was tantamount to giving him power of life and death over every member of the tribe. It was also part of the stock-in-trade practice of the sorcerer shaman. Today it survives only in the practice of lovers, one of whom attempts to control the other by keeping a lock of hair. A man whose wife leaves him can then take her hair and scatter it in the dooryard, in which case she will inevitably become a loose woman and pass from hand to hand; or he can bury it in an ant hill where it will rot away and its former owner will rot with it. Women who plan to leave their husbands will search their husbands' possessions and try to recover all of their hair. Women are still careful not to urinate in an exposed place where a man who wished to seduce them could follow immediately. This may be the reason why newly married men accompany their wives even into modern latrines. Although no superstitions attach to food, there is still strong feeling about clothing which has touched the body, and two families living together will prepare and eat their meals in common, but will never wash clothes on the same day.

The belief in *nonka* still exists with, if it is possible to judge such matters, almost unabated intensity. Here and there in the tribe are sacred objects, bundles, pipes, pouches, drums, etc., which should be treated in special ways because they are sacred. In the old days they were hung from tipi poles, but the acquisition of a many-roomed frame house was a great boon to a nervous owner of a sacred object. This is placed in a trunk, the trunk locked and stored in an empty room, into which no one but the unfortunate keeper of the bundle ever goes, and then only to perform the necessary ritual acts of keeping the room clean and "feeding the bundle" — offering up food which has been ceremonially prepared. With the loss of ritual and function, these sacred objects are believed to be even more dangerous than they were formerly. Neglect of them brings paralysis and dementia and the people point to the members of the community who have these diseases and who have also possessed or handled sacred bundles for sale. There are also two white men in the community who used to collect old relics and who have been stricken with paralysis. The young people knowing nothing of the old religion, knowing nothing of the ritual, not even cognizant of the name of the bundle or the name of the society to which it belonged are still mortally afraid of it. If it descends to them, they regard it with superstitious awe and aversion and attempt to repeat, in the mutilated and truncated form in which they have received them, the appropriate observances. Many Antlers welcome the acquisition of these sacred objects by a museum, which they feel is equipped to deal with their deadly potentialities, an equipment which the Antlers themselves are believed to have lost with the death of their old men.

As they believe in *nonka* and the potentialities for evil of the sacred objects, so the young people do not doubt any other aspect of the old religion; they do not doubt that men once saw visions, although they no longer seek them. They are convinced that in the public performance of the sorcerers' society, the missile does pass through the air and into the body of the opposing member of a pair of dancers, that the dancer can then cough up this missile and supernaturally project it back into the body of his opponent who, in turn, falls down as if shot. These young people will pay no money to learn these secrets, they hope that no sacred objects will descend to them; they believe that many of the shamans are extortioners and evil, but they do not doubt the power which they claim to possess. The old religion is out of style, but its departure is hailed with no wave of skepticism. There is only one thorough skeptic in the tribe and he is a man of fifty. His thirty-year old son recently gave a feast to the sorcerers' society, to which both his grandmothers belonged, so thorough is the son's belief in the strength of the supernatural powers of these few remaining shamans whose practices his father has been rash enough to brand as mere trickery. The old religion has died then through the elimination of its forms, not of its spirit, through the progressive outmoding of its institutions, but without any diminution in the faith and fear of the younger generation.

Just as it was the most institutionalized and integrated aspects of the religious life, the priesthoods and tribal fetishes, which disappeared first, followed by the societies, so it is the least integrated, least formalized attitudes towards the supernatural which survive longest among the Antlers — the fear of *nonka* and the beliefs and attitudes towards the dead. Innovations there have been. The four-night watch to keep the fire burning on the new grave has been commuted to fewer hours actually spent at the grave, by the simple device of putting a well filled lantern there which does not have to be watched. Mourning has been elaborated to include setting a place at the table for the departed. The funeral ceremonial itself has been integrated with the Peyote cult and will be discussed in that connection. But the general beliefs about the ghosts remain pretty constant. Because ceremonies are conducted in a more slovenly fashion, because there is less property with which to give dignified mourning-breaking hand games, because solemn feasts occur less often, the food offerings to the spirits are reduced in number. But they are still thoroughly believed in. The conception of the ghosts as lingering near at hand, shadowy and insubstantial wraiths, preserving their human shapes and floating along just a little off the ground, has been modified hardly at all by Christian teaching. Although the ideas of heaven and hell are understood, the ghosts of the dead are still believed to be close by, perhaps at the very window.

Christianity was introduced among the Antlers in the middle of the last century. The first important missionary was a Mr. G., a Presbyterian, who learned the language, even wrote hymns in a phonetic rendering of his own, founded a mission school, and evidently succeeded in impressing his personality and point of view quite sharply upon the people. The tribe was converted with a remarkable and most deceptive swiftness, until by 1890 it was possible to say they were all Presbyterian. The old mission school and buildings fell into disuse, a new mission was erected nearer to Radner, a less energetic pastor, still paid by the Board of Missions, could be sent there on the assumption that the tribe was now converted and needed only routine pastoral care. The Antlers accepted the status of Presbyterians as they accepted the status of United States citizens; it was a part of the new order which was being ushered in with trumpets. It is very difficult to tell now whether there was any religious fervor of conversion, but it seems unlikely. The parts of the aboriginal religion which the Mission would have been able to distinguish clearly for opposition went down of their own accord, because of the change in ways of life and the break-up of the tribal autonomy. No one seems to have been sufficiently impressed, or to have understood the teachings of the Mission well enough, to feel called upon to repudiate the older points of view. The assimilation of Indian concepts to Christian concepts also helped to obscure the points at issue. The name used for God in the aboriginal religion had not indicated a being, but a power with many separate and not always beneficent manifestations. A hero of folk tale was regarded as the Antler equivalent of

Christ and a trickster animal was identified with the devil. The simple prayers once offered to the four directions, to the Sun, to the Four Winds, etc., needed very little revamping to fit into acceptable Christian patterns. The Antler swiftly picked up a certain amount of Christian patter which he could use to amplify his avowed Christianity. There is no pagan group on the reservation; there is no feeling that some men are Christian and some not; all are Presbyterians, including the man who sacrificed his sick wife so that he could enter the sorcery society free, and the old woman who trades in herbs which magically produce abortion and sterility. All declaim with orthodox disapproval against the Roman Catholics and protest that they will not send their children to the Catholic school of an adjacent tribe. All bury their dead in the Presbyterian cemetery.

But as they in no way recognize the discrepancies between their aboriginal religious beliefs and aboriginal religious practices, so neither do they feel any connection between Presbyterianism and any moral code. Attendance at church seldom exceeds fifty or sixty, and consists of a handful of people who find a close connection with the Mission profitable. Most of them live near Radner. Those who attend church regularly receive some benefits, the best share in the clothes which are sent to the Mission each year for distribution, baskets of food in winter, little extra loans and subsidies and as much work as the missionary and his wife can find for them to do. Attendance is, for the most part, a matter of friendliness to the Mission or pure self-interest. But among this scanty congregation can be found a man and his two wives, old shamans of repute, the berdache who acts as procurer for both sexes, the mother of an illegitimate child who is having a well known affair with a married man. A complete gap separates the realities of their lives from either the fiction that all are Presbyterians, or the immediate fact of church attendance.

The term "Christian" means a professing convert to the Pentecostal Church. Two newer sects have come in late years to dispute the ground with the Presbyterians, but with little success. These are the Latter Day Saints and the Pentecostal Church, more popularly known as the Holy Rollers. The Latter Day Saints built their church somewhat to the south of Radner and made a definite bid for a small neighborhood group. Their claims were reinforced by the attitude of the white membership, which stressed Christian fellowship and mutual helpfulness between white and Indian. The Indian membership of the Church is small, not too faithful, but fairly stable. It can best be summed up by the remark of one Indian woman member, "Yes, I belong to the Latter Day Saints. They are awfully nice people. Last week when we went down to our farm, the white people next door who belong to the Church too asked us all over to supper and they gave us three pecks of new potatoes." This Antler group is one which feels less antagonism to the whites and is content to blur over the differences between white and Indian ways. As another of them remarked, "Those Indians in Arizona are awfully old-fashioned Indians aren't they? We are just like white people. We have a cemetery and everything." Nevertheless, only a dozen or so families claim even nominal allegiance to the Latter Day Saints.

The Pentecostal Church has had a somewhat different history. Appealing to a poorer and more ignorant class of whites, the relationship to the Indian has been different. The whites were too poor to play benevolent missionary to their Indian brethren; also, if they were to have a church, they needed contributions of sand, etc., from Indian lands. So the Indian membership was originally cultivated and welcomed. The spectacular outdoor prayer meeting caught the imagination of many of the more unstable Antlers. The sheer uncompromising supernaturalism of the Pentecostal teaching also made a definite emotional appeal which the more staid Presbyterian creed had never made. A goodly number of Antlers went into it, but the most conspicuous disciples were those who for some reason felt themselves alien to the tribal life, women from another tribe who had married Antlers, the wife and daughters of the solitary and unpopular skeptic who had quarreled with one of the leading women in the local Mission, women who had been branded as "loose." Once the bare little church building was erected, the ingrained prejudice of the poor-white group appeared. They were not going to sit on the same benches as "the greasy Indians"; no, there was to be one side for whites and one for Indians. This, combined with the high demands upon morality made by the Pentecostal creed, was the principal reason for the dwindling of the group of converts, until there were only three families left, in each of which one parent was from another tribe. The daughter of one of those is particularly adept at public prayer. She was the only girl on the reservation whom I ever heard described as a "Christian" — this because she never went to dances or talked to boys.

Race prejudice has played less of a rôle in the better established Presbyterian Church. When the white population of Radner grew, they felt that they must have a church building of their own, a wish with which even the Antlers sympathized somewhat, realizing that the long interpreted sermons must be dull for those who did not understand the Antler tongue. This building has now been abandoned. Most of the poor whites go to the Pentecostal Church; the more respectable members of the community either do not go to church at all or they maintain a nominal connection with the Mission.

So the first decade of the twentieth century found the Antlers all nominally Presbyterians. There was no emotional value attached to their allegiance, no sense of the imminence of the supernatural, no compulsion toward any particular form of behavior. Meanwhile, their old religious forms had decayed and vanished. They were ripe to receive some religious stimulation which would be germane to their older religious attitudes and yet conform to their nominal professions of Christianity, which would be distinctively Indian and yet not "old-fashioned." The Peyote cult introduced from the Black Faces fulfilled all these requirements.

No detailed investigation of the Peyote cult was made at the time of its introduction among the Antlers. Our knowledge of the history of the cult in other Indian tribes suggests, however, that the Christian elements have been progressively more emphasized in order to forestall white criticism and government opposition. It will be possible here to describe the cult only in its present form. The cult centers about the worship of God and the Great Peyote, a large sacred piece of the peyote which is never eaten, but kept for ritualistic purposes. Membership in the cult depends upon the candidates' willingness to believe and embrace a way of life called among the Antlers, "the medicine road." The principal rule of the medicine road is a prohibition against drinking; gambling and illicit sex activities also come in for disapprobation. Without becoming a member of the cult, which is expensive, individuals may attend any Peyote meeting, for, contrary to the usages of the highly exclusive, hereditary shamanistic societies of the old religion, the Peyote cult is democratic and open to all. Devotees stress this element, self-consciously using the terminology of the evangelistic sects which have attempted to missionize them. It is the Indian Church, not a society, and all are welcome. Admission to actual membership in the society carries with it the familiar aboriginal requirement of cost — the candidate must feast the entire society. Leaders of the society are designated as those who have fireplaces. These individuals keep a Peyote fireplace and a special staff in their houses and serve as priests of the society. These positions are becoming hereditary, although piety and leadership, coupled with the necessary expenditure of wealth in feasting the society, may be sufficient to acquire a fireplace. The cost of joining the society is variously estimated as between one hundred and three hundred dollars, of acquiring a fireplace as around five or six hundred dollars. This cost all lies in giving the necessary Peyote meetings, which are held when someone is ill, at a funeral, or when a wealthy member holds one in thanksgiving for his recovery. Meetings are of two types, the formal public meetings to which everyone in the tribe is necessarily welcomed, and small meetings held by a handful of devotees who have been fortunate enough to obtain possession of a little peyote.

For formal meetings there are certain definite rules. There must be four of them, although under the stress of hard times, sometimes the meetings necessary to complete the count of four are indefinitely postponed. There are special cooks, the wives or other female relatives of the leaders of the society. For a Peyote meeting, there must be all new dishes, plates, cups, and bowls, and they must all be of white enamel. If one is doing the thing properly, one will purchase new cooking utensils also. The members are served in groups of twelve — in commemoration of the twelve apostles — in a separate tent. The meeting begins at evening and continues through the night. If it is a death watch, the corpse is brought into the Peyote tent and no one can leave the tent afterwards. If the meeting is for a sick person, he attends and is made to eat peyote and drink peyote tea. Peyote buttons are passed about, and each member, beginning with the leader, takes the gourd rattle and, shaking it to the accompaniment of the monotonous, stunning rhythm of the Peyote drum, sings four Peyote songs. The meeting finishes just at sunrise. Ecstatic outburst and violent expressions of emotion are not uncommon. The visions, which are principally visual, seem to have a prevailingly sad and prophetic character among the Antlers. The meeting is over just at sunrise and a woman brings in corn and water, and standing in the center of the group, gives thanks to the Earth for these two principal gifts to mankind. The corn and water are then passed about and each member takes four sips of the water and eats four grains of corn. Then candy is passed and each member takes four pieces. This is "the Communion." Afterwards breakfast is served by the women and most of the attendants at the meeting linger until the afternoon. Prayers are sometimes interpolated in this routine. The cooks are permitted to take home all the dishes. The bill of fare is prescribed and must always include meat, pie, and fruit.

In the days of the tribe's prosperity and the new introduction of the cult, meetings were many and generous; the supply of dishes and special foods cost a great deal of money. Single meetings usually cost a hundred dollars. In those days women used to attend, not only as patients, mourners, cooks, or jealous wives, but as active participants in the religious ceremonies. The observances of the cult took up a great deal of time. The long night vigils dulled the men and made them unfit for work; the meetings meant leaving home and neglecting poultry and stock. For a few years, the cult seems to have had the special popularity of a revival, combined with a new and satisfactorily Indian form of social organization. Poverty has undoubtedly played a chief rôle in diminishing the importance of the cult; it is to poverty and the consequent difficulty of obtaining the expensive imported peyote that the Antlers themselves lay the reduced importance of the cult. It is possible also that it has become assimilated, on the one hand, to the curing-society attitude, and on the other to the laissez-faire attitude of the Antlers towards Christianity. This latter effect follows almost inevitably from the efforts of Indian politicians to reconcile the cult practice of taking peyote — which reformers have repeatedly tried to have branded as a drug — and Christian practice.[2] Under inquiries

[2] The Antler woman who went to the state capital to defend the use of peyote before the legislature advanced the following argument. "You who are Protestants would not think of going to church without your prayer books and you who are Catholics would not think of going without your rosaries. The peyote is the prayer book and the rosary of the Indian."

A very intelligent and enlightened Antler man who had never been away to school gave as his opinion: "We Indians do not know how to read. Therefore, we have to take peyote so that we can see and understand God. The young people who are learning to read will be able to understand without using peyote."

A ne'er-do-well who had been in the Navy and tried almost every type of stimulant, opiate, and narcotic which had come his way, said: "Peyote, you can't interpret. It's not like dope. I've tried all kinds of dope. I smoked opium in New

in the state legislature and conferences with the government officials, Peyote has lost some of its glamor as it has been continuously revamped into a greater appearance of Christianity and respectability. A baptism service in which the child is baptized in peyote water has now been added.

Today, therefore, Peyote is not an absorbing interest of the people; it is a principal interest of not more than a dozen of the older men, although all nominally belong. The old-time large meetings at which all were welcome practically never occur. Instead, in the case of sickness or death, a few of the "strong ones" will be invited to a small meeting at which only one table of an apostolic twelve is seated. The formal meeting is thus becoming more like the old-time private meeting where two or three ate peyote and sang the songs. The Peyote drum is often heard at night, but it turns out to be two or three men merely singing the songs without any peyote.

York in 1918. Peyote's different. The first time I went in, I watched the leader and I did just what he did. Along about midnight I began to feel different. You see lots of things which would never be in your experience. If you want a real thrill, take peyote."

An Antler politician, rationalizing the position of the Indian in a way to please the white man said: "When the white man came to this country the Indian tried to find out what he came for and he told him he came to worship God as he wished and that he would teach the Indian everything that he knew. So the Indian and the white man smoked the pipe of peace. The white man tried to educate the Indian. He built schools for him, and then this peyote came along. It took the Indian way back, hundreds of years. Now the white man can't educate the Indian any more. So now we are going to get together and frame up some laws against drinking and gambling."

A white government official: "Peyote is first a cathartic and then it produces dreadful constipation: you'd never believe some of the awful operations they have to perform on Indians that use it. But they go right back to it. One woman told me that she saw the skies open and Jesus come right down and kiss her feet. The young men tell me that they see white women come to them. It's awful, keeps the Indian from advancing."

A man who had combined his enthusiasm for peyote with experimenting with each of the other religions in town and who habitually described himself as "in the church line": "Next year I think I'll give up peyote and farm. I would have been a good farmer now if it hadn't been for peyote. I think now that I like the Pentecostal vision better. I've been to all the churches except the Catholic. I wouldn't go to the Catholic Church because the priest would rape my daughters." The same man told me on another occasion that he liked to look at the colors in my bead bag because then he "would see them when he took peyote."

Women hardly ever attend meetings as mere religious participants; when they do, they are liable to be accused of wishing
to make a rendezvous with a lover. The attempts to keep
meetings quiet, private, within small kin and society groups,
grow stronger as the people become increasingly impoverished. Things have come to such a pass that a prominent
Antler, the owner of a fireplace and a member of the chief's
branch of the Midewiwin, had to sit for four hours on a
bench in front of the Radner store before he succeeded in
finding out the place of a Peyote meeting which he knew was
under way and which he wished to attend.

But with the dwindling importance of the cult as an active
religious body, as an institution, and as a moral influence, its
importance as a cure for the sick stands out more sharply.
Any Antler questioned about Peyote invariably mentions
cures, cures of pneumonia, of typhoid fever, of epilepsy, of
delirium. Faith in the old shamans and in the root doctors
was considerably tainted by the suspicion of foul play and
sorcery, or at least of the veniality of the practitioner. Peyote cures are expensive, but in a different fashion, and the
combined strength of a group of believers is consolidated with
the efficacy of the drug in curing the sick. With medical care
as uncertain a matter as it is at present on the reservation,
with no adequate field nurse, no baby clinic, an understaffed
hospital, and a diseased population, Peyote holds the field in
the faith and trust of the Antlers. As with all religious and
magical cures, only the successful cures or the failures with
good alibis are ever quoted. In cases of illness, the whole kin
group will strain every resource to put on at least one meeting of twelve to cure the patient.

The other rôle still played by Peyote is connection with
the funeral service. The old time Antler funeral services were
simple, often providing for quick interment, a kin group
matter. Now, unless the family are wretchedly poor, the services are entirely in the hands of the Peyote leaders. Very
often two or three meetings will have been held before the

death occurs, which is probably the way in which the death-watch and actual service came to be regarded as Peyote cult duties. But even if a meeting has not been held, a deathwatch of Peyote leaders will be called whenever possible. A "master of ceremonies" is chosen by the kin, and he, in turn, chooses gravediggers from among his relatives. The usual Peyote ritual is followed through the night. The next day, after all the mourners are gathered and the grave has been dug — in the Presbyterian cemetery — the funeral feast is served. (This is a feast in addition to the Peyote feast served to the watchers.) First, water is passed to the leader and then clockwise about the circle. Then the leader smokes a cigarette and passes cigarettes around the group. Finally, the feast is served. A little of each article of food is placed in a dish and set beside the corpse. Then the leader makes a speech, thanking his helpers, condoling with the mourners, speaking of the hardness of life. Some member of the family replies to this speech and many of those present promise small contributions of money to help with the expenses. The dish of food which had been set aside for the spirit is taken out and the food is scattered to the four winds. Then a pan of burning cedar is brought in and the leader wafts the smoke to the four directions and over the corpse with the eagle-feather Peyote fan. Then he gives a signal and all the men present — the women have been outside serving food — stand up and, beginning with the man on the leader's left, they march about the casket and file out. The leader remains and continues to waft the smoke in the four directions while the women enter, file about the coffin, wailing, clapping their hands and, in the case of a child, stooping to touch or caress the face. After all have passed out, the nearest of kin makes a brief speech to the ghost, enjoining upon it a hasty departure. At the cemetery it is the leader who throws the first handful of dirt on the casket and he utters a long prayer, another exorcism of the ghost, and also makes another speech to which a member of the kin group responds. Thus without bell, book, or candle, every Antler is buried, next door to the manse but without benefit of clergy.

The integration which has been achieved between the Peyote organization and mourning and funeral ceremonies is perhaps one of the most successful adaptations which the Antlers have made. There is only one Peyote marriage on record, but it is possible that if marriage had been as completely integrated as death, instead of being left to a broken-down social system and an ill-comprehended and unsympathetic civil form, the Antlers might have preserved a greater semblance of an ordered society.

CHAPTER VII

THE EDUCATIONAL SITUATION

Formal attempts at education, aside from the usual routine instruction of children in techniques, were confined among the aboriginal Antlers to myth telling, moral exhortation, training for religious experience, and initiation into societies. This type of Plains Indian education has been adequately described in the literature and it is not profitable to recapitulate here merely a secondhand account of it.

The primary contacts with the whites brought with them a large amount of instruction in the use of tools, guns, money, cloth, etc., but this was all of an informal nature. The first serious attempt of the intruding culture to share part of its tradition with the Antlers came when the old Mission was established. Here reading and writing were taught, but a greater emphasis was laid upon speaking English, upon manners, God-fearing ways of life, and practical handicrafts, especially for the girls. The white teachers themselves came from pioneer backgrounds and they taught the Indians soap making, new ways of preserving fruit and vegetables, simple cooking, and sewing. In the same way, the boys were instructed in the simple farming methods of the period. Almost contemporaneous with the old Mission school was the attempt on the part of interested and philanthropic people to induce Antler children to go East to school. With the transportation conditions of those days, it was a long journey, and children went away to Carlisle, Hampton Institute, or Philadelphia knowing that they would spend five or six years away from home. In the summers they were sent out to work in white homes, mainly the Quaker homes of Pennsylvania and New Jersey, and this experience formed the most valuable part of their education. The girls became acquainted with the details of cooking in a home, in addition to their contact with large scale institutional cooking at school. The boys were put on farms and many of them still have friendly memories of their long exacting summers. In a few cases, they worked a year or two after they left school before returning to the reservation. This group, those educated at the old Mission and those who went East to school, formed about 15 per cent of their generation. Unfortunately, their chance of becoming an influence in their tribe was marred by the fact that most of the children who went East were orphans, children of the poor, or children of aberrant and unpopular people who welcomed the coming of a new way of life. Among a people who were such sticklers for hereditary position and validated social standing as the Antlers, this bad start was bound to militate against them. Nevertheless this group provided a leaven in the community. They taught to the younger members of their families the techniques which they had learned; they kept in touch with the white people and often profited by their bilingualism. They were and are friendly to the white people under whose roofs they had been well received. This sympathetic attitude towards white people which was engendered in this small group of Indian children, thousands of miles from home, was due largely to the spirit of mildness and racial tolerance which was characteristic of members of the Society of Friends. The young Indians with whom they dealt came from a very simple and primitive background, many of their parents still lived in tipis and earth lodges; most of them still slept only on the floor; a nominal acceptance of Christianity went side by side with all the old observances. Yet the attitude of this generation stands out in strong contrast to that of the next generation — the present parents.

The present parent generation went either to Carlisle, after it had been routinized and become a large school under ordinary government regulation, or to one or two of the large new Indian schools nearby. Here they were taught by "employees"; supervised in laundry and bakehouse, shop, and dairy, by "employees"; herded together in large numbers; forced to mix with members of other tribes; compelled to spend several hours a day in exacting labor, using machines which they would never encounter again. Harsh methods of discipline were used after these had been outmoded in the white communities. The majority of the teachers in the schools came to their tasks without the sense of consecration which had characterized the Mission teachers and the Quaker households who had received the Indian children under the old "outing system." Formerly the Indian students had gone East into communities which had no day-by-day contacts with the Indians, no business dealings with them, which had found no reason to execrate them for their unlovely habits or condemn them as poor payers of debts. A school in such a community was very different from the Indian schools of the West, in the center of the Indian country, where the white people entertain such extensive disgust, contempt, indifference, or despair towards their Indian neighbors. Instead of being missionaries to a savage and bewildered people who had been rudely uprooted from their picturesque and glamorous past, the employees in the Indian schools were paid teachers and warders of a group of stubborn and unadaptable people who unaccountably refused to accept the benefits which a kind and indulgent government showered upon them. The Antlers' report suggests that the same conditions which prevailed on the reservation prevailed in the schools of this period which they attended. The schools were administered for the most part by a group of poorly paid, uninterested employees, who lived in constant fear of exposure and dismissal. The young Antlers under their care were a generation from savagery and yet they knew no English; they had nice frame houses which the government had built for them and wells drilled in their backyards and yet they refused to keep clean! The refusal of some groups of Indian children to keep clean — the Antlers are not among these because, under the old tradition of the sweat bath, they have kept up a high standard of personal cleanliness — begat a general laissez-faire attitude in the employees, and dirt and vermin spread through the schools. The Antlers complain that their children came home with hair and clothing infested with vermin, thus intensifying their parent's indignation at school conditions.

Furthermore, with a growth in sophistication, the Antlers acquired the point of view that the government was doing them no favor in sending their children to schools where they worked half a day and only went to school for three or four hours. "They earned their keep and then some." So, under the compulsory schooling, the location and type of school, the attitudes toward employees, and the resentment of the hard work done in the schools, a completely new attitude toward schools developed on the reservation.

At the same time the lack of articulation between conditions on the Antler reservation and school training became more and more pronounced. In the early days of the Eastern schools, the farming methods at school and on the farms where the boys spent their summers did not differ radically from those which they would find upon their return home. The comments of the men of sixty upon differences in agricultural methods in the East center about the habitual use of one horse instead of a team, or the construction of the much larger and more complex Pennsylvania barns. But with the growth of modern machine agriculture, the large Indian school attended by the Antlers sought to be a self-supporting institution by putting in more and more machinery. Milking machines, elaborate harvesting and threshing machines do the work on the great school fields well and quickly. The Antler boys, sometimes interested but more often sullen, have learned to operate the machines, but the knowledge is of no practical use to them once they have left school. They come back to the primitive unmechanized conditions of the small farms on the reservation, scornful and unprepared for farming.

Furthermore, the attempt to teach Antler boys trades in the government schools has provided them merely with egotistical talking points, not with practical programs of work. Men of thirty-five will tell one that they are stationary engineers, or electrical engineers, but of course there is no employment for men as skilled as they on the Antler reservation. Aside from the inadequacy of a training which has not fitted them to enter any of the trades, the names of which they can so glibly recite, it is peculiarly unsuitable for Antler reservation life. There is no room for any trade there; there is room for a knowledge of milking a cow by hand, of plowing and harrowing and cultivating a field, for the use of the simplest fertilizers, and for very simple carpentry such as would suffice to build a small frame house or a cow shed.

Conditions among the girls are not as serious as those among the boys. The girls are taught machine sewing, an art which their mothers all know from old Mission or Eastern days, or from contact with those who learned it. It is doubtful whether they could not have learned as well from their mothers, but at any rate they are taught at school. But here again, the institutional atmosphere, the need of making dozens of boys' nightshirts and hundreds of ugly little print dresses for the small children, makes sewing a sort of factory performance, without the individual touch or the interest which would make the girls pursue sewing with interest and enthusiasm after they return home. The cooking and cleaning are of very little practical use to them. I asked one girl of twenty who had spent six years at school if she could make bread. "Yes, in the bread-making machine." Although such training might be useful were the girl to go to a big city and seek employment in a large hotel or hospital, it is of negligible value in preparing her to be a home maker with her only equipment a wood stove and a broom.

As far as it was possible to judge from observation of women of different ages, there has been a steadily decreasing emphasis in the schools upon any sort of handwork other than plain sewing. The girls who went to schools fifteen and twenty years ago learned to embroider, to crochet, to tat — all sorts of handwork which could take the place of the porcupine quillwork and the beadwork which they were ready to abandon. Although much of this training vanished in the general disintegration and demoralization of the years of plenty, still it remains in some cases to provide employment for idle hands and to give some Antler women the prestige of winning prizes at the local fairs.

I visited one of the large Indian schools which the majority of Antler children now attend. There the formal instruction in the schoolrooms was even less related to the children's lives than was the work in shop and laundry. The curriculum is a watered-down version of a characteristic public school curriculum, with subjects like Latin removed. Every classroom is handicapped by the language factor and the discrepancy in age; sometimes pupils ranging from seven to seventeen are in the same grade. Antler children remain long enough to learn to read and write and to speak a formal sort of English. Hardly any of them learn to read a book or a story and enjoy its content. History, geography, physiology, pass over their heads, leaving only a few disconnected facts sticking there.

To return for a moment to the social atmosphere of the school, there are very definite features which militate against its educational value. It will be understood that throughout the discussion I am speaking from the Antler child standpoint, although it is possible that many of these remarks are applicable to children from other tribes also. The Antlers are most affectionate and kind to their children; little children accompany their parents everywhere and can always depend upon loving consideration, unless the parent is drunk or a stepmother, in which cases violent abuse sometimes is heard. At home, they may be dirty, hungry, and cold, but they are enveloped by a warm and intimate family feeling.

Furthermore, even for the very youngest children, there is great respect for private property. A father cannot sell or give away his child's moccasins, or the little string of beads which weigh down his small daughter's braids, without her express permission. The clothes of cousins living together in a joint household are washed separately by their separate mothers. Although the living conditions are often crowded and, to a white observer, promiscuous, nevertheless, a kind of intense, although attenuated, privacy is accorded each individual. From this happy, home atmosphere, where the children accompany their parents on every excursion to feasts and funerals, small girls of seven and eight are sent to the big boarding schools. Dressed in ugly long-sleeved dresses, with the hair which grandmother loved to comb cropped to a short and unsightly length; herded together in groups of forty and fifty and sometimes more, under the care of a matron who could not possibly love them all, even if she wished to — the change is a horrid shock. Older girls are assigned to help take care of them; this is a "detail"; the girls are afraid of the matron and anxious to get through their work; they have no personal interest in their small, frightened charges, who often cannot speak one word of English. Because of the fear of homosexuality, the older girls are discouraged from showing too much personal interest in the younger ones. The children sleep in row upon row of high, narrow beds, without individuality of any sort. Their meager institutional clothes are kept in lockers. They are provided with no galoshes and no mittens so that even outdoor play in winter is difficult.

As they grow older and move to the older girls' house, they are still allowed only a modicum of individual life and personal possessions. Only the oldest girls, who speak excellent English, are in an upper grade and show great promise, are allowed to live in a room with only three other girls and have their own possessions about them. Here again, their only social contact is with a matron. All contact with their teachers is strictly forbidden them; perhaps a merciful relief for the teachers, but also another rebuff to the girls.

The whole system works so as to leave their emotions cold, insulated against sympathy with their white mentors and teachers, if not actually imbued with resentment and hatred for them. They come back to the reservation sullen, rude, gauche, without any thought of attempted participation in white life.

There is one other feature of the Indian schools attended by the Antlers which produces particularly bad results — coeducation. The schools were founded in the Western tradition of complete coeducation; the classes are coeducational; the young people are permitted to meet at socials, weekly or monthly as the case may be. There is nothing in the system itself which is inherently vicious and yet it produces a great many unfortunate results because of the background on the Antler reservation. The whole Antler sex policy is based upon bringing girls up to be modest, frightened, abashed in the presence of boys, chaperoned carefully whenever they are likely to encounter boys or young men. The boys and young men grow up believing that any girl caught alone is fair game. Just as European women are helpless in the face of attempted rape, so Antler girls are paralyzed when left alone with a boy. Coeducation changes this whole setting. The girls and boys mix freely. Their protective coats of shyness wear off. Surreptitious affairs start at school through the medium of notes, hints, glances. Once back on the reservation, the stern chaperonage and harsh rules of school are gone; the parents still trust in the blanket of modesty which their daughter should have, but have not; the young boys slip easily into the traditional Antler attitude that all's fair in the chase. The result is that each summer a new group of school girls enter a life of light dissipation, from which they return to school to excite the minds of the younger girls with their tales, or which proves so amusing that they do not return to school at all. Many of them drift into early and unstable marriages. If they do return to school, their scholarship and discipline suffer from the memories of the summer. Meanwhile, the parents blame the school, aver that the minute the girls come home from school they start "running around" so that the training at school must be at fault, while the school insists that before the girls left school they had committed no sex offenses and that the loose conditions of Antler reservation life are to blame. Both are in some measure right. The school has broken down the girl's fear-dictated modesty, detached her sympathy and affection from her parents, made her regard discipline, not as an integral part of life, but as a hostile force to be circumvented whenever possible. The parents have failed to realize the situation and have not devised any ways of meeting the changes, either by a different education for their boys or more protection for their girls.

But the life of the upper grades in the school is disrupted by the past, brewing, and future love affairs of the boys and girls of eighteen who are still in school because of their late start and language handicap, who are mature beyond the power of schools to hold them.

About ten years ago the government inaugurated a policy which was pursued with increasing emphasis until this last year — a policy of encouraging Antler children to go to day school with white children. This effort was carried even to the length of having a special officer inspect the Antler reservation and declare certain families of children ineligible for attendance at the government schools, because of adequate finances and proximity to a district school building. This move greatly added to the number of children who were attending district schools. The Federal government paid a subsidy varying from about twenty to thirty cents a day, for each Indian child, according to the class of school. This subsidy was supposed to recompense the localities for the expense of educating children whose parents owned lands exempt from taxation. The reality of the situation, that most of the Indians now live upon the proceeds of leased lands, the taxes of which help to support the local schools, is largely ignored. A computation of the present financial condition of the school in Radner showed that the government subsidy for the Indian children was almost exactly equal to the cost of the augmented teaching force necessitated by the additional number of children. The white children in the community therefore benefit by the presence of the Indian children to the extent of a narrower grading in the schools; they suffer inasmuch as the Indian children provide an unwieldy classroom element, owing to their language disability. The Federal government makes no attempt to dictate the policy of the school, to raise the requirements for teachers, or to insist upon a greater proportion of handwork or emphasis upon language.

The Antler children who go to school in Bergen are in such a minority that they really benefit from contact with the white children to the extent of learning to speak English. Where there are more Indian children, as in Radner, or in the town of the Black Faces, it is a little more difficult to evaluate the amount of education which the Antler children receive in the day schools. The same condition of great discrepancy in age and maturity exists in the local schools as in the classrooms of the government boarding schools. This is true not only of the Antler children, but also of the white children. The poor tenant farmers who lease the Indian lands move frequently. Their children change schools, sometimes every year, and are out of school much of the year owing to the condition of the roads and inadequate truancy supervision, so that there are a great number of retarded white children in the classes and the general impression of discrepant ages is as great as in the Indian schools. The Antler children are not therefore under special disadvantage because of retardation which renders them conspicuous. But the language factor does, of course, play a greater rôle in the day schools, where over half the pupils speak English as their native tongue, than it does in the Indian schools. The handicap which the Antler children suffer in competing with English-speaking children in the learning of school subjects is perhaps compensated for by the greater command of English which they acquire on the playground and in the daily contact with white children. The Indian children also change schools; they not only change from one day school to another, but also go away to boarding school a year, come back and go away again, hopelessly breaking up their educational progress. But perhaps the greatest objection to the attendance of Antler children at the day schools is the truancy situation. Despite the fact that the Federal government pays for each day on which an Indian child attends school, so that once the initial expenditure of adding to the school staff has been made, it is decidedly to the advantage of the local authorities to keep the Antler children in school, the truancy laws are not enforced.

This is due to several causes; the condition of the roads, the general demoralization of local politics in the county, the fact that the truant officer receives inadequate compensation, and the general filibustering tactics employed by the Antlers. The state of the health of the Antlers is so poor that their chronic ill health, combined with the results of exposure, inadequate clothing and insufficient nourishment, gives any parent a ready excuse for not sending a child to school. Furthermore, the Antlers' custom of taking their children with them wherever they go, means late nights for the children at hand games, gambling parties, and feasts; and children and parents sleep until noon the next day. The letter of the law is satisfied if the child appears at all; the teacher soon loses interest in children who are habitually tardy and unprepared; the child does not pass his grade, which disgruntles the parents who are all alive to the varying prestige of "low and high grades." The parents' lack of interest in getting the child to school is stiffened into active resentment of the school or of the particular teacher in question.

One further reason for the lack of control of truancy is the divided authority. The Federal government maintains supervisors of education who are supposed to combine the supervision of the children in the government schools and of the children in the district schools. As this supervisor must cover a very large territory and supervise children from several reservations, the supervision is neither very close nor very painstaking. It is sometimes a month or two before the supervisor gets around; in the meantime, the local truant officer can shrug his shoulders and wait for the Federal truant officer.

Since the government policy of sending the children to the local schools was inaugurated, there has been great dissatisfaction on the Antler reservation. Although previously there had been plentiful resentment against the insistence upon the boarding school, deprived of the right to send their children to the boarding school, the Antlers chose to regard themselves as deeply wronged. A vested right had been taken from them.[1] The root of the objection to keeping their children at home in the district schools is economic. The winter is the most difficult period for the Antlers to get through. Bad gardeners, improvident, shiftless providers, many households have very little to last through the winter. The privilege of sending four or five children off to be housed, fed, and clothed by the government represents a considerable item in the family budget. The unkind among the white critics also remark upon the saving in work when the children are away and the fact that there is no need for the mothers to get up in the morning. Although there is doubtless some truth in this last criticism, the actual relief of knowing that at least some of one's children are completely provided for during the entire winter season is undoubtedly the most important mo-

---

[1] "I don't want my child to go to the common day school with the children of renters. The children of renters use awful language. I don't want my child to learn such things."

"I went to government school and I want my children to go to government school."

"The government school belongs to the Indians."

tive. Quite characteristically the Antlers rationalize this fundamental motive into a prestige point. It was their right as American Indians to send their children to special schools which did honor to their race.

In the autumn of 1930 the Federal policy was reversed and there was a great effort made to send as many children as possible away to the boarding schools. Some of the country schools had no Indian children and there were only about 20 per cent Indian children enrolled in the town of Radner.[2] Considerable pressure was exerted to induce indigent Indian families to send their children away. Immediately public feeling veered. All the tales against the government school were remembered and recounted over and over.[3]

To summarize the actual school situation: Attendance at the local schools is so poor that the children learn very little, but the local schools provide an alibi against sending small children away to school. This alibi and the badly enforced truancy laws, coupled with the plea of ill health, combine to keep Indian children out of school until they are eleven or twelve. Entering school at this age, they stay only three or four years, only getting through the second or third grade. By this time they are physically mature and caught up in the reservation life. The local schools make very little impression upon the children except as they learn English from their white playmates. The government schools harden their spirits and breed resentment and dislike of white people and white ways, at the same time that they spend years in teaching the

[2] It is impossible to give accurate statistics here. I left the reservation during the second week of school and no registrations, either for government or local schools, were complete. Also many of the registrants would practically drop out in a month or so, if this year follows the usual pattern.

[3] The tales were told of the homesick boys who were not allowed to come home for vacation and who tried to steal a ride home so that one boy lost both his legs and later died; of the girl who was sent to school but never arrived, and the parents who did not discover she was not at school until a year later, the girl herself ultimately turning up as a prostitute in a near-by city; of the child who was silly from a blow he had received from an iron crowbar wielded by an employee; of the lack of care at school; how sick children were allowed to remain in the dormitory, etc. etc.

pupils techniques which will be of no use to them when they return to the reservation.

The language situation on the Antler reservation is peculiar. The best English on the reservation is spoken by a few old people who had many years schooling in the East. A few of these people are very sophisticated linguistically. Perhaps the most conspicuous case is a woman of sixty-five who for many years has acted as interpreter. She still delights in new words and the refurbishing of her vocabulary.[4] From these older people, there is a steady revision downward of ability in English. There are many young people of twenty who speak hardly a word. There are hardly any children under six and seven who can speak English, although a few understand it. There are only two Antler homes, where both the parents are Antlers, in which English is spoken to the children; from one of these, two of the sons have been adopted by a conservative uncle and speak very little English. In the homes in which one parent belongs to another tribe, English of a sort is spoken between the parents and consequently understood by the children. But even in such cases, the initial advantage is sometimes lost. Gains in speaking English are continually lost because of the greater vitality of the Antlers' speech on the reservation. Statistics presented in government reports concerning the English spoken on the reservation have been very misleading, because they have been presented in terms of a percentage of Antlers over fifteen who did not speak English, ignoring the fact that the English spoken by the children, nominally in attendance at school, is often of the most rudimentary sort. It is safe to say that there are not more than a dozen people on the reservation who do not al-

[4] One story is told of her which is characteristic: A prosecuting attorney, in a case in which she was interpreter for the defense, sought to attack the case of the defense by questioning her linguistic ability. (A common and stupid device endlessly resorted to by lawyers in this part of the country.) He said: "You say you understand English?" Said she: "I hope I do, Sir." "Then tell me the difference between the words *intelligent* and *intellectual*. Her answer came back like a flash: "It would take a very *intelligent* person to answer so *intellectual* a lawyer as yourself."

ways think in Antler and speak it preferentially whenever possible. Many of the children of the mixed marriages where English is spoken, understand but speak no English until they are five or six, if their mother and their mother's female relatives are Antler. The language of the reservation is still Antler, even if the banter of the young people contains occasional stock phrases such as "Oh Yeah" from the Talkies.

The English which is spoken has various stock peculiarities. The plural of "man" is always "mens," the plural of "woman," is "womens." In the speech of those whose English is very scant there is the characteristic omission of particles; confusion of tense, number, and case, occur in almost everyone's speech, and gender is continually wrongly assigned. There is also another characteristic of Antler English which is rather difficult to account for. There are young people who have learned to speak English and to read and write in the public schools; and who usually speak passable English in which only an occasional incongruity grates upon the ear, which are more often than not mere mistakes in grammar in no way characteristic of the Indian. But when they come to write letters, they revert to a purely Antler type of construction, abandoning tense, neglecting plurals, bandying gender about with complete disregard of the rules. It is strange that the compulsions of the Indian syntax have ceased to operate in the spoken word, but should still hold such sway over the written English of children who have never read nor written any language except English.

Although many Antlers know how to read, reading for amusement or for information is practically nonexistent. Antlers occasionally buy a highly illustrated magazine; newsdealers report that the only magazine which they can be said to patronize is the *Billboard*. This is explicable in the light of the Indians' view of themselves as stock figures in the show world. One woman in Radner, who belonged to a cognate tribe however, read *True Stories* and when complimented upon her knowledge of English said, "I get my education out

of the *True Story* magazine." The illustrated papers, the rotogravure sections of the Sunday papers, and the comic papers,
are as popular as actual reading matter is unpopular. All
pictures are scanned with great attention; an old comic paper
will be passed from hand to hand, and a picture supplement
kept in the tribe for months.[5] The perusal of mail-order cata-
logues is not so popular a pastime as it is said to be on many
reservations.

The Antlers' knowledge of economics and finance is as
special and as uncorrelated as the knowledge of a child who
knows the route to and from school and to and from the
grocery store, but is not able to read street signs or follow the
simplest directions. They understand the method of borrowing money by signing a note and having a friend go surety
for payment; they understand the concept of interest to the
extent that they know that one pays someone to lend one
money, but they have no idea about rates of interest or that
it is exorbitant to pay one dollar a month on a loan of ten
dollars. They know that taxes use up their lease money and
that Indians who have had land have lost it because the taxes
have piled up and eaten it up, but they do not understand
which land is taxed and which not, or why. They understand the principle of a mortgage as a way of getting money
upon something not immediately saleable, like a corn crop,
or not legally saleable like restricted land — on which unscrupulous persons will sometimes take an unlawful mortgage. They understand sale, exchange, wills, and deeding of
property, although the rules which govern their actions in
these matters belong to the old Antler set of economic ideas.
There are still some old Indians who understand so little of
business methods that they can be made to sign almost anything. They also understand special legal tricks like the me-
chanics of getting a "buy" on a bootlegger, of mortgaging

[5] From a tipi, a barefooted Antler woman once produced a three-months' old
rotogravure section and demanded the meaning of a picture which proved to be
a reconstruction of the appearance of some spiny-backed prehistoric monster.

one's car to a friend so that it cannot be seized for debt, or of evicting a tenant after he has put in and cultivated a good field of corn and is then discovered to be bootlegging. But all of these are separate pieces of information, like a knowledge of the location of different slot machines possessed by one who has no knowledge of how slot machines work or of how many more slot machines there may be. The Antler is especially ignorant of the value of money and of ways in which money may be conserved. No principle of investment or insurance has ever appeared on his horizon, and in many cases mere saving, although known to be practised by white men, is regarded as a strange and fantastic type of behavior. The very complexity of some of the economic transactions in which they have become involved tends to plunge them deeper into genuine economic ignorance. The outsider cannot credit the fact that an Antler who speaks familiarly of "putting his name on a note" will still believe that a bag of flour worth a dollar and a half is a gift more deserving of gratitude than is a two dollar bill. The Antlers were permitted to assume the trappings of complete responsibility before the value and use of money had been taught them; in the same way, they have learned to pronounce long English words while still thinking in Antler. The whole situation is a caricature of any genuine educational adjustment to the demands which white contact have made upon them.

PART II

THE INDIAN WOMAN: HER PLACE
IN THIS CHANGING
CULTURE

CHAPTER VIII

THE DEGREE TO WHICH WOMAN PARTICIPATES IN THE CULTURE

In discussing woman's participation in the Antler culture, it is necessary to remember the peculiar nature of women's place in culture the world over. With conspicuous exceptions — as when women are debarred from cooking on account of ceremonial objections, as among the Todas, or robbed of the more pleasant task of rearing their two- and three-year old children, as among the Manus — the daily routine of cooking, care of the house and care of the children, is left to the women in most societies. Although these activities are, it is true, given a definite culturally-defined form in every society, and one can place the culture to which a given cook pot, hearth broom, or cradle board belongs, as surely as one can place a bow and arrow, a canoe paddle, or a ceremonial mask, nevertheless the essential content of childbearing, child rearing, and the daily tasks which are involved in providing for the current domestic wants of a household is very similar the world over. A woman from another culture can enter a primitive society and, as soon as she can speak a few words, can find a hundred points of interest to discuss with the native women. It may be months before a man can establish a similar rapport because the white male investigator has first to get by heart the peculiar cultural preoccupations which distinguish one culture from another and which are of so much more importance to the men than are the routine affairs of domesticity. For this very reason, the breakdown of culture is almost always of more vital concern to the men than to the women. The old religion, the old social values, the old braveries, and the old vanities may be taken away from the men, leaving them empty-brained and idle-handed, but the woman must continue to bear and nurture children, to cook the dinner, sweep the house, and wash the clothes. It is impossible to strip her life of meaning as completely as the life of the man can be stripped. (There is only one condition under which culture contact may bear more dangerously upon women than upon men — where their sex is exploited by the invader. As this condition does not obtain among the Antlers, it need not be considered here.) So that when I discuss the rôle which women played in the sum total of the old culture and the new, it must be understood that the vanished traits of the old culture played a relatively smaller part in their lives than they did in the lives of the men.

Economically, in the aboriginal culture, women played a background part. The principal ceremonial, the chief interest of the tribe was focused upon hunting, the buffalo hunt in the summer and the individual hunting in the winter. Meat and furs were viewed as the principal economic goods. Inconspicuously, for the Antlers had no women's societies where counts were given on the basis of number of tipis sewed or robes embroidered, the women worked up the materials which the men brought from the hunt. They cut up and skinned the animals; dressed the hides, and made them into clothing, bedding, and tipis; dressed the meat, and made it into dried meat, pemmican meal; dressed the guts, and made them into thread and cord. They planted and harvested the maize and other vegetables; they gathered the wild fruits and berries; they gathered the beans and the nuts. Although the foods which they grew or gathered were never regarded as the most important parts of a meal, they were, nevertheless, the least perishable, the most dependable, the foods which kept the people from starvation. After the introduction of fur trading, the work which the women did on the skins came more into the foreground, for their proper dressing was as important as was originally securing them in the hunt. But primarily women's task consisted of upkeep work and manu-

facturing for domestic use. The men made the war costumes
and the ceremonial objects, so that women were allowed very
little artistic expression, beyond placing conventional and
rather meager designs on moccasins and robes.

The degree to which the aboriginal Antler women achieved
other than this routine generic rôle in their culture depended,
as has so often been found to be the case, on rank. The original lines of demarcation between men and women were cross-
cut by the lines which divided the families with important
hereditary, religious, and secular rights from those families
which were not so privileged. This influence of rank expressed itself in three ways. Rank gave importance to daughters and, more incidentally, to wives, of chiefs as a way of
ornamenting their male relatives' achieved rank. This was particularly so in the "Society of Those Blessed by the Night,"
of which the women members were those female relatives who
had been tattooed on the strength of the male members'
"counts." Daughters could inherit and pass on membership
in some of the religious secret societies. A man also occasionally bequeathed some of his religious privileges to a son-in-law,
thus elevating his daughter to a position of importance on the
road along which these privileges passed. In all of these the
enhanced importance of the women was merely a function of
the position of fathers and husbands, although when actual
society membership resulted a woman might nominally exercise important rights for many years.

But the absence of any women's societies, or of any attempt
on the part of the women to consolidate or even specialize
their greater participation due to superior rank, is significant.
Meetings of wives of chiefs are referred to in the old literature, but they seem to have been unimportant and nonauton-
omous. The one time when women did participate as a group
was in the "Society of Those Blessed by the Night." Here
rank among the women members was preserved as meticulously as among the men members, but the rank of the women
depended upon the order in which they had been tattooed

and upon the amount of tattooing which they had received, and these were both determined by the counts which had been accumulated by their male backers. The last hereditary tattooer died some twenty years ago; his place was taken, for a time, by a pretender who abandoned the old method of tattooing and used India ink. Between the women tattooed in aboriginal fashion and those who were tattooed by the upstart there is considerable individual bickering, but no definite alignment of the old members and the new has occurred. The society has now practically disintegrated, and there is no place in the aboriginal culture in which a group of women participate as women.

Women neither sought, nor were ever believed to be vouchsafed, the vision. There are a number of religious societies among the Antlers, entrance into which is theoretically based upon the obtaining of the vision appropriate to the society. Although there is disagreement between the two old authorities on the tribe, it seems probable that few women ever belonged to these societies. The authorities agree in mentioning only two women members. On the other hand, women did belong to both branches of the Midewiwin, and in both their position was frankly recognized as hereditary and people spoke of their "having taken the place of father, or sister," etc. This was so despite the fact that, although membership in the chief's branch of the Midewiwin was recognized as hereditary, membership in the sorcerer's branch was currently supposed to depend in many cases upon an individual revelation of the shamanistic tricks involved. In the case of women, however, whose membership in any religious society was merely a function of rank and in no way the result of a quest for supernatural power, all pretense of any mode of entrance except inheritance had to be waived.

The women's rôles within these two societies were pallid versions of the men's rôles. Their sex merely invested them with certain limitations; they were never grouped together as a woman's branch or women's party within the society; they had no distinctive parts to play. Women were not allowed to rise to the heights in the society which were dignified by a remission of the need to fall down, when shot in the society pantomimic dance with the magic missile. Women could shoot in the dance and be shot, but they always had to fall down and extract the missile from their bodies, by a pantomime of coughing it up. In the last year one old woman, who is a member of the sorcerer's society, the widow of a man who had died suddenly, has taken upon herself to remain standing and merely stagger as do the men of highest rank when they are hit. As the society is disintegrating and there is no longer any discipline, no one has done anything about this except to comment disapprovingly. She is a redoubtable old woman and her move seems to be merely of a piece with the way in which women are speaking up in the tribal councils, no longer afraid to talk aloud if men are about.

Most importantly, however, women were debarred from any real exercise of their nominal religious functions. Members of both branches of the Midewiwin could shoot to kill. Although the chief's branch exercised this power only as execution, the sorcerer's branch were doctors also and magically extracted the missile which they had magically injected into a victim — for a price. Women could not kill, cause illness, or cure. In the society dances they went through the pantomimic magical combats, but these could be given no reality in their lives.

When we come to discuss why society membership should have been given to daughters rather than to sons, the question is difficult to answer. The Antlers explain this with their customary gloss of the facts, as a father's lack of approval of his sons. A father is pictured as watching his sons, and rejecting one son after another on counts of irreverence, lack of filial piety, or lack of intelligence. It seems clear that this picture of a father's hesitating before bequeathing his special religious secrets to his sons is merely a rationalization of the conflict between generations implicit in the belief, which is also held, that a man dies when he gives up his secrets. But it does seem to be true that there was often considerable strain between fathers and sons over questions of inheritance; sons also have been known to refuse the onerous burden of society membership with its known penalties that one's wife and children would die before one. Sometimes also sons went away to live in their wive's households and sons-in-law supplanted them in their father's affections. When a man bequeathed society membership to a son-in-law, he sometimes bequeathed it to a daughter also, which was one way in which women entered the societies. Also a man might, on dying, have no sons alive or none near him, and then he would pass on his secrets to his daughter. Women, in recent years, have in several cases selected women as their successors, which is natural enough now that society membership is so much a matter of sentiment about the dead, rather than active functioning in the culture. The very features which made women less logical members in days gone by make them the most logical beneficiaries now, because the men have been drifting so much further from the center of the culture than have the women, less disturbed in their more routine, background position.

Another way in which women became heirs to religious secrets was through acting as assistants to aged and decrepit male relatives who needed help in practicing their doctoring arts. In the case of root doctors, anyone helping a doctor had a right to demand the secret of the root which was being used, and in this way women came into possession of various minor magical curing procedures based on roots. The roots used in the various aspects of childbirth, to produce miscarriage or barrenness, to insure an easy birth, to stop hemorrhage, were for the most part, but not completely, in the hands of women. These same women acted as midwives also. However, the old woman from whom I received the four roots which she used to produce barrenness had received the formula from her father, and she brought her husband with her to the medicine feast at which she ceremonially recited the history of her knowledge and passed the roots on to me. In thus bringing her husband she adhered to the customary pattern of a doctor's bringing his wife and children when he is asked to treat a patient.

The one way in which women acted as a group socially was in the formal games. Women played games as groups in which men did not participate, this was particularly true of the peach-stone games. Authorities differ on the point, but it seems most probable that women did not take an active part in the large ceremonial hand games in which there was extensive betting. On the other hand, it is very possible that women did join in small hand games and that their conspicuous participation today is an outgrowth of this earlier and slighter rôle.

The society was exceedingly precise in its definition of the ways in which women could participate on any given occasion. Women, as a group, were required to stay together, to sit and talk and eat together, at public gatherings, and never to mingle casually with the men. On the other hand, wives and daughters might perform special public acts by virtue of their relationship to some male. Thus the wife of the master of ceremonies, the wife of the host, the wife of the shaman, the wife of the owner of the medicine bundle, the wife of the man who was giving away property in the ring (or lacking a wife, a sister-in-law or a daughter) was permitted to play no mean rôle in the ordinary social intercourse of the tribe. By not organizing women in any way, by permitting them only individual rôles in relations to men, the society more effectively prevented women from exercising any power than if it had forced them to organize by segregation and denied them the slight trappings of courtesy rôles.

The coming of white civilization found then the position of Antler women defined as follows: They were permitted no religious privileges except such as came to them through rank and inheritance, and these they simply held rather than exercised; they were not trained for nor expected to have any religious experiences; they played no public economic rôle beyond forming occasional gift-exchange friendships with women from other tribes; they played no political rôle except such as was enjoined by considerations of etiquette upon the wives of chiefs; they owned no property beyond the tipi and a few household possessions and possibly an occasional horse; they were expected to obey their parents' wishes in marriage and to conform to their husband's preferences after marriage. At all times their behavior was to be meek, modest. They were expected to walk a few paces beyond their men and never raise their eyes from the ground.

Coupled with this limitation of social, political, religious, and economic rôles, went a theory of the nature of womankind. Women were believed to be made of frailer, more brittle psychic material than men. In contrast to the strong theoretical emphasis upon physical frailty and spiritual beauty, which characterized our period of chivalry, the Antlers conventionalized women's rôle as that of the spiritually vulnerable. Grief of any sort which would merely bow a man's head in temporary mourning, might completely disorganize a woman's life. In a sense, it was almost a stylized recognition of the narrowness of the interests which her society permitted her; while men could take refuge in the most artificial and elaborate points of cultural emphasis, women were limited in all their rewards to the field of personal relations. So a woman who loses her child and her husband both at once will be said "to be unable to stand it," "not to care any more"; "nothing mattered after that and she just went wild." All the conspicuous cases in the tribe where older women have gone definitely to the bad are explained this way. There was the case of Adam Simpson's wife. She had eight children, the oldest nearly grown. They had a nice little place and forty acres in fee patent. Neither one had been married to anyone else. The marriage had endured for twenty years. She was forty. Then in one year, their house was burned down and they lost their land because of bad crops and inability to pay taxes. From self-respecting and self-sufficient people, they became paupers, without furniture or even cooking utensils. And Mrs. Simpson deserted her husband and her eight children and became a loose woman, sleeping here and there with whatever man would have her. For a mother to desert her children is a cardinal offense in the Antler decalogue. To desert eight children, raised this offense to its zenith. But the comment today is revealing: "Some of her sons never forgave her. Adam never married again. Still, I guess it was just too much for her. She had always been a good quiet woman before and she went bad all of a sudden when they lost everything." "I guess she just couldn't stand it. The place was gone and everything burned up and I guess she just thought it wasn't any use any more so she just ran around."

There is the case of Alice. She had a nice husband and a baby, and then the baby died. "It looked like Alice couldn't never get over it. She grieved and grieved and once we all went to Y city. Her man got drunk and she went through his pockets and found a piece of her hair all tied up in a knot. Then she said, 'I guess everything will be over pretty soon. The baby's dead and I've got my hair back.' Then she started running around. She's been running around ever since. Alice ain't real bad. She's nice and kind, but she couldn't stand her baby dying and so she just got started and now she can't stop, I guess."

Even when they spoke of Agnes Willses, the most drunken, quarrelsome, dissolute woman in the community, the same note entered in: "You should have seen her when she came back from school. Such a nice quiet girl. And she married Bill Cope as quietly as could be and was going to have a baby. But he had syphilis and he gave it to her and then he deserted her just before the baby was born and married that Ellen Atkinson. And the baby died and Agnes went bad. That was more than she could stand."

Never once did I hear a similar comment made about a

man, although men among the Antlers have also lost their farms, their houses, their wives and children. It is distinctly a sex point, a cultural phrasing of the weakness of women, in terms of less power of resistance to misfortune.[1]

How has cultural contact affected the degree to which women participate in the Antler culture and has it changed the form of their participation? The proportionate rôle of men and women has changed radically as the culture has been shorn of its more distinctive emphases, because it was in the most intense cultural development — in the buffalo hunt and its ritual, in the secret societies, in the war dance, and the rituals of war — that women had the least part. Now that all of these institutions have vanished, or are rapidly vanishing, and nothing remains but a set of attitudes, a vocabulary which expresses a point of view towards activities which are no longer engaged in, the women who were passive believers and spectators, while the men were actors, have almost as great a share in the past as the men. Society secrets were guarded very closely and uninitiated men knew no more of the secrets of the Ghost Society than did uninitiated women. Now that there is only one member left alive and he has no one to talk with about the old ritual, the Antler women know as much about the Ghost Society as do all but one of the Antler men.

So the memory of the buffalo hunt and its attendant ritual lives only in the memories of the very old, and both old men and old women tell their grandchildren tales of the hunt, and young men and young women alike know it only as history; both may experience it equally in imagination. In fact, it is now often the women who treasure the past, in which they would have been so much less important actors, more fervently than the men. This is particularly striking where women are not permitted to be the custodians of medicine bundles.

[1] A similar attitude is said to obtain among the Pima, where women express excessive grief for the loss of children by going to pieces and turning to promiscuity.

In the old days, this was men's work; men fed and tended the bundles and, if a wife participated, it was as a wife, an assistant, only. Today the largest collection of sacred objects in the tribe is guarded and cared for by an intrepid, hatchet-jawed, childless old widow, whose husband held an important ceremonial position. She has inherited his sacred duties in relation to the ritual of a particular society and also she keeps medicine bundles of people who are only remotely connected with her, because she is not afraid of sacred things, and has sufficient obstinacy to oppose any offers to buy them from her. The guardianship of the heirlooms of the past is no longer an absorbing activity, fit to take up a large part of a grown man's time. It has faded to the ghost of an attitude and the women, less disturbed by cultural change than the men, are as fitted, often better fitted, to discharge it.

The next important change which the transition has wrought in the lives of the women is an economic one. The distinctions between rich and poor, which include women equally with men, might be said to be analogous to the distinctions formerly existent between those of high or low rank. But whereas formerly women's rank was but a function of the rank of father or husband, today, when wealth, not rank, is important, women's position as rich landowners is not a function of the position of some male connection. Various factors have contributed to the conservation of the land owned by women: women were less approachable by unscrupulous white men; less easily tempted into the cities and into expensive habits; more liable to invoke a protective response in the government officials. Requests from women to sell their land were usually made on the following grounds: to raise money out of which to buy farm implements or to improve farm and living quarters on land farmed by husbands or sons; to raise money to go to the Southwest to be cured of tuberculosis, or to take a tubercular child away. The first of these requests has been viewed with considerable suspicion by government agents. Although such requests when coming

from men are usually open to the suspicion of white interference and exploitation, nevertheless the case is not so clear
for the government agent. He may be morally certain that
a petitioning male Indian will not make good use of his new
equipment; he may even be convinced that the Indian has
already made a deal to resell what equipment he purchases
with the results of his land sale. Still the request for sale will
be drawn up in good order; the farm in question will be in
conspicuous need of better equipment. Where, however, the
notably impoverished husband of a rich woman persuades her
to petition the Indian Department for a right to sell part of
her lands, the agent's case is clearer.

   To take a case in point: Alec Randolph is a dissolute, lazy,
slightly neurasthenic Indian of about forty. He went East to
school and is proud of boasting that he could be an electrical
engineer if he wished — "he is trained for it." He enlisted
in the Army and after discharge from training camp, came
back to the reservation. He has one sister who is married to
a man of small income, and he lived with them. His mother,
who had been a woman of loose character — Alec's male
parentage is unknown and very probably white — had remarried in a near-by city. He married Louise Morgan, who
had no property but lived with her parents on the rent of
thirty acres. They had two small children. Alec drank and
abused his wife and, wearying of the small income, deserted
her. At this time Sallie Jones came home from school, a slender inexperienced girl of seventeen. Both her parents had
died of tuberculosis, and she and her half-sister, Grace, came
from a long line of tubercular ancestors, so that each of them
had inherited large amounts of land. Sallie was slight and ill
even then, and her guardian, Tom Strong, an old time Antler
who spoke no English, conserved the religious practices of his
forefathers and disliked all white ways, insisted that she stay
at home and rest for a year. Alec Randolph surreptitiously
courted her and eloped with her. Then began years in which
Alec bent every effort to sell his wife's lands. They had one

child after another, until now they have seven, the oldest of whom is eleven. Three times the agency authorized the sale of part of Sallie's inheritance and set the family up in a house on Sallie's land, complete with horses, wagons, farm machinery, furniture. Piece by piece it would all vanish: Alec did no farming, but gambled and drank on the proceeds of the illegal sale of one article after another which had been bought with his wife's money. Finally the agency gave the matter up as a bad job. Sallie had sold 120 acres. She had 120 left. This 120 the administration insisted should be kept for her and the seven children. Meanwhile, a Federal school inspector came through and declared that Alec had sufficient property near the school, and was able-bodied; he should be able to work and send his children to the district school. The next week Alec fell ill of a mysterious abdominal complaint. He claimed that this was the result of an injury received in training camp and went to a government hospital. When he returned, he succeeded, through the help of a local politician, in getting a pension, and he now receives twenty dollars a month. Meanwhile, Sallie's health has become steadily worse. She is now pronouncedly tubercular. Alec finds twenty dollars a month and the rents from 120 acres of land very insufficient for his needs. His family lives in Radner, in a house which they rent for five dollars a month. Sallie's health does not permit her to make a garden, so all their food has to be bought, begged, or borrowed. They live in a miserable little shack, holes patched in the walls, no furniture except one single bed, two chairs, and one table. Alec has one shirt. Now he is playing his last card. Sallie obviously has tuberculosis. She should be sent to Arizona. To do this he must sell some of her land. Sallie, devoted through years of beatings, unfaithfulness, despoiled home life, signs the petitions. She and he both go over to the agency and rave and swear at the farmer. Meanwhile, the wife of a shopkeeper in Bergen lends them her car and drives them to the agency at Black Face Town. She is said to have taken a mortgage on the land to which they have not yet gotten fee patent. Meanwhile, they live on credit from her store. If the appeal goes through — and the appeal of tuberculosis is a powerful one which employees, ever sensitive to public criticism, are afraid to resist — it is safe to prophesy that Sallie will never breathe the healing airs of the Southwest. Most of the money will be owing to the shopkeeper and Alec will blithely use up the rest.

There is another case on the reservation where the wife's land was sold so that she might go away to be cured. This is Helen Stone, the wife of Steven Roberts. Steven is a tall, good-looking, young ne'er-do-well, notoriously unfaithful to his thin, prematurely aged wife, who has borne four children while suffering from tuberculosis. She had eighty acres, forty of which she was permitted to sell, so that the whole family might go to the Southwest. Steven bought a big car and spent weeks driving about the reservation, showing no signs of setting out. Finally, he ran out of the initial allowance and the agent said there would be no more money until the family really started. They set out and got to a city across the state border where they stayed until the next installment ran out. When they received a new one, they moved on to another city where they spent the winter, Steven gambling and drinking, and Helen getting thinner and thinner. In the spring they sent for the rest of their money and came back to the reservation where they still were.

This situation, in which a woman's land has been sold on the plea that she is tubercular and the money dissipated by her husband, recurs and recurs. I could find no record of any case where an Indian woman had been cured by the brief trips to the Southwest permitted by such programs of home expenditure. It is a good illustration of the conflict between citizenship and wardship, between an ideal standard of administration and present-day conditions. According to current American standards, an Indian woman who owns lands and is suffering from tuberculosis should have a right to sell her land, take the money, and try to get well in a good climate. An agent who vetoed such a procedure would be an easy target for the politicians skilled in mobilizing liberal sentiments to further their devious plans. But although the agent may give or withhold the recommendation which will probably bring a fee patent from Washington; although he may exercise a certain amount of control by doling out the money, he cannot sufficiently coerce a free American citizen to see that the money is really spent for the woman's health. The docility of the average Indian woman in the face of her husband's plans and demands is amazing and increases under the ravages of disease. Sallie Jones, Grace Jones, Helen Stone, to mention only three of these diseased women, all sat tamely by while their husbands abused them, spent their patrimony and beggared their children. The tradition by which a man was master of a woman is not broken down merely by giving a woman legal rights to her property. The legal rights are no safeguard when the husband wishes to realize on his wife's property.

I will cite two more cases to illustrate how little power wealth has given to women. One is that of an old woman who died about three years ago. She had no children of her own, only a niece and two nephews and various more distant relatives. She was rich, and every month the office would honor orders against her rent and land-sale moneys. During the two or three days around order time, both of the nephews would appear and demand a share of the money; even take their aunt home with them and treat her rather royally; once the money was spent they would take the helpless old woman to the home of some unwelcoming, distant relatives and leave her there. Theoretically, this old woman had a great deal of power. She was the only source of income of the three high-living young people. Theoretically, she could have disinherited them and refused them any money while she was alive. But to do this, she would have had to contravert every rooted feeling of her upbringing; grandmothers give to needy youth when they ask for food; money was in the same category to her. The pattern of conspicuous consumption as a means of evading the demands of relatives is very slightly developed among the women; is hardly exercised at all by old women who have no husband to put it into practice for them. The result is the paradoxical situation where some old woman, ailing, in need of care, is neglected and put upon by the young people whom she feeds now and to whom she will leave her property when she dies. There is only one record of an old woman, so neglected and flouted by her heirs, who did revenge herself by making a will and leaving all her property to her thirteen-year old grandson. But such behavior is felt to be most reprehensible from the Antler point of view. Money and land are not privileges which may be bequeathed singly, like a hereditary privilege; they should be divided among the heirs.

There has been some attempt to break away from this custom of permitting the law to take its course and divide inheritances according to the state law on the subject. This is the custom of deeding, discussed earlier, which seems possibly to have been introduced by a disinterested Indian agent who was aghast at the wholesale granting of fee patents to Antlers who, he was sure, would be unable to continue to pay the taxes. He attempted to conserve some of this foolishly freed land by persuading the holders of the fee patents to deed the land to their children. His prudent foresight was rendered sterile when a speculator finally purchased a large number of the tax certificates on land of this type and the state supreme court held that land once held in fee patent, although if deeded it might not be attached, could be sold for default of taxes. Meanwhile the custom of deeding lands to individual heirs has held. It is sometimes also used in marriage settlements, as when old Sampson Carter persuaded Angeline Balber, twenty years his junior, to marry him by settling forty acres of land on her, and Marie Holt's mother persuaded Timothy More to marry her daughter and father her daughter's illegitimate child, by making a similar settlement upon him. But as often as not, this deeding pattern merely falls under the old categories and children persuade their parents to strip themselves of the last shred of power by deeding their land away during their lifetimes.

A striking example of the lack of respect which a wife with money can enforce is Sallie Jones Randolph's younger sister, Grace. Grace was married when she was fourteen to a much older man, named Matthew Patterson. He had no land at all and they lived entirely on her money. Matthew was very rough with his young wife, who was a heavy, unattractive girl, already tubercular. He imported a family of other-tribal relatives to work for them (the fiction under which members of other tribes are imported into households on a different reservation). All of them slept in the same room and Grace heard him rise in the night from his place at the head of her bed and go to sleep with the daughter of the other-tribal couple. The next day the girl lay in bed and would not get up or do any work. Still the young wife did nothing. After a while, the other-tribal family left and Matthew used to go off and stay with them for quite awhile at a time; then he would return and beat his wife cruelly. She went to stay with Sallie, and Matthew went to the agent and complained that Sallie was alienating his wife's affections. In this case, the agent took the woman's side, and Grace got a divorce. Matthew married the other-tribal girl and went to live on her reservation and Grace married John Harmon. John was the eldest son of a hard-working family. His father was a leader of Peyote and a good farmer; his mother, Bertha Harmon, was an excellent housekeeper and gardener. There were eight children. Bertha had sold her land to put improvements on her husband's forty acres, and although he was a conscientious farmer by Antler standards, they were often hard put to it to feed so many mouths. Grace's income, which came to about seven hundred dollars a year, was a godsend to them — even though John put part of it into a car in which he was always going to take Grace to the Southwest. Occasionally they went for short trips, but always returned. Grace had three babies and all of them died. She was always ailing. John in his fine new car began running around with other women. As Grace told her sister, she knew that John was running around, went to all the hand games and left her at home, but still she didn't complain. The Harmons were kind to her; they didn't scold and they didn't make her help with the washing. All she had to do was her own washing. And she contributed at least half of the income to the household, was mistress of her own money and could have divorced her husband for adultery under the state law at any time. Instead, she was grateful to his family for not making her help with the washing.

It is true that many of these cases are of tubercular women. But women with large amounts of property among the Antlers are the descendants of sickly lines, most of the members of which have died, many of whom have died of tuberculosis, so that this particular conjunction of wealth and tuberculosis is not an accidental one.

On the whole it may be said that Antler women have not taken any conspicuous advantage of their nominally improved economic status. Conservatively rooted in old habits of thought, they remain dependent and uninitiating, even where the law of inheritance has given them property and the potentiality for power. This is due, I think, to the lack of any pattern by which women may enforce their wishes economically. If it is compared with the Zuñi pattern, for instance, where the wife as house owner may and does evict the unwanted husband, it is clear that the Antlers have not yet developed attitudes which permit the women to exert their economic power. Merely conferring property upon them under the law and permitting them legal resources equal to that permitted men does not ensure them any independence of action whatsoever.

When we turn from the place of woman through the ownership of property to her place as housekeeper and mother, again a change of emphasis is seen. In aboriginal times, her contributions did not exceed those of the man, although it is probable that she spent a larger proportion of her time in satisfying basic needs for food, shelter, and clothing, than did he. It is, of course, a corollary of the fact that women play a smaller rôle in the institutional elaborations of culture — in their religious and social forms — that they play a proportionally greater rôle in basic and economic activities. Now that the Antler man has ceased to pay much attention to his old cultural institutions, and in a great majority of cases plays no economic part in the new culture, woman's part is correspondingly greater.

This can be illustrated if one takes as an example either a home where the Indian husband attempts to farm, or one where the family lives on rents or results of land sales. Let us take the household of Fred Peters, for instance. He had no domesticated animals, except two horses. His work consisted of caring for the horses, plowing, cultivating, and planting corn on some twenty-five acres of ground, and harvesting and marketing it in the fall. Even these activities were not carried on alone; his wife helped with the horses and, in the fall, she and her mother and their fourteen-year old daughter assisted with the harvest. The fourteen-year old daughter also helped her father plow. But the twenty-four year old son, although he could occasionally be bullied into helping for a day or so with building a fence, or similar emergency work, was off most of the time, riding about in cars with dissolute cousins, or living with the relatives of some girl with whom he was having a temporary liaison. He was a skillful rodeo performer and sometimes went away to rodeo shows, but his family did not profit from this; instead they usually had to send him money to get him home after he had spent all his earnings. Meanwhile the grandmother, the mother, and the daughter cared for the chickens, raised a garden, and dried the vegetables, prepared the hominy and sweet corn, gathered berries, fruits, and nuts, made the clothes, did the washing, prepared the food, and kept the house. Even though these tasks were divided among three women, the three of them were far oftener busy than was the husband. As he was one of the best singers and drummers in the tribe, and was also a conspicuous Peyote man and a member of the now practically extinct branch of the Midewiwin, he did put a certain amount of time into tribal activities which made the household to some slight degree approximate an aboriginal one.

In contrast to this household let us put the family of Harvey Stanton. Harvey Stanton had graduated from one of the higher Indian schools with athletic honors, and a position had been secured for him as disciplinarian in a government school. He married Beatrice Sands, whose mother had been a member of another tribe and whose father was an Antler who had left the reservation and gone away to the city to work. The mother was dead. Beatrice spoke no Antler and Harvey preferred English to Antler. After two years he had tired of his position as disciplinarian, had become overbearing and quarrelsome, and finally was discharged. He returned to the reservation with his young wife and one child. Soon the little money which he had brought back was spent; piece by piece he sold his fine clothes until finally he had only a couple of shirts and a pair of overalls. They lived first with one relative then another, with no income except Beatrice's rents from her other-tribal lands which amounted only to about two hundred dollars a year. Another child was born and then another. For a whole year, they shared one room with Beatrice's brother, a fairly hard-working young farmer, and his wife. Then Harvey inherited several thousand dollars from a land sale. Immediately they rented a house in Radner and bought a large car. Beatrice had lost one of her children and now was expecting a fourth baby. They went out to all of their meals. But Beatrice still had the task of clothing and washing for the children. Harvey had nothing to do but drive the car, and he even resigned this labor to a youth named Frank Coffey, who came to live with them, nominally as chauffeur. After the new baby was born, Beatrice had to keep it clean and neat. So, although the household represented a minimum of economic responsibility on anyone's part, still Beatrice had some economic rôle to play and Harvey had none.

The only social events which remain are hand games, and the various preparations for powwow. In the organization and administration of the hand-game groups, women now play as conspicuous a rôle as men. Women are often secretaries and treasurers of the groups — there is, as a rule, no president, but the former officers are necessary to record the forfeits which are pledged for the next meeting. As hand games no longer depend upon large stakes of horses and blankets, but primarily upon sufficient small contributions of food to feed all comers, the women's real rôle in the games is more important than the men's. A man and a woman always head the game; the contributions are always announced by a man; and if food is offered to the spirits, if speeches are made or prayers offered, this is done by the men. At funerals, however, women members of the bereaved household are permitted to make speeches in exactly the same fashion as men.

Powwow is still nominally in the hands of men. The members of the committee are men, although there are open committee meetings in which women are now allowed to stand up and speak openly in the presence of men. This is, however, done only by old women or mixed bloods. Young Indian women would still be too shy to do so. They speak aloud in the presence of a mixed group only if they are drunk. (It is noticeable that it is the women even more than the men who tend to become noisy and exhibitionistic when under the influence of liquor.)

One group of women who have considerable power and influence in tribal affairs are the mixed bloods.[2] This is again

[2] There are among the Antlers a couple of mixed-blood families who have so far surpassed the standard and experiences of the Indian group as to defy comparison. A few members of these families have made auspicious professional records in the white community. Their experiences are too unique for detailed consideration in a study such as this which seeks to preserve the anonymity of its subjects.

only a result of the greater conservatism of the women. Mixed-blood men tend to move away from the group as completely as possible. If they marry white women, they try to dissociate themselves from Indian affairs and mix with whites and become active participants in the local white culture. There are, of course, some mixed-blood males who have been brought up so completely in the Antler tradition that they do not differ in outlook and behavior from their full-blood relatives. These men, in common with the full-blood men, drift, and play slight rôles. There was one exception to this, a young mixed blood who had had considerable experience with rodeos and fairs and who for several years had successfully run powwow. But he had left the tribe, married a rich mixed blood from another tribe, and never now returned to the reservation. But on the Antler reservation there was a group of some seven or eight mixed-blood women, some of whom had married full-bloods, some had married white men and were now widowed. They were hard-working women, thrifty, close-handed in everyday life. For this they were respected by the white community, regarded as "not like Indians." But they still retained many Indian points of view. It was their pleasure to give away elaborate presents in the ring and then dance in costume on the strength of their donations. They feasted the drummers, feasted the singers, hobnobbed with white politicians, and met Indian politicians on a slightly different foothold from that of their own women. Their advice was sought and heeded in all tribal affairs, for they were esteemed for their generosity and loyalty to Indian things. One of them made a speech at a local gathering in which she loudly berated the terrible white man who had come from over the sea to take away the land and inheritance of "my people."

I will quote a comment of another to illustrate the extent to which Indian attitudes still dominate their thinking. "Yes, there are some things that the Indians will never give up. I've got a lot of that sacred stuff out at my house, though don't you tell anyone I have. And I try to take care of it just the way my mother taught me. I can see her now, a real old woman sitting with all her things around her. One of these sacred things I have is for making rain. And I broke the drought with it. You can just ask Gregory Slack and his boys if you don't believe me. They was all there at the time. And I got it out and I said, 'Now boys, you all come with me. I am just as solemn as if I were reading a page out of the Bible.' And we went out and hung it up and that night rain fell. And I know that was why. Oh yes, there are some things, that the Indians will never give up."

Yet the power of this little group, although it is in a sense dependent upon their femininity, upon their combining the conservatism of their own sex with the thrift of their white inheritance, is also quite limited by their sex. Nevertheless, the position of the mixed-blood women is in a sense revelatory. Their transition from Indian standards to white standards has simply meant a tightening of their habits of life, not a total change. As wives of white farmers, they have cooked, and gardened, borne and nurtured children, sewed, and washed clothes, just as their full-blood relatives are doing. There has been no violent occupational break, no important cleavage in interest between them and the Indian women. And similarly they have stepped as unobtrusively into the confidence of the white women whose interests are similar to theirs. Against the Indian man who "goes white" there is tremendous resentment on the part of his Indian relatives and considerable contempt and amusement from his new white associates. One side regards him as a traitor, the other as a parvenu. But the Indian or part-Indian wife of a white husband meets with exactly opposite treatment. The Indians do not resent her defection because, after all, a wife must do as her husband says; the whites admire the pluck with which she adapts herself to a situation dictated by the necessities of matrimony rather than by sheer assertiveness and vanity.

In the earlier days of white contact, the mixed-blood male

played an important part. The Antlers had not yet learned to mistrust and hate the white man; they aspired to learn white ways and benefit by white contact, and the mixed blood had the necessary linguistic ability and understanding to make a bridge between the old life and the new. But with the intensification of the economic struggle and the failure of the original optimistic approach to white culture, this part could no longer be played by the mixed blood male. Today he has very little choice between getting away completely or deprecating his white blood as much as possible and living as a full-blood. Here again it is because the interests of the Indian male and the white male are so much more diverse that the clash between them outlaws the mixed blood from both cultures, while the mixed-blood woman, spared the burden of the conflict, remains a possible force for acculturation in the mixed Indian-white community.

To take a specific example of this: There is a young mixed-blood Antler woman married to a member of an immigrant community about twenty miles west of Radner. During the harvest season she permits the Antlers who come to work for the neighboring farmers to camp on her place. While the men are away in the fields, and after the slight housekeeping of camp life is finished, the Antler women take their babies into the kitchen of the mixed-blood woman and as they gossip together, they help her with her preserving, or sewing. Without this friendly stronghold, which means a desirable camping ground, good water, food from the garden, the Antlers would find working in the harvest fields a more onerous and unfriendly business. Their enthusiasm for the heavy, exacting work is slight at the best, and one eviction from a white man's paddock, one unpleasant experience in an attempt to get drinking water, and the whole of the group would be likely to abandon the work. Here the mixed-blood woman, still in strong sympathy with the Indian women, bridges the gap between Indians and whites and makes them function economically in the same community.

The position of women from other tribes and of white women married into the tribe also affords illumination of woman's rôle. In those cases where the wives have come from tribes which were more assimilated than the Antlers and have endeavored to put over points of difference upon their husband's kindred, the household, if it has endured, has become definitely alienated from the tribe. There are some striking examples of this. Take the case of the two other-tribal girls who married as school girls Elmer Carver and William Driver. Both were better educated than the average Antler woman; neither attempted to make common cause with the women of the tribe. Mrs. Carver, now the stout mother of eight living children has proclaimed her sense of difference by dressing differently, by preserving her fruit and vegetables by the new "cold pack" method, rather than by the old kettle method, by making a hundred small points of manners and minutiae of everyday life. As a result her husband is alienated from the men of his tribe also; her children are looked on askance with the exception of Richard, the eldest, who has married Elsie Gordon and gone to live in her father's conservative, polygamous family. The younger children are disliked by the community and neither Elmer nor his children would expect much help from the Antlers in case of need. His wife has further emphasized her separateness by joining another church and alienating Elmer from the church of which he was once a member.

William Driver's wife has similarly held out against her neighbors and maintained her husband and child against the community. She is a comely thrifty woman, with a great deal of white blood, who was brought up in the East. The sight of the name of some New York shop stamped in a garment sets her to sighing of her girlhood. Her thin little husband helps her a little about the house, and goes out to work for a living when he can. Meanwhile she works hard for various white people, and bears the economic burden of the household. Both she and Mrs. Carver are as important to their families, eco-

nomically, as any of the other women; they play the domi-
nant rôles in the household and the households are as un-Ant-
ler as they can make them.

On the other hand, there are a fair number of marriages
with cognate tribes where the other-tribal wives have made
only Indian points, instead of seizing upon bits of white manners and outlook as ways in which they could define their
differences from their husbands' peoples. Although if these
women come from any other tribe except that most closely
related to the Antler, English has to be substituted for Antler
in the home, nevertheless the essential solidarity of the household is not broken. Only if the women from other tribes
dramatize their temporary sense of tribal difference in terms
of the white-Indian conflict do they succeed in alienating
husbands and children from the tribe.

White women married into the tribe have to stand the
same test. They are not required to learn the language nor
wear the costume of the Antler — it would be regarded as a
foolish piece of affectation, an attempt to claim blood to which
they had no right, if they did. But they must order their
households, especially as it affects their husbands, in Indian
fashion, cook, and eat in Indian fashion. Although there have
been a number of such marriages, only three survive at the
present time; one is the case of an invalid husband and a
mannish white wife who runs his farm for him (neither have
much to do with the other Indians); the second white woman
took her husband away to the city to work — this is what
they almost always attempt to do; the third was a woman of
exceptional native intelligence, a widow with young children,
who married an Indian with a salaried position, and adapted
herself as fully as possible to Indian ways.

There is a further paradox of the Indian woman's position
today. Although her participation in the aboriginal culture
was slighter, although she played a more generic, a less cultural part than did the male, today she is far more conservative than her husband. The social situation at a hand game

symbolizes one of the reasons for this. The old men sit apart, some of them still with long hair, sunk in their meditations over a lost past. They view with horror the young people who now take hands when they dance. "These young people," they say, "they are neither white nor Indian. They have lost their road." The middle-aged men cannot remember the buffalo; they have never sought the vision; they know no society secrets; they know that some of the old men are very sacred and powerful and they shrink away from them. They gather about the drums and sing for the dancers or talk quietly of powwow, of sending a representative to Washington to get a new bonus for the tribe, of the latest political scandal. They no longer wear long hair, like some of the older men; but occasionally they wrap blankets or sheets around their waists in the fashion in which broadcloth robes were worn. In their dress there may be seen some of the fantastic survivals of the time when the Indian made a colorful pageant of the materials which he bought from the white man. The crier, a man of between forty-five and fifty, wears a bright cerise shirt. Other men, dressed in old worn blue shirts and patched overalls, wear scarlet or pink feathers in their broad-brimmed hats. They speak only Indian, without any sprinkling of English words. Meanwhile, the young men drive up in cars, casual, bold, no longer respecting their elders, wearing sport clothes, striped white trousers, and sweaters with school letters, delicately matching colored shirts and ties, if they are rich; conventional overalls without a single bizarre touch if they are poor. They do not cultivate the society of the older men; they have nothing to learn from them. The old who governed so long by their superior skill in hunting and their knowledge of the tribal tradition, by their traffic with the supernatural and their jealously guarded religious secrets, have nothing now by which they can intimidate the young men. In very many cases they have not even any land. At any rate the pattern of equal inheritance of land is still too strong to make the young men fear disinheritance. A still

separate group are the small boys who race about, undisci-
plined, unmindful of the older men or of the women, only
returning late in the evening for the food which their mothers will save for them. Meanwhile, without respect for the
quiet dignity with which a hand game is still conducted, they
throw blazing firecrackers among their seated elders. It is,
throughout, a picture of discontinuity, each generation careless of the preceding one, and yet no generation fired with
the enthusiasm of those who would make a new point of their
own: From the standpoint of the males of each age group,
the last age group is out of style; but the bitterness, the antagonism, the fanatic advocacy of the new, which so often
distinguishes the conflicts between generations in a changing
culture, is absent. Without any fire of rebellion in them, the
young men shrug their elders aside; it is a discontinuity of
lack of interest, of failure of tradition, not of active rebellion
and change.

Meanwhile let us reconstruct a little more vividly the scene
of the hand game. Out of doors, under the trees, near one of
the lodges, the three-sided square of blankets has been spread.
The grass has been worn thin by horses' feet and in many
places resembles a traveled roadway. No matter; the ground
plan of the three-sided square must be spread with old blankets, quilts, horse blankets. Sometimes the blankets are taken
directly from around the women's shoulders. Outside the
square, horses are tied to the tailboards of the wagons, or
tethered loosely so that they may crop the bushes. Earlier in
the afternoon, before all of the people were gathered, the
women and children have gone for gooseberries and the tin
lard pails of gooseberries are now packed away in the wagons.
Here and there a battered old automobile is standing, but
most of the people who have cars come late. At the center of
the middle side of the hand-game ground plan is the place of
honor; here a man and his wife, or sister-in-law, sit to preside
over the hand game. At the right of this couple is the men's
place, at the left, the women's. The right is filled very scant-

ily, some half dozen older men sit there. A little way off, leaning against trees, and not showing by any sign whether they intend to participate or not, are little groups of men. Another group, mostly of young men, are tightening up the drum by the heat of a small bonfire, at which several women are cooking the great kettle of stewed meat or chicken which is to provide the feast later. Here and there in the cars sit groups of young people, several boys and a girl or so who have long since lost all claim to a good reputation.

The left of the master of ceremonies is broken up into groups; it does not present the picture of a solid side ready to take part in an evening's game. It is otherwise with the right. Here sit, not six women, but forty or fifty, old grandmothers, mothers with baby boards in their arms and small girls hiding behind their skirts, young girls in groups of twos and threes with interwined arms. Although all wear cotton dresses, there is some difference in the costumes of the women of different ages. The skirts of the grandmothers are fuller, more heavily ruffled; there are those among the young women who have made their dresses in one piece, abandoning the customary loose blouse and tight banded skirt of their mothers, the young girls wear store-made cotton dresses, cheap, gay, and in the height of fashion. The short skirts reveal their long silk-stockinged legs. Most of the small girls are dressed in home-made clothes with short skirts also. Yet beneath this dissimilarity of costume, there is a sense of solidarity in this large group of women of all ages, huddled close together, with their dishes, their babies, their water jugs around them, talking to each other in soft low voices.

And when the game begins, when the lots have been drawn and the small pebbles given to one pair of players while those of the other side guess, the chosen watcher guards against cheating, and the master of ceremony keeps the count with feathered sticks, laid straight on the mat in front of him, the women take part eagerly, solemnly. The men have to be drawn in from their separate little groups, only to fade away again as soon as they have been guessed down. Finally one side has won a count, the gourd rattles are given to the losers; they have danced with them and pledged their two chickens or their ten cents for the next game; then the drummers carry the drums into the central space and begin to play for dancing and, one and all, the women rise to dance. The fashionably-clad young girls borrow the shawls of their decrepit grandmothers and drape them over their modish store garments, become suddenly too conspicuous and inappropriate; small girls of eight and ten years old dance, pressed close together, three under a shawl. If one watches the feet, which move so slowly, in such perfect time to the drum beats, while the voices follow a different rhythm with their song, one sees moccasins, worn shoes, and high-heeled slippers, purple and red and green; one sees old cotton and woolen stockings in the style of fifty years ago, and the latest black-and-white silk fad, all moving in perfect accord to the drums, and over the whole group rest the shawls. From old women to smallest toddler the women are one, their differences in generation and outlook forgotten in the dance.

And this dancing group is strictly symbolic of the rôle of women, as a group, in the Antler culture of today. The institutions have gone and only the memories and attitudes remain. The social elaborations of gens, chieftainship, society, war police, have vanished, to leave only the household and the social dancing lodge; it is the women who are now the core of Antler culture. It is the women who are able to teach their daughters the dancing steps, the household arts, which are all that is left of the culture. The men are Indian by virtue of blood, language, and a disinclination to accept the economic behavior and economic attitudes of white society. But the women are still Indian in positive terms, in a multitude of details which bind mother to daughter and both to the grandmother. All three have fastened their babies on a cradle board, all three cook the same food and order similar households. Meager though their inheritance is, a matter of rules about who should sleep in the one feather bed in the household or how to wash a sliver from the baby's eye with mother's milk, nevertheless it is a tradition taught by one generation to the next, binding the group together in a set of positive habits which distinguish them from other peoples and give to them a sense of security and meaningfulness which their husbands and brothers lack.

Chapter IX

THE ORGANIZATION OF THE HOUSEHOLD

In the tables in Part III, I shall present Antler society in terms of households, defining household as a group of people living under one roof and pooling their economic resources to some extent. Although this picture is considerably more·reliable, and far truer economically than the census picture in which parents and children are listed together regardless of their residence apart, or as a unit of a larger household, and in which all unmarried people over twenty-one are listed without reference to any household, still it leaves something to be desired. For these households are defined more by house sites than by personality; they are actually the groups of people who live in any given residence. I have listed as the head of the household the person to whom the residence belongs, with some exceptions, as when the owner is a minor, or a man's wife. (A man who lives in a house owned by his wife is felt to be the head of the household.) In aboriginal times, the organization of the household was far tighter and clearer. If several families lived in a tipi or earth lodge, they were either mother and daughters and their husbands — in which case the sons-in-law showed all deference to their father-in-law, or of mother-in-law and daughters-in-law, where sons showed deference to a father. The defined position of the elders served to organize and clarify status within the family group. The women made or built the house and owned it; the men organized the hunting, the distribution of meat, the social life of the household. A daughter or daughter-in-law left home to build her own tipi, or build a new lodge with some other woman. The economic life, gardening and hunting, which supported each went on, undestroyed by change of residence. Garden sites were separated from residence sites

and a change of dwelling did not necessarily mean the abandonment of a half grown garden or the breaking of new land
for the next year. Strict etiquette governed relationships between different households and no family was subject to continual abuse of hospitality from others. The dwellings were
crowded close together and the general atmosphere was one
of public village life.

Modern conditions have changed all this. On practically
every allotment the government supervised the building of
a frame house. Some of these are two stories high, almost all
have three or four rooms, a cave, a small barn, a privy. The
houses can accommodate more people residentially and fewer
people in a gathering than could the old earth lodges. No new
convention requiring a bed or a chair for each guest has grown
up to make the frame house more exclusive than the old
dwelling. It is customary, when land is leased, to keep the
house. Usually, although not always, the owners of the leased
land continue to live in the house. It is also customary to
keep enough land for gardening. Occasionally these isolated
houses will be leased to white tenants or to other Indians who
have no homes, or in the case of the wealthy, poor relatives
will be permitted to live in them for a nominal rental — but
the former is the rule.

These houses are scattered over the reservation; some of
them, especially since the increase in white settlement, are ten
and fifteen minutes' walk from the nearest Indian dwelling.
They were originally erected in relation to an economic plan;
the four- or five-room house was to shelter the family which
owned and farmed the attached eighty or one hundred and
sixty acres. Leasing the land without the house has nullified
this relationship. The houses have become merely places of
shelter, sometimes made more desirable by the presence of
fruit trees, berries, dogs, and chickens, at different points in
a widely scattered area. Residence within them is now based
on a number of new factors; besides relationship, there are
now considerations of income. The newcomer is a burden

or a blessing, if a male, not in terms of what he can do, but of what he has. Meanwhile the housewife, gardening for one of these households, cannot plan for any definite number; any day five or six people may be added to the household. Perhaps they will be wealthy wanderers with a car and a fair amount of clothes but with no permanent abode; or they may be a young male relative and an eloping bride, or a female relative who has left her husband and come with three children for shelter. A white farming household with its habits of plenty, large garden, well stocked preserve shelves, and full corn bins, could stand such unreliable and shifting populations better than the far more hospitable but poorly equipped Indian household of the renting Indians. For where the man of the house does not farm, there is nothing to keep him at home on the isolated little patch of ground where his wife should be gardening, but where he has no alloted tasks or interests. His one impulse is to hitch up the team if he has one, jump into the Ford if he has one or, failing that, walk to a neighbors and get a lift to town. The excessive possessiveness of Antler husbands and wives, coupled with the peculiar sex ethics which makes any woman caught alone the helpless prey of the man who so finds her, makes husbands unwilling to leave their wives at home alone, or alone except for small children. So when the husband goes to town he takes his wife with him. Day after day, the wife leaves home early in the morning to return late at night. As a result, there is very little and very poor gardening done on these scattered homesteads; lacking farms and garden, the household is but poorly prepared to meet the shifting influx of visitors. What is true of the scattered dwellings is of course doubly true of those Antlers who live in Radner or Bergen. Their houses are twice as desirable as stopping places, being near hand games, shinny and gambling games, or radio and movies, as the case may be. But the space about these little town cottages provides only for very small gardens, even if the owners are not too disheartened to care for them.

In discussing the household organization, I have mentioned the renting households first because they represent two-thirds of the households which I have analyzed in Part III, below. If the first 15 households which are separately listed as "wanderers" be included, the Antler households which do not live by the direct practice of agriculture reached a total of 115 out of 165. This tendency to live by other means than agriculture is steadily increasing with extended leasing of land and the diminution, through the sale of heirship lands, of the amount of land owned. The situation of those few families who have no means and yet very few members is analyzed in Part III, below. The situation of the bulk of Antler households, in which a large group of people live in a house with only garden land attached and subsist from the rent of forty to eighty acres of land — which means an income of from fifty to two hundred dollars a year — slight inheritances, casual earnings, or windfalls, is the far commoner case and the one towards which the whole tribe is drifting.

Of the 50 households supported by farming, it is possible to make the following generalizations. In 7 cases young men farm the land for their parents; in 5 cases, for their fathers, and in 2 cases, for their mothers. There is one case of a son-in-law farming his father-in-law's land. In 4 of these 50 households supported by farming, the farmer either has no land suitable for farming or has rented it but, for whatever cause, 4 farmers are farming on rented land. Excluding the cases in which sons farm for their parents, there are exactly 12 men under forty who are farming their own land. Yet allowing for the approximate nature of the age figures due to faulty statistics, there are about 170 young men in the tribe between the ages of twenty and forty. So that it is reasonable to regard the non-farming population as typical and as likely to become even more typical.

Once having given up farming it is very difficult indeed for an Antler to get back on the land. He will have sold his farm machinery or left it to rust in the rain. He has no implements, no seed, sometimes he has neither horses nor wagon; in other cases he may have held on to these last. It takes a long and uphill fight, without capital, without encouragement, against tremendous odds, to return to a type of work in which he is at best only mildly interested. To take an example: Peter Ross was one of the better educated Indians. He could read and write, was not given to women, although he did drink and gamble to some extent. He had forty acres of land and he married Addie Caldwell, whose mother, Ethel Caldwell Plumber, was a very rich woman by Antler standards. She had had forty acres of her own, and from her second husband she inherited forty acres. Her son inherited another forty acres and died soon after leaving it to her, so that she had now eighty acres from the estate of her second husband. Addie was Ethel's only daughter. Peter and Addie had four children. They lived on his forty acres well assisted by the rent from the mother's eighty. Forty acres of her land was unimproved, low-lying, along the river.

Peter's farm lay in the northern part of the reservation, towards Black Face Town. For a generation the drift of residence has been south, so that finally he found himself the only Indian farmer within a mile or so. His children were the only Indian children in the district school. He was not a very good farmer, but with the help of his mother-in-law's rents and also of her pension — for she was the widow of a government employee and received thirty dollars a month pension from the government — they got along fairly comfortably. The grandmother had never quite recovered from her resentment at Peter and Addie's marriage, as they were members of different sub-gens of the same gens. The three older children were sent away to school, and in the spring of the year of the big payment, when every Antler received a bonus of about two hundred dollars (a pro-persona division of an old interest payment which local politics had succeeded in pushing through Congress), the middle son died. Both Addie and Peter took to drink, quarreling over the disposition of the money. Without the bonus of the dead son, which they received later, they had $850 in cash. The summer was spent in drinking and quarreling. There was enough money to get through the year without planting a crop. Peter drank the entire year, and the next year he lost his farm through an unpaid mortgage. Addie, already sufficiently unnerved by the death of her son, left her husband and went through a period of promiscuity. The grandmother rented a small house in Bergen and took the children to live with her. After several months she persuaded Addie to come home to her, to give up her dissolute life and return to Peter, who had been consoling himself with drink in the interval.

The debauch was over, but Peter had lost everything he owned. He had neither horses, nor farm machinery, nor house. He, his wife and his three children were dependent on the bounty of the grandmother. After a couple of years, he began to prove a piece of her land, land which the grandmother had already deeded to the three grandchildren. He and his wife put up a tipi and he cleared and began to cultivate the land. There were no farm buildings; wagon and farm implements, bought by the grandmother, were unprotected. He had started, but never gotten very far, with a log house. (The government insistence upon frame houses has become such a matter of prestige that no Antler is any longer satisfied to build himself a log cabin.)

Meanwhile the household possessions, sewing machine, bedding, shawls, which had not been sold with the place, had vanished through another leak. The only son Andrew, was an idle waster of twenty-two or so. He came and went as he chose in his grandmother's house, and whenever he was short of money he took some one of the household possessions which he could sell or pawn in order to raise ready money. The helplessness of the entire household before these continued thefts is significant of the present situation of the Antlers in regard to any protection afforded by law. An Antler will seldom take another to court unless it is a question of illegitimacy or of jealously between two women. But for one to take a member of one's own family to court is inconceivable. Yet Andrew Ross's behavior was a product of modern conditions and the Antlers had no methods of their own with which to deal with it. I once suggested to his mother: "Why don't you make his grandmother refuse to give him money, unless he behaves better?" The mother only shrugged helplessly: "Oh, then he would take everything which we have. Now he only takes *some* things." There is no form of family discipline, no sort of religious punishment, with which the Antlers can meet this delinquency; yet they steadfastly refuse to invoke the law to protect themselves.

This then was the situation of the Ross family in the summer of 1930. Peter had rallied from his period of drinking. Addie had come home sober and ready for quiet from her months of license; Peter had worked hard, according to Antler standards, to prove the new land. But they had no house, only a tipi, and a pair of horses bought with the bonus of the dead brother. The grandmother's thirty dollars a month was spent before it arrived. She borrowed it in advance from the man from whom she rented her house, paying one dollar interest per month for every ten which she borrowed. Her rent money went to pay larger debts at the store. Furthermore, she was an enthusiastic gambler and a good deal of money was lost that way. In any event, sufficient money would never be saved to build and furnish a frame house. Therefore, the family daydreamed; if the grandmother could only sell some of her land, there would be money enough for a house, a car, furniture, everything the heart could desire. Would the agency permit it? Here the agency was not in quite so clear a position as they would have been had the old woman had no pension for life. It was not a question of providing for her, but of conserving the land for her grandchildren. But before I left the reservation, I was assured that her petition to sell her land would be unfavorably reported to Washington. Peter will not get his frame house and his car;

it is more than probable that he will weary of his uncomfortable venture and give up farming altogether, content to live miserably on the grandmother's income, part of which will, of course, stop when she dies. Then a new situation will arise. There will probably be four heirs, Addie and her three children. All of them will be enthusiastic about a land sale. If they are denied it, they will live poorly on the rents; if it is granted, they will probably be penniless in a few months.

So much for the situation if an Antler once gives up farming. Peter's situation was not nearly so desperate as many; he had his mother-in-law to depend upon for support and shared her income with only four others. But even so, it was impossible for him to get back upon his feet economically, in terms of the standards of behavior among his group. He was not a good enough farmer to earn a surplus; he was too proud to live in a log cabin.

Let us now take the case of a young Antler, Alfred Judson, who had been educated at a government school, had spent two or three years as chauffeur for some rich Indians, and now returned to the Antlers reservation, married and prepared to settle down. Judson owned forty acres of farm land which he rented and a cottage and forty acres at the other end of the reservation, also rented. He had neither surplus funds, implements, furniture, horses, or live stock. If he were to occupy his cottage and farm his forty acres, he would obviously have to sell some land. Giving him credit for a maximum exercise of caution and prudence, and granting that he did not spend the bulk of his land-sale money for a car, new clothes, and trips about the state — which temptation it is unlikely that he would resist — were he to stock and equip his farm, the struggle would have only begun. His cottage was on a remote section of the reservation away from friends, relative, movies, hand games, all sorts of gaiety. Neither he nor his wife had had any experience of loneliness. She had been in school and in Bergen all her life; he had been in school, or leading the pampered life of a chauffeur for the Oil Indians.

All he knew of farming was what he had learned at school — at a school equipped with electric milking machines and all the other apparatus of a large scale power-driven farm and dairy. His wife did not know how to milk nor how to take care of chickens. She knew next to nothing about cooking. She knew very little about sewing. The chance of these two young people, so completely unequipped for the rigors of life on a small farm, persevering all alone so far from everyone, would be very slight indeed. But there was a further complication. Judson knew that if he did succeed, if his wife did grow a good garden and have luck with her little chickens, if he did get a cow and succeed in keeping it, he would be working, not for himself and his wife and children, but for all of their relatives on both sides. They would sit down to the table not two, but ten, and although the middle-aged and old might have some chance of making such guests work, what chance would a twenty-year old boy have against a father, father-in-law, uncles, and their wives?

Now let us consider Judson's alternatives. His rents brought him about one hundred and fifty dollars a year. This would be enough to clothe himself and his wife and permit them a few good times. If he went to live with either her relatives or his, he would be able to make some slight financial contribution to households well in need of it. He would not have any work to do. He could loaf in front of the store, or play shinny, go to hand games, and ride around in some one of the cars which a land sale brought temporarily to the reservation. Or, if he were really industrious and willing to work, he could go and work on some farm on shares. This course would depend upon finding someone with whom he was willing to live. Fortunately, his wife's uncle was one of the outstanding thrifty farmers of the reservation; one of the few Indians who "put money in the bank." The uncle had no children and his wife had always been fond of her niece. Judson and his wife went to live with them. This was his best choice. Here he will gain experience in farming; here, if nothing goes wrong between himself and his wife, if she does not die, or the babies do not die, or if she does not take up with other men; if the uncle, who farms rented land, does not fall ill or die; if no one takes to drink; if Judson does not sell one of his lots of forty acres and dissipate the money, and so on through the hundred "ifs," he may learn to take up his land again, with a better, but not a good, chance of seeing the venture through.

I have chosen men who were well situated, who either had wealthy relatives or land in their own right, to illustrate this question of the return to farming, once it has been abandoned. The moral pointed by the difficulties of the wealthy is of course all the more sharp for the poor. The more usual case is for a man to lose everything and come to share, with some half dozen others, a little rent money. No land sale could relieve this situation. The bulk of Antler young men do not have, as did Judson, land which they can sell and still have a house and land left. Instead, they are luckier than the average if they have a third interest in the rent of eighty acres. Nor have they any adequate way in which to protect this interest. The government might survey off their third, but what could they do with it? If it had woodland on it and log houses were not out of style, they might put up a log cabin, beg a little seed, start a garden, borrow horses to plant a little corn, and gradually, with enormous thrift and industry, such as is shown by the hard-bitten white immigrant who labors tirelessly to acquire and improve his land, become independent. But log cabins are out of style, and such thrift and industry is bred only of generations of European land hunger, not made overnight under Antler reservation conditions.

And there are an increasing number of young men who have no land at all, not even a fourth interest in forty acres. These have the following alternatives: they can go away to work, which means going into the stockyards and packing houses of the large cities and doing the heaviest, the roughest, and the most ill-paid work; they can stay at home, but make occasional forays away from the reservation to rodeos, fairs, etc., if they are clever at rope spinning or riding bucking steers; if they are exceptionally clever at any of these entertaining devices, they may make a living for themselves and their families out of it (there are three cases of this); they may stay at home and pick up occasional odd jobs, work at harvest time, pick wild grapes and sell them to the immigrant farmers for wine making, beg money to gamble and make a small profit. Staying at home has various other ramifications. They may nominally work for a living, farming for some rich relative or relative-in-law, or drive a car for such a one; they may simply live upon their relatives or relatives-in-law.

Marriage fits into this pattern of partial or no economic responsibility in various ways. With the growing number of landless young men, all demand that a man should be able to support his wife has disappeared. The relatives of both boys and girls may do their utmost to prevent marriages which will bring more dependents into the family and to further marriages which will bring income into the family, but their failure to do this is of course, frequent and not accompanied by any set of social attitudes concerning the duty of a man to support his wife and children. The marriage of one's relatives is simply a lottery in which one may win or lose income, but no one considers that the young people should be permanently debarred from marriage simply because they have no way of supporting themselves and their families.

But marriage does very definitely affect a man's economic choices. If he marries a woman from another tribe who has money or land, this may be a definite inducement to him to leave the Antler reservation permanently. If he marries a woman from another tribe, he will find it increasingly difficult to find shelter among his kin without working for it, and he may be driven to assume some economic responsibility by virtue of his slightly alienated state. If he marries a white woman, he will ultimately face the alternative of working or divorce, and although the latter is more frequent, there are cases where white women have succeeded in making their Antler husbands leave the reservation and go to work. But all of these are the unusual cases. If he marries, as he does in forty-five out of fifty cases, an Antler woman, his economic choices become at once more circumscribed. Antler women will leave the reservation only under very special conditions. They will consent to go into the oil country if they or their husbands have rich friends there with whom they can live in luxury and for whom they can nominally work. The coming and going between the Antler reservation and the Oil Indians is casual but continuous, and there are usually some half dozen families living for months at a time with rich Oil Indians. The Antler women will also leave the reservation if they marry white men or men from other tribes. But they are unwilling to go away with their Antler husbands so that their husbands can work in the cities. A couple of weeks' camping during harvest is accepted, but not a prolonged absence from their kinsfolk, where they are forced to accept alien living conditions, continuous hard work, and the risks of poverty and unemployment amid strangers.

The average Antler household on the reservation is neither self-supporting nor self-sufficient. The Antler housewife is never accustomed to having to find money whenever she needs salt, sugar, or a spool of thread. She is not accustomed to having to care continuously for her own children; instead, there are always relatives with whom she can leave a child. A life of partial responsibility in a wide relationship group, where the cares of each are divided by the many, is the domestic situation in which she has been reared. Trying to make ends meet in a large city, on seventy-five or one hundred dollars a month is a task for which she is unequipped and which she has no possible motive for wishing to undertake.

The result of these various tendencies is an ever-increasing number of young married couples who form a sort of drifting population of the reservation. The widowed without land form a similar sort of free-floating group, and there are some cases of old couples who shared in the original allotments but were granted fee patents and so lost their land.

The fewer the children the more migratory the couples will be, although in some cases the older children will be scattered about among relatives, while husband and wife and a child or so drift from place to place. The economic urges to such drifting, failure of food in one place, slight temporary employment in another, the chance of borrowing from a relative who has just received rent money or a payment from a land sale, are all reinforced by the social factors. The isolation of so many of the dwellings, the desire to see other people and attend hand games, all combine to make the population unstable. To take an example: Ted Slaughter and his wife and two children live in a place which belongs to his brother, and pay five dollars a month rent. They have a team of horses. Ted works during harvest and his wife puts in a garden. Their place is quite a distance from any of their relatives. There is to be a war dance over at a lodge near his father's, so Ted and his wife and two children take the team and go over and stay at his father's for a week. Then they get tired of staying there — there are too many people there, and Elizabeth, Ted's sister-in-law, says if they will bring their team and help her plow her garden, they can come and stay with her for a bit. So they move to Elizabeth's for a week. The Andersons, who live next door to Elizabeth, offer to let Ted have some wood from their wood lot if he will take his team and do the hauling for them. So Ted helps Jack Anderson get wood, and then his brother plows his garden. By this time, they have reached the week before powwow. Having worn out their welcome at Elizabeth's, they go down to Ted's wife's mother's — she has married again and lives on her husband's land — and stay a week, until time for powwow. They haven't any tent for powwow, but they drive the stepfather and mother in, in their wagon, and stay in their tent, although it is pretty crowded. Ted has gotten a couple of days' work which gives them money to pay for some groceries during powwow. But after powwow they go home. The garden is choked with weeds and someone has stolen the last three chickens. There is nothing to eat in the house, only corn and beans. Anyway, they want to go to the fair, which is next week. Ted hears that a mixed-blood family in Radner is going to move to a larger house and asks them if they would like to buy a bed and table for two dollars each. This leaves them with only one cot bed and a tiny deal table, but they can manage well enough. With the four dollars they go to the fair. These young people were, however, in a better position than many, for they had a little rent money; Ted did work occasionally, and they had a team. But the absence of any specific employment for the husband meant the lack of any definite tie to their nominal residence.

Antler parents may reasonably hope to escape the burdens of support of their children from the ages of seven to eighteen or nineteen if they are permitted to send them to government school, but they must then anticipate caring for them for the rest of their lives. If the parents had an earning power or an income on a par with the white population, this shift in the ages of dependency might not mean so much greater economic burden. They are not properly able to support their children at any age; this support of adults is far too heavy a burden.

In Part III (p. 282), I present the minimum clothes budget and the minimum budget of purchases from the store if a family depends primarily upon purchased food. Accepting this minimum, a family of seven has to have between $300 and $350 a year to get along by even minimum Antler standards. Nor must this be regarded as the necessary money income of a farming population where eggs, milk, pork, berries, fruits, vegetables, wood, etc., come off the farm. Of the 160 Antler households, only 50 are supported by farming. Only some 15 of these are good farms, well stocked with cows and chickens. From these must be subtracted the 5 or 6 good farms whose "owners live like white people" and are not willing to contribute endlessly to friends and relatives. These few good farms, and the thirty or so poor farms, do not form a sufficient reserve to supplement the inadequate incomes of the Antlers who do not farm and who live on insufficient rent money.

The deficit each year between the income earned by the group or received from rent moneys and the actual consumption of the group is met in various ways. The principal way is through drawing on capital through land sales. Land sales are of two types: sale of land of a living owner, the proceeds of which are nominally restricted and devoted to special purposes such as repairs, purchase of new farm machinery, etc.; and second, sale of heirship land which has become too involved for administration. In the majority of cases such money is not restricted and is paid over to the heirs on the instalment plan. (It is restricted if it belongs to minors or to dependent older women, and occasionally if it belongs to old men or anyone who can be called an invalid.) These heirship payments buy clothes, horses, furniture, which are used for a year or so, and are then in turn sold for small cash values to meet the urgent demands for ready money. The Antler's preference for expensive clothing stands him in good stead here, for he invests in durable materials. A certain amount of the money brought in by an authorized land sale, especially if made by obtaining a fee patent instead of by selling through the office, also finds its way into current purchases which are later translated into income. Thus the tribe for the last twenty years has been living partly upon capital. Then a certain amount of clothing finds its way into the tribe through extensive gifts from the Mission — which this year gave away several hundred garments, only a portion of which are suitable for use, however — gifts from mixed-blood and white connections, gifts from individual white people of worn-out clothing. Food is supplemented by attendance at feasts which are provided by contributions from the better-situated Indians, or by gifts from politicians or local shop-keepers. Powwow brings some thousand dollars into the tribe, most of which is spent upon food to maintain the camping group during the two weeks of powwow. Contributions to funeral feasts and the payments made during mourning also bring in small amounts from those who have friends to those who have not. Similarly, expeditions to visit the Oil Indians bring back blankets, shawls, and other articles of clothing. School children who go to the government schools are partially clothed during the school year.

Even with all this assistance, the standard of living is so low that it definitely affects the health and happiness of the Antlers. Many young men have only one pair of overalls, and have to go to bed while these are being washed. Whole families live for weeks in the winter without tasting meat, or milk, or eggs. Once during a cold winter a few years ago, sixty grown men turned up to dig a baby's grave, for it was rumored that a pig was to be killed for the gravediggers. Attendance at the public schools suffers because the children do not have shoes or warm, or even presentable light, clothes. Or a child will be required to buy a tablet for school and stay at home for weeks because the necessary nickel is not forthcoming.

Within this curious economic frame, of poverty, sudden slight wealth, pauperism, and feasting, the housewife attempts to organize the domestic economy of her family. Housewives may be roughly divided into three types, according to the economic status of their husbands: wives of farmers who themselves share in the routine activities of the farm, wives of renters who have money enough to live upon and help others, and wives of those men who are so poor that they cannot even provide a roof for their families. Those in the first group vary as to whether they take the business of farming seriously and raise chickens and have good gardens — there are some nine or ten of these — or urge their husbands to put all of their efforts into corn, which is a money crop, but actually pays far worse than raising chickens and live stock. The wives of renters are put to continual makeshifts to conserve the small money income and to supplement it in as many ways as possible. Whether such families are fairly comfortable or definitely miserable depends upon whether the wives grow good gardens and levy as heavy a toll as possible on the wild berries and wild fruits and nuts in the neighborhood. Here the division is primarily one of age; there is no woman under thirty on the reservation who is herself a good gardener; neither do the younger women gather the wild fruits. Years in school have not given them any knowledge of gardening and has made them too nice for the day-long scrambles after gooseberries.

The more either a farming or a renting household depends upon money income, the more difficult is the problem of the housewife. When there is money, if she puts it into flour and sugar and other staples, she has then the continual fear of a horde of relatives descending upon her and consuming the whole supply. Under such a threat many families dissipate money for pleasure, rather than invest it so precariously. One family whom I knew rented their house from people who had seven children. Every month the landlord brought his whole family to collect the rent. The house was in Radner, while the landlord habitually lived with his son on an isolated farm. Taking the rent money, eight dollars in this case, he and his wife would join a gambling group in the village and gamble as long as the money held out. If it held out for several days, the unfortunate tenant's family had ten additional people to feed throughout that period. The tenant's wife would empty the flour barrel, leave only a few scrapings in the sugar tin, and hide every possible bit of food in an attempt to discourage the unwanted guests. But guests of this type are shrewd in rooting about for hidden supplies. One woman told a story of her husband's aunt who was just the "meanest, stingiest person" imaginable. She and her husband went to visit the aunt who met them with the customary insincere lamentation that she had nothing but the scraggly end of a piece of salt pork on which to feast them. But the young wife went upstairs and hunted about until she found almost the whole of a freshly killed beef, hidden away under a quilt. She went down and whispered the news to her husband, who presently informed his aunt that he would like a little of that beef she had upstairs. The old woman attempted to hide her embarrassment and rage under mumbled remarks about the steer having died of some disease and her thinking they wouldn't want to eat such meat. This story went the rounds of the reservation.

Groups of relatives gather wherever there is known to have been a money payment, or where a gossip reports that the household has just bought a bag of flour. The more food a family has the quicker it disappears, and only those with an almost empty larder are sure of consuming the dregs of their supplies. What is true of food is also, to some extent, true of clothing, bedding, etc. These are always being requisitioned by the needy relative, so that no housewife will store a pile of extra blankets on her shelves; she knows too well that they would all be begged away from her. The minimum standard of living is therefore doubly dictated, by the meager income and the impossibility of conserving supplies.

The wife in the household where there is a money income has primarily a conserving, planning task; the wife of the poor, on the other hand, has actually to find shelter for herself, her husband, her children. It is impossible to say whether the present-day pattern, by which it is always the duty of the wife's relatives to shelter her and her children, is a result of the old matrilocal residence in which the dependent son-in-law lived with his wife's relatives, or whether it is an answer to new conditions. With an increasing number of homeless people, either husband or wife must make the bid for help from the relatives. Actually, it is the wife who makes it, who implores shelter, or food, or clothing, for herself and her children. This may be due to the old standards by which men were supposed to care for women, so that the women can more swiftly make a sentimental appeal than can the men, or it may be due to the peculiar position which women occupy in the non-farming households. On the few well managed farms, the men are interested in taking on young and strong men who will help on the place, but in the renting households the men have fewer economic, and no practical, stakes. It is the woman of the house who will bear the brunt of planning for the newcomers, and she is more willing to give shelter to a woman whom she likes and trusts than to the wife of some male relative. This follows the aboriginal pattern in which mother and daughter, or two sisters, so often made their homes together. Analysis of the residence further shows that where men do seek and find the home (I am excluding here residence of sons with fathers, which is not regarded as seeking shelter), it is most often with a woman relative that they seek it. Wherever it is a case of a favor to be asked, it is usually also the women from whom and by whom it is asked. Desperately poor families present a dilemma to a woman before they do to a man; she must somehow find food for her children, by gardening, by working, or by begging shelter. The lack of responsibility felt by men today exonerates them from any such sense of urgency.

Opportunities for women to work are very slight. During the summer I found the following occupations followed by Antler women:

Cooking for gamblers	8
Preserving	5
Housework	2
Clerk	1
Interpreting	2
Fees for assisting prohibition agents	4
Working in a laundry in city	1
Seamstress	2
Laundry	4

Only four of these women had steady employment; the rest simply earned a small amount of money now and then, possibly supplementing the family income by twenty-five to seventy-five dollars. Furthermore, several of these occupations overlapped, so that the list does not represent the number of women employed, who were only sixteen in all. The one place in which a woman can definitely care for her children is the home. Furthermore, if she seeks shelter with a woman relative, she is exchanging loneliness and want for companionship and less want. She has the same washing, ironing, and cooking to do as before, possibly a little more, but not enough to change her way of life seriously.

But the young man who goes to live with relatives, receiving for himself and his family a promised share of the crop in return for his labor, is in a different position.

Let us take a few of these cases. A young man with a wife and two children went to live with his uncle, on the understanding that he was to farm the place and receive a third of the crops as his. The uncle had a wife and four unmarried daughters. The nephew put in the corn crop and cultivated it once, when the uncle's married daughter came home with her husband and two children. The uncle thought this was too many mouths to feed, the daughter had the stronger claim, and the nephew and his wife and children were turned out. The nephew received nothing for his months of work. In disgust, he let his wife find them a home with her relatives and gave up all pretense of working.

Another instance is that of a seventeen-year old boy who went to help his half-brother farm. The half-brother lived with his wife and child on his wife's mother's forty acres. After the corn was well up, had withstood the drought, and promised to be a good crop, the old mother and her son decided that they wanted to take a trip. They prevailed upon the son-in-law to mortgage his corn crop and buy a car. Meanwhile the younger half-brother was deprived of his share in the crop.

Or take the case of Jerry Maxwell. He was one of the many men who had been living casually with Jean Saunders, a widow who was living on the forty acres she had inherited from her dead husband. When she became pregnant, she claimed that the child was his and persuaded him to marry her. He went to live on her place and helped substantially in planting the forty acres in corn. It was a large and miscellaneous household consisting of his wife, their baby, her three children by her dead husband, his wife's mother — who after several years of loose living had married at sixty-five an old *roué* of about the same age — his wife's younger sister, his wife's stepfather's daughter, and her temporary young husband. After the corn was cultivated and growing well, dissension grew in the household; his wife took to attending hand games and returning to her former promiscuous existence, and when he objected he was thrown out of the house, losing all share in the corn which he had assisted in planting. The custom of making contracts has penetrated very slightly into Antler life; and even where these are made, the cost of prosecution would debar the injured Indian from obtaining any legal redress. Within the present flimsy pattern of living, a man no longer has any guarantee of receiving his due return for his work unless he has planted on his own land. There are several conspicuous cases of older men who have gotten different young men to come in each year and farm for them, only to cheat them in the end. The fact that they can still find new recruits is abundant testimony to the straits of the younger generation.

So it remains simpler to permit one's wife to beg shelter from her relatives and not to invest labor where there will probably be no rewards in any event. Meanwhile, with important planning made impossible economically and socially, the lives of women living on rent money and the lives of completely dependent seekers of lodgings do not differ materially. The daily routine of cooking, washing, ironing, sewing, mending, goes on in one household very much as in another. But each year, with the sources from which the depleted incomes are reinforced grown scantier, the task of the women to make ends meet becomes more difficult. And coincident with the loss of capital, there is an equally fatal loss of skill which makes the younger women far less able to cope with the difficult conditions than were their mothers and grandmothers.

Chapter X

MALADJUSTMENT AS AN INDEX OF CONFLICT

Conflict between Antler sex standards and present day reservation sex laxity is the most important factor in producing delinquent women. The Antlers are essentially puritanical in their attitudes towards sex.[1] Women were expected to be passive, unresponsive, never initiate sex activity nor courtship in any way. There was no standard of positive behavior for lovers; the desirability of a husband or a lover was judged in terms of minimum demands and of gentleness. Courtship was adorned with a few sentimental flourishes in the old days, but these were meager and very stylized. Young girls were bred to modesty and fear, and chaperoned on all occasions. Wives whose husbands were away from home, divorced women, and widows, had to be exceedingly circumspect in their behavior, as they had lost the protecting cloak of ignorance and fear, and at the same time their relatives' stake in their chastity had been removed. The puritan attitude toward one misstep is only partly present. A woman who leaves her husband for another man has to make a quick decision between institutionalizing her new relationship or becoming promiscuous. Unless she goes to the home of her new lover, appears with him in public, and is accepted by his relatives, all the young men in the community will regard her as legitimate prey if he is absent from her side for a moment. From this condition of promiscuity there is no escape until she meets some man who is willing to give her protection and status. The attitude of Antler men is that of the company in

[1] My discussion of sex among the Antlers is based upon the testimony of women exclusively; the youngest girl informant I used was seventeen, but still a virgin. The attitudes of men and of children are unrepresented, owing to the short duration of the investigation. This has very definite drawbacks; it is impossible to discuss the subject developmentally.

De Maupassant's story, *Boule de Suif*, who resented so fiercely the prostitute's claims to her right to choose upon whom she would confer her favors. The right of the virgin or the legally wedded wife or the very circumspect widow to preserve her chastity is granted by the bulk of the male community and in fact will be enforced upon the unregenerate young by the more responsible male relatives of the woman. However, the failure of such women to go adequately chaperoned, which may be simply remaining alone for a short time in a house, walking along the street alone, or going about in the company of another woman of poor reputation, are all considered to lay the woman open to proposal or attack, depending upon the setting. A characteristic of virginity is believed to be such an extreme form of modesty that it amounts to panic, immobility, and helplessness, in the face of attack.

While a virtuous woman may with propriety repulse an attack, if she is fortunate enough to be able to do so, it is far otherwise with a woman who has had several lovers or one who has borne an illegitimate child. The Antlers manifest the customary inconsistent attitude that it is worse to bear one illegitimate child to one lover than to have taken many lovers without pregnancy ensuing. Early authorities on the tribe mention the child's inalienable right to membership in his father's gens. This has sometimes been recognized today by giving an illegitimate child his father's English surname. But analysis of the twenty-three cases of living illegitimate children shows that among them there is only one child the responsibility for whose care has not fallen upon the mother and the mother's kin. This fact and the opprobrium showered upon the unmarried mother and the illegitimate child form a consistent picture.

The Antlers have one corollary of their Puritanism which is found in other primitive societies on other points as well — that is, short memories. The unmarried mother, the mother who deserts her children for temporary promiscuity, the girl with a conspicuous record of promiscuity, are all able to marry and settle down and become respectable members of the community again. Should the daughters of such women, in their turn, become indiscreet or promiscuous, or should their husbands leave them, or other bad luck in personal relations befall them, their old derelictions will be recalled and cast up against them. Such mothers today have great difficulty in controlling their daughters, and where there are no other relatives who have influence over them, the daughters of mothers who have lived promiscuously are very likely to follow in their footsteps.

Despite the rigid standards for women, and the lack of standards for men — except the injunctions against interfering with the wives and daughters of other men — and despite also the lack of premium upon sex technique, Antler women seem to have viewed sex with pleasure. Homosexual sex play among children is reported and this may partly account for the lack of frigidity in adult women. Once the customary standards of behavior under which a woman is always passive are let down, the women and girls play an important initiating rôle in making sex proposals. Among the unvirtuous, it is more often the girls and women who send the messages for assignations, while the men treat their companions in casual sex-activity as loose women, unworthy of respect or consideration. The intersexual situation today is aggravated by the fact that such a large proportion of the women under forty have been promiscuous at some period and so forfeited the consideration of the opposite sex.

The complete double standard and the absence of all limitations upon the men, except those of property, carry with them the opprobrium from the man to his partner, and the right of a brother, himself involved in illicit sex activities, to censor his sister. This is one of the principal ways in which girls become embroiled with their families today, now that the old chaperonage has dwindled in the face of the automobile, and its attendant freedom. Brothers and sisters tend to encounter one another on mischief bent, but the double standard prevents the brothers from shielding their sisters from parental wrath.[2]

Instruction to the young girls from their grandmothers is considerably complicated by the tremendous changes which have occurred within the grandmothers' lifetimes. Aboriginally, the Antlers institutionalized menstruation; there was a menstrual hut with separate bedding and dishes; menstruating women were believed to be a menace to a hunter, a warrior, or a buffalo doctor — the latter could lose his curing power through contact with them. Even ordinary men, if they came in contact with menstruating women, were in danger of having the evil emanation of the women enter their bodies in the form of a missile of clotted blood, which made them weak and ill, and had to be withdrawn magically, as the missiles of the sorcery society were withdrawn. With the building of frame houses, when the present grandmothers were children and very young girls, the menstrual hut was abandoned. It disappeared over a period of about ten years, an amazing collapse, which is difficult to explain,[3] of what

[2] The following was the most flagrant case of this kind. The berdache, because he was able to pass without comment from the girls' groups to the boys' group was a favorite go-between. He was asked to take a message from a young man whose wife had just left him, to a girl who was his (the berdache's) classificatory niece. Such services are usually paid for in cigarettes, and the boy for whom the message is being carried watches the go-between until it is delivered, and then pays the cigarettes. So the berdache delivered the message, telling his young "niece" who was a quiet little virgin, carefully chaperoned by an efficient grandmother, that Tom Tilden wanted to "talk to her." He then returned to Tom with the girl's reply that she "didn't want to talk to him," and collected his cigarettes. Had the girl been unrelated to him, this would have closed the incident. In this case, however, the berdache sent word by the girl's brother to her parents that Tom Tilden had been sending messages to her. It is characteristic of the unfairness of the whole situation that the parents then gave the girl a terrific scolding because Tom Tilden had been sending messages to her, completely disregarding the fact that she had sent a negative reply.

During the period when his young wife was in the hospital having a baby and during the ensuing weeks when she sat in the car with the baby while he circulated about at hand games, Sam Snyder had many a passing intrigue with the younger girls. Yet, when he found his younger sister talking to her Black Face lover, he immediately reported her to his father.

[3] It is interesting to compare this modification of cultural behavior, in response to a change in material culture, with other changes which occurred. In aboriginal times, the tipi in which death had occurred was given away; this could not be

appears to have been a strong cultural attitude. The disappearance of. the menstrual hut was accompanied also by a complete abrogation of the old taboo against intercourse during the four days of menstruation. It is, of course, impossible to tell whether this was an observance formerly honored more in the breach than in the practice and whether the people did not welcome a chance to do away with an institution which no longer corresponded to the realities of individual behavior. It is possible also that the principal emphasis in the menstrual taboo was upon its relationship to hunter, warrior, and wound doctor, and that as these occupations were dimmed in importance it was easy to eliminate the taboo also.

The Antler also had the old attitude characteristic of adjacent American Indian tribes that it was indecent to have too many children, that it implied lack of restraint on the part of the parents. Whether the menstrual taboo and the attitude toward unspaced births were connected in aboriginal times, it is impossible to say. Certainly today those older women who were brought up to preserve the old taboos which, however, vanished in their girlhood, expend all the emotion aroused by the idea of intercourse during menstruation upon what they regard as the result of such improper behavior — too many children.[4] This attitude they embody in a teaching to their granddaughters that intercourse during menstruation results in pregnancy. Curiously enough this teaching, so definite, is given long before the girl receives any instruction as to the cessation of menstruation which occurs with pregnancy. From this emphasis upon the menstrual

done in the case of the house. The presence of a medicine bundle infected the entire tipi or lodge; after the building of partitioned frame houses, the medicine bundle was segregated and its presence infected only one room. Although the old central fireplace disappeared, the arrangement of a dining room or meeting room in an Antler house, the etiquette of seating, passing in front of persons seated, etc. still conforms to the fiction that there is a central fireplace.

[4] As one old woman graphically put it: "When we were young we kept away from our husbands for four days, now this is no longer done and look at the young women today, they have a child so high and so high and so high, and one hiding in their skirts, one on their backs, and one in their bellies."

taboo as birth control, rather than as something to protect the power and skill of the men, the onus is placed upon the women to reject their husband's advances, whereas under aboriginal conditions it was the woman's duty to protect her husband by giving due notice of her state and retiring out of reach. It is interesting to note that a certain amount of emotion, a sense of penalty and danger resulting from intercourse during menstruation, has remained, while the whole content, institutionally and ideationally, has radically changed. The stubbornest element in the complex has been feeling. So completely have the men given over their old attitudes that her husband's desire for intercourse at this time which she fears will result in pregnancy is now regarded as one of the difficulties which an Antler woman has to face. Today the Antler women also know about a "safe period," but this is most probably due to cultural contact, as in the old days they relied upon magical doses to bring about immunity from pregnancy.[5]

Young people among the Antlers have fairly abundant information concerning the facts of sex although they are sometimes less well informed about the facts of pregnancy and birth.[6] The isolated living conditions do not provide every child with the same type of experience of birth and death. The facts of defloration were once surrounded with sufficient fear and shame to be a good deterrent from experimentation. Undoubtedly this aura of fear was far more complete in the old days before school, and when all young girls were equally sheltered from experience.

[5] The use of protective mechanical devices against disease has also penetrated Antler knowledge, but the birth control element is completely disregarded by the men. The women report that unless the fear of infection is present there is no hope of enforcing its use.

[6] One young girl told me that she once heard, as a child, her mother discussing with another woman a Caesarean operation — new then even to the adults — and she had believed for years afterwards that all children were born in this way. This is the type of misunderstanding comparable to those which occur among white children and probably similarly caused — no experience of birth in the home and a new type of delivery which was sufficiently new to call forth discussion from the adults.

The breakdown of this old modesty has been partly considered under the results of coeducation. Perhaps equally instrumental in its destruction has been the increasing number of loose women and promiscuous young girls in the social group. In aboriginal times, their number was far smaller, social disapproval was much stronger, and the influence of such women on the group was relatively slight. Women of sixty can remember only two loose women in their youth. This is, of course, the proportion of public sexual laxity one would expect in a culture as puritanical as the Antlers where a man could stamp an illegitimate grandchild to death without being censured for it, and where one of the tales tells of strapping an unmarried mother and her lover to a raft and setting them adrift on the river. As long as the culture was a coherent, consistent whole, very few people would succeed for any length of time in flouting convention. But for the last twenty-five years there has been a steady deterioration of behavior among the Antlers, which differs from the shift of standards in the white community in one marked respect. Although there is not perhaps a greater discrepancy between the sex behavior of the last generation and of this generation among the Antlers than among the whites, the white community has gradually shifted its attitudes as well as its practices. But among the Antlers, with the old controls breaking down and no new ones taking their places, public opinion has not adapted itself to changing practice as it would in a less disorganized community. Instead, the attitudes of the grandparents remain crystallized, meaningless, serving to set up conflicts rather than to control the behavior of the young. There is no one in the tribe, not the loosest women nor the most accomplished rake, who does not believe that all sex activity is a little indecent, and who does not believe that all extramarital activity is wrong for women and wrong for men to the extent that they are partners in a sinful act, although the double standard preserves the men from feeling their behavior as strongly as do the women. Men who engage in illicit sex activity with women of loose reputation are not censured severely unless they are married men and are therefore being unfaithful to their wives. What censure there is, is disguised under imputations of venereal disease. "I wouldn't want my daughter to marry him. He's slept with every loose woman on the reservation and he certainly has syphilis." As the Antlers are notoriously careless in taking precautions against disease,[7] or in investigating the future spouses of their children, it seems probable that such remarks as these disguise moral reprobation under a gloss of practical concern.

Yet with every woman deviating from the code being disapproved of by men and women alike and feeling herself a sinful person, nevertheless the majority deviate. This produces an essentially maladjusted society in which all are sinners and everyone points the finger of scorn. A part of the inevitable conflict between standard and behavior is solved by the myth that the white man is responsible for all of the Indian's sins. The following tale is typical of this attitude:

An Antler boy went away to school and after many years he graduated and came home to the reservation. His father wanted him to take up the medicine road, but he refused. He said, "I have graduated and now I am not going to live like an Indian any more. I am going to live like a white man." So he went away to the white man's town. Presently he passed a saloon where everyone was drinking. His heart told him not to go in, but his legs were too strong for him, and so he said, "Well, I am graduated so why shouldn't I do everything that the white man does?" So he went in and got very drunk. Then he went along the road again and came to a house where some people were gambling. Again his heart said that he should not go in, but his legs were too strong for him, so they took him in, while he said: "Well,

---

[7] This is a typical comment. "My cousin told me not to go with Harry Ransome. He's got that syphilis, she said. But she went with him. I guess she's just jealous."

I might as well go in for I have graduated." Finally, he lost most of his money and he came out of the gambling house and went along until he came to a brothel. Now he said again, "I should not go in here." But his legs were too strong for him and they took him in. After he came out of the brothel he had lost all his money and he was disgusted with everything. So he went back to his father and said, "Father, I have traveled the white man's road and it is all evil. Now I have come back to travel the medicine road of my forefathers."

This rationalization which exonerates the Indian by virtue of his race from all responsibility for the social evils of his present-day life, serves as a partial solution of what would otherwise be an impossible conflict. It permits the most dissolute members of the community to retain some self-respect, for this evil to which they lend themselves is not of their making, but is a foreign intrusion. As one old Indian phrased it: "While you have been here, you will have heard much bad and much good of us. All that is bad was brought by the white man."

Over and above the conflicts, based on changing standards, between disciplinary parents and delinquent young people, there remains the Antler attitude which enfolds and protects its criminals and sinners because they belong to a much abused and sadly decimated race. Over and over again one hears such expressions as the following: "But after all she's an Antler and there are so few left." "You have to let every one come because there are so few left." "Well, what can you expect of the poor boy, he hasn't any land, he was born too late." "Well, poor thing, she has syphilis; she got it from X, who brought it back from the War." (This comment ignores the former existence of widespread infection, although this too is, of course, known to be due to white contact.) Law and order are no longer upheld by the Antlers themselves; they have been stripped of all real authority. Law and order, moral demands for sobriety, for industry, for thrift, for marriage — now that it is "legal"— no longer Indian — all come from the white man and his government.[8] Yet the white man is also conceived as a monster of cruelty, who has robbed the Indian of his self-respect, of his lands, of his happiness.

But although the Antler can use to solve his worst conflicts, this concept of a noble race debased externally through contacts, nevertheless his sense of race solidarity tends continually to spread moral dissolution within the group. This is most noticeable in the attitude towards loose women and delinquent girls. At a hand game, the staid modest young wife will dance side by side with a rollicking, drunken, syphilitic who shouts obscenities as she dances. The quiet, inexperienced little girls of fifteen sit in a row which also includes girls little older than themselves who are notorious. A community to which the presence of delinquents is so new and which blames its delinquency upon an external cause is not equipped to deal with them. They are Indians, they are Antlers, they should have the right to share with the remnants of their persecuted race the simple pleasures of the hand game and the dance. After the dance is over, the young men may drag away the drunken shouter of obscenities and subject her to the final indignity of mass assault, finally turning her loose naked to find her way to shelter as best she can. But this does not represent a moral punishment dealt out by the community; instead it is an expression of annoyance on the part of the young men because a woman had been bad-tempered, arrogant, or uncompliant.

Meanwhile at the hand game, good and bad, modest and obscene, mingle together. And here again an old standard of values definitely conflicts with the new difficulties. The old standard of behavior from which women judged women was concerned primarily with amiability, good nature, generosity. In the absence of divergent practices, these aspects of char-

[8] As one old Antler said, "in the old days there used to be punishment for adultery. Now there is only the law."

acter were determining in making friends. Furthermore, the old primitive premium on kinship, by which one's own kin had a first claim upon one's interest and companionship, prevailed. Now, in the case of girls who have run away in stolen cars, who have spent days out in the woods, picking berries and waiting for a series of boy lovers to come to them, these old standards prevail. If the delinquent girl is kind, unassuming, generous, she will be valued as a human being by her own age-sex group, even though they know she "runs around and bothers the boys." Furthermore, if she is a relative, the sternest parent does not have the face to forbid her child from associating with her. And yet every delinquent girl in the Antler community is a definite plague spot, a source of infection to the other girls because of the whole social attitude toward sex.

To illustrate, let us take the cases of Jane and Lillian, who were bosom friends. Jane was twenty and Lillian was seventeen. They had been friends at school and still paired off at every hand game. They were still good girls, sticking close together. Their minor sins were only whispering an occasional word or two to a boy, sometimes sneaking away with another girl to smoke a cigarette in a barn. Jane had been kissed several times. Lillian only once at a hand game two years before by a boy who had gone south immediately afterwards. Jane engaged in slight flirtations, all very swift and surreptitious, for a girl may not be seen talking to a boy without losing her reputation, nor could Jane absent herself for long from a watchful mother. Both girls hoped to get married at the same time. Jane had had a slight flirtation with a cousin, but announced that she would respect the exogamy taboos and would not marry him. Both girls were modest, easily embarrassed, flushing quickly, given to giggling and losing their tongues.

At the Black Face powwow, the girls were allowed to wander about from booth to booth, watching the side shows and drinking pop. Here Jane for the first time talked to

Philip Lamb, who was wandering about aimlessly because Marie Griffith, his temporary mistress, had gone off for the evening with Stephen Roberts, resplendent in the new car which was to have taken his tubercular wife to the Southwest. Philip was a good-natured, unattractive youth who had spent the summer dissipating, with the help of various girls, an inheritance of three thousand dollars. For three weeks now he had been living with Marie Griffith, an unmarried mother, who had been married to a Black Face, divorced him, borne a child to another, run off to the city with a white man, (in Antler phrasing) had deserted him, and come back to her family. She and Philip had been living with a cousin and his wife and children. As Philip and his cousin had both been beneficiaries of the same inheritance, they were spending it together. Marie had wheedled a couple of hundred dollars out of Philip and fifty dollars to get clothes for her little boy. But she had wearied of him after two weeks and gone off for the evening with Stephen Roberts. Philip felt much abused, and ready to assert his superiority over womankind in some way. He encountered Jane and Lillian and drew them behind his car to tell them his wrongs. At the same time, Frank, who had been Lillian's boy at powwow two years before, appeared. The two couples edged apart, still sheltered by the big car, and while Frank and Lillian renewed their acquaintance, Philip had time to ask Jane if she would marry him, marry him properly, asking her parent's consent. Someone turned the searchlight of a car on the group and they separated, Jane and Lillian returning arm in arm to their parents, Jane whispering to Lillian that Philip wanted her to marry him and she thought she would, though, she added, it wouldn't be for looks. (Antler girls recognize two categories of choice —"looks" which includes charm, physical appeal, etc., and "money"). Philip had a big car — although gossip said he had already mortgaged it and counter-gossip said it was only a dodge so that if he did get in debt, his creditors wouldn't take the car — he must have some money left, and he owned forty acres besides. Lillian whispered back that if Jane got married, she would get married too, to Frank, who had said he still liked her, in the two minutes conversation they had had. But both girls reckoned without Jane's parents, who were rich and lived comfortably on two hundred acres of land, a small section of which was farmed by Jane's married brothers. They pronounced Philip no match at all, his money was almost gone, he would never start farming his forty acres, his car was mortgaged, and in no time he'd be going afoot. Sullenly Jane accepted their dictum. Weeks dragged by and Jane had only time to whisper to Philip that her folks were unwilling. Meanwhile, Philip had gone home and sent Marie off, telling her to pack her clothes and get out, that he done everything he could to please her, but it hadn't been of any use. He sulked and consoled himself with Sadie Farmer who was, however, too easy game to console him thoroughly as she was shamelessly willing to come to him in the daytime.

Then came powwow. Lillian had almost decided not to marry Frank, who had not expressed himself very definitely in any case beyond saying he still liked her. If Jane were to remain single, so would she. In the shadows of the powwow grounds, she and Jane slipped about, talking for a moment to one boy, then to another. Wednesday night Lillian saw Frank for a moment and he tried to persuade her to slip away with him, but she stayed with Jane. But two nights later, Lillian's brother came into the tent and slashed her across the face with a sweater, declaring that he had seen her out on the shinny grounds with a boy. Lillian flew into a boiling rage, returned his blows, the parents interfered and took sides, the father with the son, and Lillian, her mother, and grandmother left the tent for the night. In the course of her aggrieved mutterings over the bad behavior of her husband and son, Lillian's mother remarked that she didn't care what Lillian did.

That night, Frank and Philip met Lillian and Jane and an

elopement was discussed. Jane knew that it was useless, that her parents were determined that she shouldn't marry Philip and would only follow her and drag her home. Lillian's father had on several occasions given her different advice: "If you ever run off with a boy, you stay with him. Don't you dare come home, a shame to us all, or I'll beat you up." Frank hadn't counted on getting married, he was only eighteen and had thought of returning to school. Still Lillian was very desirable and very determined. Finally, Lillian and Frank decided to run away to his aunt's, a good two miles' walk in the rain. Jane was then faced with a choice; should she go with Philip knowing that she would be brought back, or should she remain soberly at home? She was mature and fearless. Years of surreptitious light love making had worn down her modesty and fear. She took a chance and ran off with Philip. Later that night, when her parents discovered that she was missing, they went to Philip's house and ordered her, shamed but defiant, to come home. She went. An Antler girl cannot afford to flout a rich family completely for an unsanctioned union upon which she may not be able to depend for a month. Jane's family were divided. The grandmother wanted to bring her back, furious because she had married her classificatory "son." Father and mother, who had themselves married within the gens, felt that it would be better not to. Brought back, she might have a bastard child, or in any event she would most certainly take to running around.

Now let us shift the scene to a hand game two weeks later. Lillian and Frank, who have been legally married through their parents' agency, are not there. They are still too shy to face their comrades and so they stay at home, too shy to talk to each other, also, but quietly contented. Jane, however, is there, no longer the quiet, giggling modest Jane, who walked arm in arm with Lillian, but a loud-voiced, hand-on-hip Jane, who publicly smokes cigarettes, accepts drinks from hip flasks, goes away openly to sit in dark cars with anyone who asks her. Jane had become a "bad girl." The whole community knows that she slept with Philip and was dragged home by her parents. No longer a virgin, careless of public opinion, her parents as helpless to discipline her now as she was to flout their final decree about her marriage, she drops every restraint. At the next hand game, she took with her her sister, Mildred, hitherto a well chaperoned quiet girl, and her sister eloped with one of the most notorious young wasters in the community. They escaped in a car and in a few days returned to Mildred's house where the outraged parents made him so uncomfortable that he speedily left and returned to his noisy middle-aged wanton mistress, who had evicted him in a fit of temper. Now Mildred, like Jane, would run around, fair game for any man.

If Mildred and Jane continued on this course, if they took to drink as they probably would, if they contracted syphilis, if they became involved in any car thefts, brawls, or other difficulties with the law, then the law might step in and send them away to a reformatory. The Antlers phrase this as, "Oh, her folks got tired of her and so they sent her to reform school." As long as the parents are sufficiently interested to take charge of the girls, pay fines for them, if necessary, go surety for them in court, the girls usually remain on the reservation.

This is a typical case of the way in which delinquency spreads though the group. Lillian's parents were sober and hard-working; she had been well chaperoned. Jane's parents were even more upright and much richer. Years of casual initiation into smoking, petting, etc. by other girls who were cousins had broken down Jane's reserves sufficiently so that Philip, completely without responsibility and trying to make his wealth compensate for lack of personal attractiveness, found her easy prey. Once Jane went, it was impossible to protect Mildred.

Two weeks later two other girls in the same age group eloped, one with a youth who did no work, was notably vicious, the other with a boy who had lived a most dissolute existence. His sisters were all conspicuously delinquent. The mother and stepfather of the first girl compelled her to come home again, as they had done on three previous occasions, because she was not of age and they were living on her income. She had returned, bitterly resentful, and more ripe for adventure than ever. The other girl spent a few weeks in the riotous household of her lover's sister in Bergen; he then quarreled with her and she had to return to her father. Her mother was dead. About a month later, little fifteen-year old Evelyn Guthrie eloped with her cousin. Her mother, a member of a cognate tribe, was a careless, pleasure-loving woman, and she did not chaperone Evelyn properly. Evelyn was allowed to go about with a divorced syphilitic woman who was living in a quasi-servant capacity with a neighbor. Her sixteen-year old lover replied to her shy demurrer that they were relatives by announcing that he was going to live by "white ways." [9] Evelyn was the granddaughter of one of the most conservative old men in the tribe; her uncle was a distinguished secret society member. The whole family were enraged and pursued her and dragged her home from the boy's family, who had received her very coldly because they too were conservative and disapproved of broken exogamic rules. Now Evelyn was added to the list of probable delin-quents. In the section which follows, I present a set of twenty-five case histories of notably delinquent women and girls. This does not exhaust the number of promiscuous women in the tribe, but it merely selects the most conspicuous about whom I was able to obtain full data. Fifty years ago

[9] "Going by white ways" is often used as an alibi to do something of which Indians disapprove and does not necessarily, as it did in this case, refer to a real cultural difference between whites and Indians. So I have heard a man say that he would talk to his mother-in-law were she living, because he went by "white ways," and received an account of the same man's asking a woman to have intercourse with him in the back seat of a moving automobile shared by others, because he wished to "go by white ways." Similarly, a boastful young married man announced that he meant to take out other women, even if he was married, because it was the "white way."

there were two loose women in the tribe; today there are about forty women at any given time who are living equally loose lives. The twenty-five whom I selected for special study merely showed more continuous maladjustment than the others. I have excluded from consideration here women who are merely carrying on an occasional affair, young girls whose lovers cannot be named on both hands, grandmothers who in the opinion of the entire tribe are living in temporary sin.

When these twenty-five cases are considered in detail, the result is a significant comment upon the present social system on the reservation. The causes of delinquency are chiefly the same as those in contemporary American society; broken homes, bad influences from relatives, alcoholism, unmarried motherhood. This means that Antler society as such, no longer exists as a coherent social fabric; it has been replaced by a series of discontinuous, non-comparable disunited Antler homes. Just as in the modern American city the social worker finds the home, in the absence of any group life, any group standard, the determining factor in character building or character marring, so it is among the Antlers. In a genuinely homogeneous society, there are many factors which can overcome the influence of the individual home, should it chance to be defective. The child, whenever it leaves the home is confronted by coherent and consistent social standards; the influence of age mates, more constructively reared, is continually brought to bear upon the deviating child in terms of ridicule, abuse, ostracism, etc. There is no standard of good or bad beyond the standard of the social group, and the delinquent parents have no way of successfully proving an alibi for their own or their children's bad behavior.

In postulating that Antler society once approximated to conditions which have been found characteristic of other primitive societies, a certain amount of caution must be observed. It has been remarked at several points in this study and has been most clearly demonstrated in a recent ethnological study [10] on this tribe, that great divergence between theory and practice is so prevalent in different aspects of Antler culture as to be correctly termed a trait of the society. In religion, there was a theory of free vision and a practice of strict inheritance of religious privilege; in politics there was a theory of free accession to chieftainship by potlatch [11] and in practice there was strict inheritance; in economics there is a theory of free distribution of gifts for which no return is expected, and in practice most of the gifts are returned. These are all aspects of the aboriginal culture pattern which I quote here, on the basis of another detailed work, for purposes of argument. To this array it is possible to add one current divergence, the series of inconsistent attitudes on sex which make everyone in the society delinquent from the standpoint of everyone else. It is open to question whether this is a new phenomenon. Certainly I believe that the theoretically arranged marriage was far more often the post-elopement validation of the choices of the young people. Similarly, the theory that women went to the bad [12] after a great grief seems to be an aboriginal phenomenon. But the ferocity of Antler aboriginal attitudes on such subjects as infidelity and illegitimacy leaves in my mind little doubt that the present high percentage of delinquency — in terms of Antler and local American standards equally — is a recent condition.

It would be possible to recognize this unprimitive approximation to current American conditions and yet not predict an increase in delinquency among the Antlers, were it not for the existence of other factors, absent in the white community, which combine with these conditions, such as lack of standards for boys and men, relative exposure of unprotected women to assault, the aboriginal reliance upon fear

[10] To the author of which I am exceedingly indebted for all points of detail bearing upon the aboriginal culture situation in its formal aspects.

[11] Potlatch — validation of privilege by public distribution of wealth.

[12] Throughout this study I use moralistic terminology which accords with Antler feeling.

and its breakdown under conditions of coeducation, and the failure of the group to isolate its delinquents so that they do not become a source of infection to their age mates and younger relatives. All of these hold overs from a puritanical primitive régime serve to aggravate the more familiar background for delinquency. Furthermore, the Antler home, as the only social form left which can be relied upon to give character training to Antler children (I am disregarding here, of course, the government schools, the missions, etc., none of which have sufficient relevance to Indian attitudes to have much present effect), is in an even more infelicitous position than the average American home. Because the differences and points of likeness are so striking, it will be profitable to compare them.

The American home finds it difficult to provide growing children today with a firm and reliable character development because of the following conditions (among others): the transitional phenomenon of differing standards between parents and children; the phenomenon of heterogeneous standards within the community, which makes different homes present different standards to their children; and the shifting residence and divorce conditions. The Antler home suffers from similar handicaps, many times exaggerated; the conflict between the parents and children in standards of conduct is far greater — the most liberal Antler on the reservation still insisted that he would not permit his daughters to receive young men callers even in the presence of their parents. Parents consider the fact that their daughter has been addressed, either directly or through an intermediary, by a man, as cause for punishing her. The exchange of any private conversation between young people of the opposite sex is still regarded as reprehensible. The children, on the other hand, have conceptions of love making, note writing, gathered at school, influenced by the automobile, the standards of the moving pictures, and the behavior of cognate tribes who have become more assimilated to current white practice. Yet Antler parents still disapprove most strongly of a boy and a girl touching hands in a modified form of the old dances, into which features of the Virginia Reel and the Paul Jones have been introduced among other tribes and recently imported into the reservation. The second great difficulty of the American parents, heterogeneous standards within the community, is replaced for the Antlers by two other complications, the fixity of Antler moral theory which has been accompanied by an almost universal breakdown in practice, and the divergence between old-time Antler, modern Antler, mixed-blood, other-tribal, and white, practice. From all these various groups, divergent moral standards are being presented to the young people; also they are continually forced to recognize in the behavior of their own parents a discrepancy between precept, and past, if not present, practice. To take one example: If an Antler girl smokes cigarettes, she is immediately branded as "bad." The only young women who smoke openly are the openly promiscuous and the temporary wives of men who are too dissolute to care about their wives' behaviors. Yet the older women whose children are grown may smoke with impunity. So a smoking mother forbids her daughter to smoke; the girl knows that five years ago her mother deserted her father and herself and became promiscuous for a period of several months. This produces a mother-daughter situation partly compounded of a difference between the Indian standard by which older women may smoke and girls may not, partly compounded of the marked contrast between the mother's exhortations and her known behavior. Another factor for delinquency among the white population, bad economic conditions, is becoming increasingly a problem among the Indians. With land sales and shrinkage of available houses, overcrowding and insufficient economic bases for households is becoming more and more a feature in the lives of the growing generation. The majority of the young married people have no land and very slight expectation of inheriting enough to support them. This means more divorces under pressure of crowd-ing, poverty, and interfering relatives, and a greater crop of post-marital delinquents. It also promises a poorer home back-ground for the children who may become delinquents ten and fifteen years from now.

From the case records it will be seen how often the delin-quent girls were reared by grandmothers. Although there are too few cases from which to draw conclusions, this is never-theless suggestive of the gap in custom and thought which would be expected between grandparents and granddaughters in a transitional situation. But a word of warning concerning the overinterpretation of this material is in order. It has already been stressed that upon the Antler reservation there are no such alignments between old and new, such as those between one generation and another, pagan and Christian, Peyote cult and the old religion, Protestant and Catholic, Indian-speaking and non-Indian speaking — as are found on so many reservations. The impact of white civilization upon the Antlers has been so prolonged, so badly and sporadically organized, from the standpoint of the missionizing and accul-turating agencies, that there has been no consistent Antler response to white influence. Although by and large the grand-parent generation is less acculturated than the parent, and they less than the adolescents, this is only relatively true. There are grandparents who speak much better English than their grandchildren; there are grandparents who have been to Washington or to California, and young people who have never left the reservation. There are grandmothers who have worn Paris gowns and granddaughters who have never worn anything except the drab school uniform and the conventional two-piece calico of the reservation. There are men of sixty with long hair who have been to New York and boys of twenty who can drive large automobiles, but who speak no English. There is a grandfather skeptic and a son who fears most actively the old religious societies. With-in each family there is a different alignment of interests and experience so that it is impossible to generalize beyond the fact that the family setting is intensely important because every other type of setting for character training has vanished.

In order to illustrate more concretely this tremendous variety of family setting, I shall give here briefly a sketch of one family whom we will call Gordon. Considering the children under ten as the fifth generation and counting backwards, there are now three generations alive. I shall discuss only the immediate ancestors and the living members of the family, omitting the past generation members of collateral lines who have died out. The grandfather in generation one was a war priest, an important member of a special priestly class. He had three sons, one of whom married into a French mixed-blood family, the middle son married a woman from another tribe which was linguistically completely diverse from the Antler, although belonging to the same general culture area, and the third son married a mixed-blood Antler.

The first son who married the granddaughter of the original French-Antler cross had three children, Alice, Thelma, and Carl. Alice married a full-blood Antler, Peter Anderson, a slender, pious little man without important society privileges of any kind, who characteristically took to Peyote with great special enthusiasm when it was introduced a few years after his marriage. He had been East to school and had received a fairly good craft training. He spoke English with considerable fluency, wore store clothes with a distinctly ministerial air, and gave a strong impression of acculturation. He was therefore one of the first to receive a fee patent to his land, which he sold except for ten acres of woodland. He had five children, of whom the eldest, Tom, got into a quarrel at school and was sent home. At nineteen, after several years of loitering about and learning a little of the trade which his father practised in a very desultory manner, he married Edith Green, the daughter of parents who were strongly addicted to gambling and drinking. Peter had reared his children very strictly and looked upon the marriage of his son at nineteen to a member of the Green family as a terrible event. Alice had also had ambitions for the boy, a mild, soft-spoken, unenterprising youth, whose spirit had been completely broken. She never forgave her daughter-in-law for having married her son.

The second child was a daughter, Sarah. At school she had been assigned the special task of acting as domestic servant to one of the chief officials. The official's wife had taken an interest in her, had taught her to cook, and more especially to sew, had given her an interest in fancywork, in ornamental sewing beyond the plain sewing taught in the dull routine of the school. While she was at school, during her holidays on the reservation, she had begun a sly, undercover flirtation with Sydney Roth, a young returned soldier, who had a bad syphilitic infection. But during her last two years at school, he went to live with Catherine Emmons, a violent-tempered young woman who had been deserted the year before by her first husband. Sydney Roth's mother and sisters (he came from a wealthy, landowning family), had counted on the slight attachment between Sarah and Sydney maturing, and they frowned heavily upon his alliance with Catherine. He could not marry her by the state law because she was still married to her deserting husband; his family refused to let him bring her home or to make any gifts which would have given Indian validation to the marriage. After he had lived with Catherine, in her house and on her rent money, for about thirteen months and after she contracted syphilis from him and when she was eight months gone in pregnancy, Sarah came home. Sydney's sisters were her friends and they privately urged her to take him away from Catherine, whom they disliked. Sydney renewed his covert flirtation with Sarah and, finally, he and she eloped to the county seat. Catherine heard about it and, renting a car, rushed over to attempt to stop the marriage, but her efforts were unavailing; she was the legal wife of another man and Sydney and Sarah were legally free to marry.

Catherine challenged Sarah to a fist fight and both of them rolled in the mud in the center of Radner. The young couple went to live with Sydney's parents and Sydney took regular prophylactic treatments. After four years they had one child. During this period Sydney and Sarah lived with Sydney's parents and with Sarah's parents, who lived in a house belonging to Alice, which they later lost in a mortgage foreclosure. Peter did a little work at his trade, but enjoyed his joint position as a functionary in the Mission and much more in Peyote, and explained his failure to work by declaring that no one was willing to hire an Indian. When any work on government property was given to a white artisan, Peter found an acceptable alibi for doing no work at all for at least six months.

The next younger brother is subject to epileptic seizures and stays close to his parents. The two younger children, a girl of seventeen and a boy of fifteen, are still in school. The girl was seduced quite violently two years ago, but is still vigorously debarred from attendance at dances by her strict parents. This is a stricter ruling than that of any Antlers except the one household in which parents and children are all members of the Pentecostal Church. About two years ago, Sydney had a chance at a slight job which carried with it four rooms in a double frame house belonging to his employers. He and Sarah and their two-year-old child moved in here. For the last five years neither of them had done any work to speak of; they had lived with their parents, Sarah had helped with the dishes and done her own and Sydney's washing. Both of them drank and gambled whenever opportunity offered. But now, coming into closer contact with a benevolent employer and his interested wife, they sobered down. The white woman discovered Sarah's old training as a seamstress and utilized it. She also employed her to work in the house, lent her patterns, gave her old clothes, encouraged her to put her house in order, embroider herself bedspreads, dress her child attractively.

Sydney held his job and the family were just settling down to a cheerful and industrious life with a well-planted garden and well-stocked pantry shelves, and Sarah making quite a little money from her sewing, mostly by sewing for Indians.[13] Then Alice and Peter lost their house and Alice, Peter and the three unmarried children came to live with Sarah and Sydney. Sydney was making twenty-five dollars a month and his rent. About a month later, Tom and Edith and their seven-year-old child came there also, having exhausted their welcome at Edith's parents, who had used up all of the rent money in gambling and had only about half a bag of flour left.

This impossible situation of eight people in half of a small house smoldered sullenly for about three months, and then one day Edith quarreled violently with her mother-in-law, Alice. She bundled up her bedding and her dresses, took her small girl and marched off to live with a widower with five children whose other-tribal wife had just died leaving him a large interest in some oil lands. This deceased wife had acquired by a previous inheritance from a deceased husband, forty fine acres on the Antler reservation. The widower commiserated with Edith over her poverty and crowded quarters with a disagreeable mother-in-law, and promised her a car, fine dresses, etc. But after a day in town, he informed her that his lease on a small house in Radner was up, and he and his children all moved in with her parents; he, however, contributed most of the ready money from his income. The small seven-year-old child stayed with her mother. She was in the fifth generation from the original Gordon whose descendants we are tracing. Her mother and *soi-disant* stepfather soon came to blows; Edith was unused to the arduous work of caring for so many children; people laughed at her at hand games as she tried to dispose her newly acquired brood

---

[13] Antlers always prefer to wash or sew for Indians rather than for white people because they will always "pay better"—the old prestige point of being proud of an expenditure.

about her. Her widower had been denied permission to sell his land, from the proceeds of which he had hoped to buy a car; and, in a sudden fit of caution and annoyance at his new mistress, he deeded all his valuable oil lands to his children. At the same time, it became increasingly evident that he was suffering from tuberculosis, which manifested itself as galloping consumption, and he died nine months after Edith eloped with him. She was now in an indeterminate position, living at home with her improvident parents. Tom made no attempt to claim his child, declaring that as Edith had deserted him without cause she could have the trouble of rearing her. He admitted that his former parents-in-law had been cruelly harsh to his former wife's sister's child which they were also rearing; still, after all, what could he do? He had no money, no trade, no land. What could he do with a child? So here with a deserted, quasi-widowed mother and a pair of gambling grandparents, we will leave this one member, five generations descendant from the original Gordon.

After Edith ran away, the crowded living quarters still remained unendurable; Peter got a slight job repairing the house of another Indian and decided to build himself and Alice a log cabin on the ten acres of woodland still remaining to them. He erected a temporary shelter there for the summer months while he finished his employment, and got money to buy nails, screening, etc. Meanwhile, Sydney and Sarah and the child went to camp about ten miles away on the farm of a mixed-blood married to a white man, while Sydney worked in the harvest fields. In the autumn, Alice's two youngest children went back to school. This accounts to date for the descendants of Alice Gordon and Peter Anderson.

Thelma went to government school and learned to speak excellent English. She married a full-blood and bore him three children; he died when they were quite young, and she married again, an other-tribal full-blood, who had formerly married an Antler and inherited land from her. This land he traded for a house in Bergen. He died a few years after marrying Thelma and the daughter by his first wife inherited the house in Bergen. This she exchanged with Thelma, her stepmother, and moved to Thelma's forty acres, when she married a mixed-blood, also of other-tribal affiliations. Meanwhile, one of Thelma's children died of tuberculosis and the other two girls showed signs of pulmonary weakness. Thelma's second husband's sister had married an other-tribal Indian and was living in the Southwest. With money gained from the sale of some inherited land, she took the two girls to the Southwest to stay with her sister-in-law. The older daughter became well enough to return to school and eventually married a man from a cognate tribe. The younger daughter remained with her aunt in the Southwest and finally married an Indian from the same tribe as the one into which her aunt had married. The second daughter, Minnie, and her other-tribal husband lived on in Bergen in Thelma's house. Thelma divides her time between her two daughters, having become very much attached to her daughter's affinal relatives in the Southwest. Minnie's husband, having no land, and away from his tribe, works as a laborer and supports his wife and three small children. The older daughter has no children, so these three children are the only members of the fifth generation.

Carl, the third child of the eldest son of the original Gordon progenitor, married a white woman. He himself was only one-eighth white. His wife was an enterprising woman and they moved to another state and he went to work. He had three sons, two of whom moved still farther away and married white women. Although their names are still on the roll, they have very little contact with their Antler relatives. But the youngest son married an Indian woman of a cognate tribe and lives with her tribe. However, he has continued in the pattern set by his father and runs a small business for a living. A fourth son is unmarried and working in a factory on the Pacific Coast.

This ends the tale of the three children, Alice, Thelma, and

Carl, children of the oldest son of old Gordon by the daughter of the French-Antler half breed.

The youngest son of the old war priest married a mixed-blood woman and had two children, a boy, William, and a girl, Margery. Each of them inherited eighty acres of good land. Neither of them went away to school, but both speak a little English, William speaking more than Margery, who is confined to a few very mutilated scraps of English. William is an aberrant Antler in many ways. He is far more industrious and active than most of the other men, and immensely more imaginative. He has had an individual vision, but from this he received, not the traditional trick which is only claimed from the vision and really inherited, but a supernatural sanction to do a bit of surgery, of medieval type, it is true, but none the less surgery, not an empty shamanistic trick. For his assumed skill he is sometimes called in even by white men, and is also called to doctor members of other tribes. He has also improved, by melting up metal and by the use of modern tools, on the traditional method of manufacturing the musical instrument of this region. He is also the only Antler who does much fishing and he has learned to make a type of splint basket; these he sells to white people. He has asserted his individuality against changing custom in one other respect — by marrying two sisters. By the first wife, he had six children and by the subsidiary wife, he had one. The eldest of the six came home from school and became involved with a woman of very poor reputation, who had been leading a dissolute life for many years. The old man, William, refused to tolerate his son's choice in the house, and finally she proved so quarrelsome and unmanageable that the son left home to join a rodeo show. He has been gone about a year. The second girl was so fair that she felt ill at ease with her more copper-colored brothers and sisters and refused to come home from school until she was grown, so that she finally came home speaking practically no Antler. She married a boy about her own age whose father had become very much alienated from the tribe by his marriage to a woman of a completely different tribe who had never learned to speak Antler and had reared her children to speak only English. The two young people were drawn together by their common plight, a sense of separateness and a lack of understanding of Antler speech or of Antler ways. But after their marriage they went to live with old William under whose roof there was always plenty to eat, and the young son-in-law began to take over much of the heavy farming work from the aging father-in-law. At the same time both husband and wife began to learn to speak Antler, and the aggresively non-Indian mother of the son-in-law began to bewail the fact that her son, reared to English-speaking and white ways, was regressing to Antler beliefs and even taking bits of food out to feed to the ghosts at night. This is a particularly good illustration of how deceptive assimilation still is as a prophecy for the next generation. This young husband and wife gave every evidence of having been weaned by circumstances of temperament and upbringing from the old tribal custom. By an accident of residence, economically dictated, they were both being drawn back into the intricacies of Antler tradition.[14]

The three younger children of the senior wife and the one child of her younger sister were all in school. William had as yet no grandchildren.

His sister Margery married a full-blood and had two children, Truman and Patricia. After she had been married only a few years, the daughter of her older brother was deserted by her husband's parallel cousin. The niece Marian, took refuge with her paternal aunt, and was taken as a subsidiary wife by her aunt's husband who was also the cousin of her deserting first husband. This arrangement continued until

[14] The brother of this young man married the granddaughter of one of the most conservative old women on the reservation, a member of the sorcerer's society, who still makes moccasins, hunts for mice caches, and makes soap. They are at present resident in his home, but should they move to hers, he will very likely return to Indian ways just as his brother has.

the niece had borne one child, when she left the household, practically forced out by the resentfulness of the senior wife, Margery, and married again. We shall return to her case again when we consider another set of descendants. Margery's two children grew up, with very few years of school and speaking very little English. Truman married a full-blood girl who bore him five children and died. One child, who is crippled, lives with him; the others spend all their time at school. He inherited forty acres from his father, but was fraudulently persuaded to deed it away, without realizing what he was doing. He then married a very young girl of only seventeen and went to live with her grandmother. He and she have one child, a little boy of two. He, his wife, his crippled child, and his youngest child are pensioners in a household which contains fifteen other people and towards which neither of them contribute anything. The other child of Margery, Patricia, married an unenterprising youth, son of a mother who had no English name — this is usually significant as an index of little schooling or contact with white ways — and a father who, while quite well schooled, was one of the most adamant in the observance of old sorcery custom. He also, by the contrariness peculiar to the Antler situation, was more than a usually attentive church member. This young man, whom we will call George Sanders, lived on forty acres of his father's which he farmed in a shiftless, desultory manner. He and Patricia have seven children none of whom attend any school or speak any English. A few years ago George's mother died, and Margery, the mother of Patricia, married the father of her daughter's husband. Besides being now husband and wife, they are members of the same sorcery society. They live on his forty acres, the farming land is rented, and rent from her eighty acres also goes to support the household.

To return to the original ancestral line again: Wilbur, the second son, married a woman from another tribe, speaking a different language, but having a culture somewhat similar to the Antler's. She bore him two girls, Ruth and Marian, and died. The father married again, this time a descendant of the same French-Antler cross into which his brother had married. But his second wife's mixed-blood father had married a woman whose mother was one-half Negro, which made the wife of this second Gordon's son a quarter Negro. This stepmother did not like her husband's two daughters and treated them very unkindly, so that when a government agent wanted to send little Marian, who already showed promise of great intelligence, East to school, there was slight objection. Marian was away at school among Pennsylvania Quakers for six years and came back proud of her English accomplishments, versed in the housewifely secrets of the Quaker women with whom she had lived during the summers. But shortly after her return home, she eloped with a young man who deserted her after she had borne one daughter. She then took refuge with the husband of her paternal aunt, as previously described, and bore him one son, Philip, and subsequently left him and married a rather down-at-the-heel old widower with one son. Her daughter died as a young girl and her son, Philip, married a white woman, who quarreled with her mother-in-law and deserted her Antler husband, taking their one child with her. Philip then married a woman who had been living as a quasi-second wife of a married man, and had borne him a child. They live on her land and he farms it passably well and also works for a wage during the harvest season. The second son, by Marian's third husband, married a wealthy and dissolute young woman from whom he finally separated. They had no children and he died a violent death soon after. The fourth child, also a son by the third husband, also married a wealthy young woman, who under Marian's influence became a good housekeeper and a great success at preserving and gardening. This marriage was arranged by the girl's aunt and uncle, who invited the young man to the house and told him that they proposed to have him marry their niece. Two children were born and then he died. The father, Marian's third husband, had died some years previously, leaving her practically destitute. Her son's wife married again at once, and the children remained with the aunt and uncle who had reared her son's wife. Then Marian married again, this time to a very old man who had been married four times previously. This marriage, late in time, had a very precarious existence as Marian and her daughter-in-law, with whom her decrepit old husband lived, did not get on well together.

The second sister, Ruth, had much less schooling than Marian and never went in as thoroughly for white ways. She vacillated between two husbands, now taking on one, now the other, until she finally earned a reputation for promiscuity which was later to involve a young niece, Lila, who will appear later in this narrative. She ended her life under the shadow of promiscuity.

This completes the account of the two daughters of the second of the original Gordon sons and the other-tribal woman. We now come to his children by the partly-negroid, mixed-blood wife. There were three of these: Ralph, Maxwell, and Elizabeth. Elizabeth married a relative of her sister Marian's third husband, and bore him seven children, all but one of whom died. He died from after affects of a war injury. He had been a most conservative Antler in many ways, retaining membership in one of the societies. She now, with her one remaining child, lived on a pension in the house of relatives. The elder brother went East to school and married on his return a girl who had also gone East to school and who had, by virtue of the summer outing system, received an excellent education in domestic economy. They married, living at first with Ralph's father, who was one of the first and few Antlers to make a success of farming. After his death, they inherited a good deal of land. Speaking excellent English, they had no difficulty in getting patents to their lands and they sold and spent, spent and sold, until nothing remained to them but a house. Here they and their four children, all of whom have spent many years in school, live. The eldest girl has an illegitimate child and is promiscuous. The other three children are still in school. The mother is articulately pessimistic about the hard lot of the present-day Antler. Although she is trained as a seamstress and could make a little money in that way, she does nothing except keep the tiny house neat and clean. Ralph works occasionally and takes a prodigious interest in religion.

Maxwell's life has been more colorful. He was sent away to school, but got on the wrong train and ended up somewhere in the far South, whence it took him three months to get back to the reservation. After leaving school, he worked for quite a while at various semiskilled jobs in the East. He married a girl whose parents had been violent and drunken. She very shortly became unfaithful. Nevertheless, she did her best to prevent his enlisting when war was declared, by laying information that he was a deserter. After he went to war, she became promiscuous and his mother took the one child. On his return from the War, he married again, this time a most conservative woman, the niece of one of the few women members of the sorcerers' society. His wife makes moccasins, does beadwork, dresses in strictest Indian fashion, and goes very few places, while he is of a jolly, roving nature and sometimes leaves the reservation for months, following rodeos, fairs, wrestling matches, etc. They have three little children and live on the proceeds of the rented eighty acres belonging to his wife's aunt. He often takes advantage of the mother-in-law's privilege of abusing her son-in-law by addressing an unconscious child on the subject of its father. Occasionally he does a little work harvesting, or picking wild grapes to sell for wine making, but usually he lives as he says, "like a rabbit, holing in anywhere I can find a wind-break." His daughter by his first wife came home from school, became involved in a family quarrel for which he beat her savagely, whereupon she finally ran away to her mother and a few months later was sent away to a reformatory as incorrigible. This concludes the tale of the living descendants of the original old war priest, (modified here and there so that the description may not be identifying).

On this note of particularity it is appropriate to end this study. Here in this one family history we find samples of many of the types and conditions which have been discussed in previous sections; there is the innovator, the man who leaves the reservation, the man who reverts to old custom, the good farmer, the shiftless farmer, the renter, and the man without any income at all; also those who have house roof only. There are all types of marriages: white-Antler, mixed-blood-Antler, negro-Antler, and their descendants, and inter-tribal marriages. There are two cases of polygamy, which it should be remarked, is higher than the average history will show. There are two illegitimate children and several dissolute women, at the same time that there are women of thrift and sobriety. There are old people who have been well schooled and young people who speak no English. It is a heterogeneous picture more diverse, less amenable to strict analysis than would be the histories of individuals in any average small-town American community. It illustrates the tremendous diversity of experience which cultural breakdown and culture contact have forced upon the Antlers, removing all the old sanctions, leaving only this differentiated precarious family life as an educational background for the next generation.

In the problem of Antler women, their adjustments and their failures, I consider these conditions which have made, are making, and will make, for increasing delinquency, to be the most important. In the case of the adjustment of Antler men, the economic dislocation is probably equally important, but for the women, I consider it secondary. Although it is true that young women are playing a decreasingly important economic rôle, parallel to the loss of old techniques, the introduction of store buying, and also to the decreasing rôle of their husbands, there remain sufficient economic tasks for any married woman with children. If their moral fiber, their sense of responsibility to a code, their habits of life, were not corrupted by the existent standards of sex ethics and sex behavior, their ultimate adjustment might be predicted with considerable more hopefulness. Under existing conditions and existing trends, there is reason to believe that the increase in delinquency during the last generation will continue. With the changing standards within the Indian group so dependent upon white attitudes, it is not possible to say that with the death of the older generation and the removal of the conflict between the standards of the old and the standards of the young, conditions will improve. The tendency to retain theory, to retain the outward and visible structure though immeasurably shrunken, is characteristic of Antler society, in religious, social, and economic behavior, as well as in sex behavior. If this tendency continues, the greater freedom of this generation of young mothers will not argue for greater tolerance, but merely for less control over their daughters. Meanwhile the double-edged interracial situation — white society standing for a cruel code, Indian society standing for an amelioration of racial injustice, an Indian situation reflecting changes in white sexual behavior but not changes in white sex attitudes — will continue to operate.

Yet one solution of the present situation, the gradual amalgamation of the Antler into the white population through scattered residence and absorption into various industrial pursuits, depends upon the adjustment of the women. As long as the women are so conspicuously unwilling to leave the reservation to take up the challenge to attain and maintain a higher standard of living, the group, no matter how decimated by disease and economically impoverished, may be expected to remain together. Yet the present situation of reservation life promises to produce, with each decade, women of less moral fiber, less willingness to struggle, with fewer reliable habits.

I should like to conclude this account with an analogy. A

coherent primitive culture may be likened to a dwelling house, within the protecting walls of which generations are born, live to old age and die. Some parts of the structure may be much older than others. Although the architecture conforms in a general way to the type of architecture peculiar to its geographical area, yet it will have idiosyncrasies of its own which give it individuality. The design for some parts of the structure may be similar to the design of other parts of neighboring houses. A room used for one purpose in other houses may serve an entirely different purpose in this house and may be modified in response to this new use.

Such a house will not be a perfect dwelling; it may be asymmetrical, inadequately adapted to current needs, a little cramped, or too rambling. But each part of it will bear some relation to the lives of those who live beneath its roof. If they live there long enough, they would probably tear down an unused section here or build there for new needs. Between the house and the individuals who live in it there will be a definite relation.

Compare now the state of a house which is being wrecked. The house wrecker is guided by no consideration of use, of intimate relation between the house and the way of life of its inmates. The part of the house which remains after the house wrecker has been at work upon it, but before the house is completely leveled to the ground, has no coherence, no necessary relationship to anything. The inhabitants may be sleeping in the kitchen or cooking in the bedroom. Nor will the house wrecker proceed in the same way on successive houses which fall beneath his wrecking tools. He begins to demolish that section which gives him the best vantage point. He may start with the roof, or the woodshed, or the veranda, or merely lop off the kitchen.

Figures of speech are always dangerous, particularly so in science, when they are too often taken for more than they are worth. But the process of cultural disintegration in which the inevitable progress of the more complex culture gradually breaks down the native culture is as meaningless, as random, as is the collapse of a house before a wrecking machine. It is not possible, as it is in a homogeneous society, to study the individual in relation to a definite social background. Far less is it possible to find any set of social forms which govern and regularize, dignify and define, the life of the individual.

Some of these social forms are completely gone, others are mutilated beyond understanding of their earlier forms, and still others are skewed to new and anomalous uses. Within this disintegrating social structure, the individual develops a formless uncoördinated character.

In the centers of modern civilization it is possible to find those who have developed individual standards of behavior which permit them in some measure to live without a background of coherent social form. Individuals with such cultural sophistication, with such a degree of self-conscious integration, may offer proper subjects of study both to the individual psychologists and students of culture. But among those unfortunate primitive peoples, only a generation or two from a coherent primitive background, no such illuminating self-consciousness occurs. The student finds neither formal order and the typical behavior characteristic of homogeneous societies, nor the self-conscious individualization of cosmopolitan communities, nor does the investigator find sufficient numbers to afford statistical control of his material. It is possible only to record the complete fortuitousness of the process — by which the primitive culture breaks down and the individual member of the primitive society is left floundering in a heterogeneous welter of meaningless uncoördinated and disintegrating institutions.

PART III

TABULAR AND DIAGRAMMATIC TREATMENT
OF RAW MATERIALS

CHAPTER XI

HOUSEHOLD ORGANIZATION

A complete analysis of 160 households was made and the data compiled. The following system of abbreviations has been devised for the presentation of the data.

KEY

The initial number is the number of the household. The series of numbers simply indicate the number in the household, 1 always being the nominal head of the household.

Sex
M — male
F — female

Age [1]
c — child, 1-10
a — adolescent, 10-20
y — young adult, 20-30
ma — middle age, 30-50
o — old, over 50

Relationship
h — husband
w — wife
m — mother
f — father
s — son
d — daughter
b — brother
si — sister

Modifications of relationship
( ) — relative is dead, e.g., f(si) — father's dead sister
dv — divorced
wd — widowed
Numeral preceding h or w refers to that person, e.g., f 2w — father's second wife
il — illegitimate
Parentage is indicated by c (d or s) 1, 2 — child of 1 and 2
If one parent is dead — c 2 (1 w) — child of 2 and his deceased first wife
If the other parent of an illegitimate child is living — il c 2 f — illegitimate child of 2 by a living father
? after husband or wife indicates a temporary relationship
st-step. e.g. — st d 2 — stepdaughter of 2
ot — other tribe, *i.e.*, member of some other tribe
hb — half breed
wh — white

Economics
* — income or property   *** — income or property and also works
** — works

1 (household number)
 1. F(emale) o(ld) w(i)d(owed)
 2. F(emale) m(iddle) a(ged) d(i)v(orced) st(ep) d(aughter) (of) 1
 3. M(ale) (adolescent) s(on) (of) 2
 4. F(emale) il (legitimate) d(aughter) (of) 2

[1] All ages are approximate.

Households Studied

1.
1. F o * wd
2. F ma dv st d 1
3. M a s 2
4. M c s 2
5. M c s 2
6. F c il d 2 f

2.
1. M o *
2. F o w 1
3. M ma h (d) 1, 2 **
4. F c d 3
5. M c s 3
6. F c d 3
7. F c d 3
8. M c s 3
9. F y d 1, 2
10. M y h 9 **

3.
1. M ma **
2. F ma w 1
3. F a d 1, 2

4.
1. M y
2. F y w 1 *
3. M c s 1, 2
4. M c s 1, 2
5. F c d 2 (h)

5.
1. F ma wd *
2. F y d 1
3. M y ot h 2
4. M c s 2, 3
5. F c d 2, 3
6. M c s 2, 3

6.
1. M ma *
2. F ma w 1
3. F y d 1, 2
4. M ma h 4
5. F c d 4 dv h
6. M c s 5 (w)
7. M c s 5 (w)

8. F c d 5 (w)
9. M c s 5 (w)

7.
1. M o wd *
2. M ma s 1
3. F ma ot w 2
4. M c s 2, 3
5. F c d 2, 3
6. F a d 1
7. F a d 1

8.
1. M ma ***
2. F ma w 1
3. M y s 2 (1w)
4. F y w 3
5. F a d 2 (1h)
6. M c s 2 (2h)

9.
1. M ma ***
2. F ma w 1
3. M a s 1, 2
4. F a d 1, 2
5. M c s 1, 2
6. F c d 1, 2
7. F c d 1, 2
8. F c d 1, 2
9. M c s 1, 2
10. F c d 1, 2

10.
1. M ma **
2. F ma w 1
3. M a f 1, 2
4. F c d 1, 2
5. M c s 1, 2

11.
1. M o *
2. F o w 1 *
3. F ma d 1 (w)
4. M ma h 3
5. F c d 3, 4
6. F a d 3 (h)
7. F c d 3 (h)

12. 1. M o *
2. F o w 1
3. F y d 1 (w)
4. M y h 3

13. 1. M o
2. F ma w 1 *
3. F y d 1, 2
4. M y h 3
5. F c d 3, 4
6. M c s 3, 4
7. M ma h (si) 2 b 4
8. M y s 7 (si) 2
9. F y w 8
10. F a d 7 (w) d (si) 2
11. F c d 7 (w) d (si) 2

14. 1. M o *
2. F ma w 1 *
3. M ma s 2 (h)
4. F ma w 3 *
5. M c s 3, 4
6. F c d 3, 4
7. F c d 3, 4
8. M c s 3, 4
9. F y d 2 (h)
10. M y h 9 *
11. M c s 10, 9
12. M c s 9, 10

15. 1. F ma *
2. M ma h 1
3. F c d 1 (h)
4. F c d 1 (h)
5. F c d 1 (h)
6. M c ils 1, 2
7. F o m 1 dv h
8. M o h 7 **
9. F a d 7
10. F y d 8
11. M y h 10 s 2

16. 1. M ma *

2. F ma w 1
3. F a d 1 (w)
4. F a d 1 (w)
5. F c d 1, 2
6. M c s 1, 2
7. F c d 1, 2
8. M a s 2 dv h
9. F c d 2 dv h

17. 1. M ma *
2. F y w 1
3. F c d 1, 2
4. F c d 1, 2
5. M c s 1, 2
6. M o wd f 1
7. F o wd m 2 (part time)
8. F y d 7 si 2
9. M y h 8
10. F c d 8, 9

18. 1. M ma ***
2. F ma w 1

19. 1. M o
2. F ma w 1 *
3. F y d 1, 2
4. F y d 1, 2
5. F a d 1, 2
6. F a d 1, 2
7. F c d 1, 2
8. F y d 1 (w)
9. M y h 8 ***
10. M c s 8 dv h

20. 1. M o wd *
2. M ma s 1
3. F y w 2
4. M c s 2, 3
5. F c d 2, 3
6. M a s d 1 ot
7. M a s d 1 ot

21. 1. M ma ***
2. F y w *

22. 1. M o wd *
    2. F y d 1 (w)
    3. M y h 2
    4. F c d 2, 3
    5. F c d 2, 3
    6. F c d 1 (w)
    7. F c d 1 (w)
    8. F y d 1 (w)
    9. M y h (8)
23. 1. M ma
    2. F ma w 1
    3. M a s 1, 2
    4. F c d 1, 2
    5. M c s 1, 2
    6. M c s 1, 2
    7. F c d 1, 2
24. 1. M o
    2. F o w 1 *
    3. M ma s 1, 2 **
    4. F y w 3
    5. M c il s 4 f
25. 1. M ma
    2. F ma w 1
    3. M a s 1, 2
    4. M a s 1, 2
    5. F c d 1, 2
    6. F c d 1, 2
    7. F c d 1, 2
    8. F ma d b f 1
    9. M ma h 8
    10. M a s 8, 9
    11. F a d 8, 9
    12. M c s 8, 9
    13. F c d 8, 9
    14. M c s 8, 9
    15. F c d 8, 9
26. 1. F o wd (2h) *
    2. F ma d 1 (1h)
    3. M ma h 2 *

4. F a d 2, 3
5. F a d 2, 3
6. F y d 1 (2h)
7. M ma s 1 (1h)
8. F y w 7
9. M c s 7, 8
10. M c s 7, 8
11. M c s 7, 8
27. 1. M ma *
    2. F ma white w 1 **
28. 1. M ma *
    2. F ma w 1
    3. M c s 1, 2
    4. F c d 1, 2
    5. M c s 1, 2
    6. M o wd f 2 *
    7. M y s 6 b 2
29. 1. F ma dv 2 h *
    2. F c d 1 dv h
    3. F c d 1 dv h
30. 1. M ma ***
    2. F ma ot w 1
    3. F a d 1, 2
    4. F a d 1, 2
    5. F a d 1, 2
    6. M a d 1, 2
31. 1. F o wd
    2. M y s 1
    3. F y w 2
    4. M y s b (h) 1
    5. F ma w 4
    6. M a s 4 dv h *
    7. M a s 4 dv h *
    8. M c s 4 dv h *
    9. M c s 4 dv h *
    10. M c s 4, 5
    11. M c s 4, 5
32. 1. M o *
    2. F o *

3. M y s s s 1 * *
4. F y w 3
5. M o wd no rel

33. 1. M ma * *
2. F ma ot w 1
3. M a s 1, 2
4. F a d 1, 2
5. M a s 1, 2
6. M c s 1, 2
7. M c s 1, 2
8. F c d 1, 2
9. M y s 1, 2
10. F a w 9

34. 1. F o *
2. M ma h 1 *
3. F y d (s) 2 (2h)
4. M ma h 3
5. M a s 3, 4
6. F c d 3, 4
7. F c d 3, 4
8. F y d (s) 2 (2h)
9. M y h 8
10. M c s 8, 9
11. M c s 8, 9
12. F a d (s) 2 (2h)
13. F a d (s) 2 (2h)
14. F a d (s) 2 (2h)
15. M c (s) 2 (2h)
16. F ma 1 w (s) 2
17. M ma h 16

35. 1. M ma *
2. F ma w 1
3. M a s 1, 2
4. F c d 1, 2
5. F c d 1, 2
6. F c d 1, 2

36. 1. M ma *
2. F ma w 1
3. F a d 1, 2

4. F c d 1, 2
5. F y d 1, 2
6. M y h 5
7. F c d 5, 6
8. F y d 1, 2
9. M y h 8 *
10. M c s 8, 9
11. M c s 8, 9
12. F c d 8, 9
13. M y s 2 dv 1 h **
14. F y w 13
15. M c s 13, 14
16. M c s 13, 14
17. F c d 13, 14

37. 1. M ma *
2. F ma w 1
3. M c s 1, 2

38. 1. M ma *
2. F ma w
3. F a d b 2 (white woman)
4. F c d (s) 1

39. 1. M ma * * *
2. F ma w 1
3. M y s 1, 2
4. M a s 1, 2
5. M a s 1, 2
6. F a d 1, 2
7. M c s 1, 2
8. F c d 1, 2
9. M y s 1, 2 **
10. F y w 9
11. M c s 9, 10
12. M c s 9, 10

40. 1. M ma wd * **
2. F ma w 1
3. M a s 1, 2
4. M a s 1, 2
5. M y s 1, 2

6. F y w 5
7. F c d 5, 6

41. 1. M ma wd *
    2. M y s 1 (w) **
    3. F a d 1 (w)
    4. M a s 1 (w)
    5. F c d 1 (w)

42. 1. M y ***
    2. F y w 1
    3. F c d 1, 2
    4. F ma m 1
    5. F a d 4 (h)
    6. M ma h? 4

43. 1. M y ***
    2. F y w 1
    3. M c s 1, 2
    4. M c s 1, 2
    5. M c s 1, 2
    6. F ma m 1
    7. F a d 6 dv ot 4h
    8. M ma h? 6
    9. F ma dv si 2
   10. M c il s 9 f

44. 1. F o wd *
    2. M y s 1
    3. F y w 2
    4. F c d 2, 3
    5. F c d 2, 3

45. 1. F o wd *
    2. M ma dv s 1
    3. M a s 2 dv w
    4. F a d 2 dv w

46. 1. M o *
    2. F o w 1
    3. M ma s 1, 2 **
    4. F ma w 3
    5. F a d 4 (dv 1 h)

47. 1. M ma wd ***
    2. F a d 1 (w)

3. M a s 1 (w)
4. F c d 1 (w)
5. F c d 1 (w)

48. 1. M o **
    2. F o w 1 **
    3. F ma d 1, 2
    4. M ma h 3
    5. F c d 3, 4
    6. M c s 3, 4
    7. F c d 3, 4
    8. M o wd b 2

49. 1. M ma ***
    2. F ma w 1
    3. F c d 1, 2
    4. F y si 2
    5. M y h 4
    6. F c d 4, 5
    7. F c d 4, 5
    8. M ma f 5 dv w
    9. M y s 8

50. 1. M ma
    2. F ma *
    3. M c s 1, 2
    4. M c s 1, 2
    5. F c d 1, 2
    6. F o wd m 1 (part time)
    7. M y b 1 s 6 (h) **
    8. M c b 1 s 6 (h)

51. 1. M ma **
    2. F ma w 1 *
    3. M c s 1, 2
    4. M c s 1, 2
    5. M c s 1, 2
    6. F c d 1, 2

52. 1. M o **
    2. F ma hb w 1
    3. M c il s (d) 1, 2 f
    4. F y d 1, 2
    5. M y ot h 4

6. M c s 4, 5
7. F c d 4, 5
8. M c s 4, 5

53. 1. M ma **
    2. F ma ot w 1 ***
    3. M a s 1, 2
    4. F a d 1, 2
    5. M a d 1, 2
    6. F c d 1, 2

54. 1. M ma ***
    2. F ma w 1
    3. M a s 1, 2
    4. M a s 1, 2
    5. M a s 1, 2

55. 1. M y ***
    2. F y w 1

56. 1. M ma ***
    2. F ma w 1
    3. M a s b 1
    4. M y s b 1
    5. F a w 4

57. 1. M ma *
    2. F ma w 1 *
    3. M y s 1, 2
    4. F y w 3
    5. F c d 3, 4
    6. M c s 3, 4

58. 1. M ma ***
    2. F ma w 1
    3. F a d 1 (w)
    4. F a d 1 (w)
    5. F a d 2 (1h)
    6. M a s 2 (1h)
    7. M a s 2 (1h)

59. 1. M ma *
    2. F ma dw 1
    3. M a s 1, 2
    4. F a d 1, 2
    5. F a d 1, 2

6. M a s 1, 2
60. 1. F o wd *
    2. F ma d 1
    3. M ma h 2 **
    4. M y s 2, 3
    5. F a d 2, 3
    6. F a d 2, 3
    7. M a h 6 *

61. 1. M ma ***
    2. F ma w 1
    3. F a d 1, 2

62. 1. M ma
    2. F ma w 1 *
    3. M a s 1, 2
    4. F y d 1, 2 ***
    5. M y h 4

63. 1. M ma ***
    2. F ma w 1
    3. F ma d si m 2
    4. M ma h 3 **
    5. M a s 3, 4
    6. M c s 3, 4
    7. M c s 3, 4
    8. M c s 3, 4
    9. F a d dv s b m 2
    10. M a s wd b 2
    11. M ma wd b 1 *

64. 1. F ma *
    2. M ma ot h 1
    3. M a s 1, 2
    4. M c s 1, 2

65. 1. M ma
    2. F ma w 1 *
    3. M y s 1, 2
    4. F a d 1, 2
    5. F y d 1, 2
    6. M y ot h 5
    7. F c d 5, 6
    8. F c d 5, 6

9. M o wd b 1 *

66. 1. M ma
    2. F ma w 1 *
    3. M c s d (d si) 2

67. 1. M ma (ot) ***
    2. F y w 1 *
    3. F c d 1, 2
    4. M c s 1, 2
    5. M c s 1, 2
    6. M y b 1 *
    7. F ma si 2
    8. M ma h 7
    9. F a d 7, 8
    10. M c s 7, 8
    11. M a s 7 dv h

68. 1. M ma wd *
    2. F a d 1 (w)
    3. M a s 1 (w)
    4. M a s 1 (w)
    5. F c d 1 (w)

69. 1. M ma *
    2. F ma w 1 **
    3. F a d 1, 2
    4. M a s 1, 2
    5. M y dv s 1, 2
    6. M y s 1, 2

70. 1. M ma
    2. F ma w 1
    3. M a s 1, 2
    4. F a d 1, 2
    5. M a c 1, 2
    6. F c d 1, 2
    7. M c s 1, 2
    8. M o wd f 1

71. 1. M ma *
    2. F ma w 1
    3. M a s 1, 2
    4. M c s 1, 2
    5. M c s 1, 2

6. M c s 1, 2
7. F ma si 1
8. M a s 7 dv h
9. F a d 7 dv h

72. 1. M ma *
    2. F a w 1
    3. M a s 1, 2
    4. M a s 1, 2

73. 1. M a *
    2. F a w 1
    3. F ma ot m 1 (f) *
    4. M ot b 3
    5. F ma w 4
    6. F c d 4 (w)

74. 1. M ma
    2. F ma w 1
    3. M c s 1, 2
    4. M a s f 1 (wh w) **

75. 1. M o **
    2. F ma wh w 1 **
    3. F a d 1, 2
    4. M a s 1, 2
    5. F c d 1, 2
    6. M c s 1, 2

76. 1. M o dv *
    2. M ma s 1
    3. F y w 2
    4. M a s 2, 3
    5. M c s 2, 3
    6. F c d 2, 3
    7. F c d 2, 3

77. 1. M ma **
    2. F ma ot w 1 *
    3. F a d 1 dv ot w
    4. F c d 1, 2

78. 1. M ma wd *
    2. F o wd m 1 **
    3. M a s 1 (ot w)
    4. M a s 1 (ot w)

5. F c d 1 (ot w)

79. 1. M ma *
    2. F ma w 1
    3. F y d 1, 2
    4. M a s 1, 2 **
    5. M a s 1, 2 **
    6. M a s 1, 2
    7. F a d 1, 2
    8. F a d 1, 2
    9. F c d 1, 2
    10. M c s 1, 2
    11. M c s 1, 2
    12. F y d 1, 2 dv
    13. M c s 12 dv h
    14. F y d 1, 2
    15. M y h 14 **
    16. M ma b 1
    17. F ma w 16
    18. F c d 16, 17
    19. M c s 17 (h)

80. 1. M ma **
    2. F ma ot w **
    3. M c s 1, 2

81. 1. M o wd *
    2. M a s 1 (m)
    3. M a s 1

82. 1. M ma
    2. F ma w 1 *
    3. M y s w b 2 (h)
    4. M ma wd s (b) 2

83. 1. M o ***
    2. F ma w 1

84. 1. F ma wd ***
    2. F c d 1 (h)
    3. F o s 1 dv **

85. 1. M ma *
    2. F ma w 1

86. 1. F o wd ot *
    2. M o h? 1

3. M y s (d) 1
4. F a d (d) 1
5. M a s (d) 1

87. 1. M ma **
    2. F ma w 1 *
    3. M a s 1, 2
    4. M a s 1, 2
    5. M o wd b f 1

88. 1. M ma
    2. F ma w 1 *
    3. M y s 1, 2
    4. F a d 1, 2
    5. F a d 1, 2
    6. M a s 1, 2
    7. F y d 1, 2
    8. M y h 7 *
    9. M c s 7, 8
    10. F c d 7, 8

89. 1. M ma *
    2. F ma w 1
    3. F a d 1, 2
    4. F c d 1, 2
    5. M c s 1, 2
    6. M y s 2 (h)

90. 1. M ma ***
    2. F ma ot w 1
    3. F a d 1, 2
    4. M a s 1, 2
    5. M c s 1, 2
    6. F c d 1, 2

91. 1. M o *
    2. F o w 1 *

92. 1. M ma ***
    2. F ma w 1
    3. M a s 1, 2
    4. M a s 1, 2
    5. M a s 1, 2
    6. F c d 1, 2
    7. M c s 1, 2

8. F c d 1, 2
9. F c d 1, 2

93. 1. M ma
2. F y w 1 *
3. F c d 1, 2

94. 1. M ma ***
2. F ma w 1
3. M y dv s 1
4. M c s 3 dv w

95. 1. M ma ***
2. F ma w 1
3. M a s 1, 2
4. M a s 1, 2
5. F c d 1, 2
6. F c d 1, 2
7. M y dv s 1, 2
8. M c s 7 dv w
9. M c s 7 dv w

96. 1. M ma ***
2. F ma w 1
3. F a d 1, 2
4. M a s 1, 2
5. F a d 1, 2
6. F a d 1, 2
7. M c s 1, 2
8. M y s 1, 2
9. F y w 8 *
10. M c s 8, 9
11. F c 9 dv h
12. M c s dv d si 1 dv h

97. 1. M ma ***
2. F ma *

98. 1. F o wd *
2. M y s 1 (h) *
3. F a d b 1

99. 1. M o
2. F o w 1 *
3. M ma s 2 (dv h) **
4. M y s 2 (dv h) **

5. M a s 2 (dv h) **
6. M a il s 2 f

100. 1. M ma *
2. F y 2w 1
3. F y d 1 (w)
4. M a s 1 (w)
5. F c d 1, 2
6. F c d 1, 2

101. 1. M ma *
2. F y* w 1
3. M c s 1, 2
4. F c d 1, 2
5. M c s 1, 2
6. M c s 1, 2
7. F c d 1, 2
8. M c s 1, 2
9. M c s 1, 2

102. 1. M ma *
2. F ma w 1
3. M a s 1, 2
4. F c d 1, 2
5. F c d 1, 2
6. F a d 1 (1w)

103. 1. M ma *
2. F ma w 1
3. M s 1, 2
4. F d 1, 2
5. F d 1, 2
6. F a d 1 (1w)

104. 1. M ma *
2. F ma w 1
3. F c d 1, 2
4. F a d 2 (dv)
5. M y ot h 4

105. 1. M o *
2. F y w 1
3. M o f 2
4. F ma w 3
5. M a s 3, 4

106. 1. M o *
    2. F o w 1 *
    3. M a s (s) 1, 2
    4. F a d (s) 1, 2
    5. F c d (s) 1, 2
    6. F y d d m 1

107. 1. M y ***
    2. F y w 1
    3. F c d 1, 2

108. 1. M o *
    2. F ma w 1 *
    3. F y d 1, 2
    4. F y d 1, 2
    5. M y s 1, 2

109. 1. M y
    2. F ma *
    3. M a s 2 (1h)
    4. M c s 2 (1h)
    5. M c s 2 (1h)

110. 1. M ma ***
    2. F ma w 1
    3. M c s 1, 2
    4. M c s 1, 2
    5. M c s 1, 2

111. 1. M y ***
    2. F y w 1
    3. M c s 1, 2
    4. F c d 1, 2
    5. F y s 2

112. 1. M ma **
    2. F y w 1 **
    3. F c d 1, 2

113. 1. M ma **
    2. F ma w 1 *
    3. F a d 1, 2
    4. F c d 1, 2
    5. F c d 1, 2

114. 1. M y *
    2. F y w 1

    3. F c d 1, 2
    4. M c s 2 (1h)

115. 1. M ma **
    2. F ma w 1
    3. F a d 1, 2
    4. M a s 1, 2
    5. M c s 1, 2
    6. F ma si 2
    7. M ma h 5
    8. F a d 6, 7

116. 1. M ma
    2. F ma w 1 *
    3. F c d 1, 2

117. 1. M ma **
    2. F ma w 1 *
    3. M a s 1, 2
    4. F a d 1, 2
    5. M c s 1, 2
    6. M y s 2
    7. F y w 6
    8. M c s 6, 7
    9. M c s 7 dv

118. 1. F o wd *
    2. M y **
    3. M y **
    4. M y **
    5. F y w 4

119. 1. M ma wd **
    2. M a s 1 (w) **
    3. M a s 1 (w)

120. 1. M ma ** *
    2. F ma w 1 *
    3. M a il sd si 1 (white man)
    4. M ma wd h (si) 1
    5. M a s (si) 1 4

121. 1. M ma
    2. F ma *
    3. F a d 1, 2

4. F c d 1, 2
5. M c s 1, 2
6. M c s 1, 2
122. 1. M ma
2. F ma w 1 *
3. M a s 1, 2
4. M a s 1, 2
123. 1. M ma
2. F ma w 1 *
3. F a d 1, 2
124. 1. F o wd *
2. M ma s 1
3. F ma w 2
4. M c s 2, 3
5. F c d 2, 3
6. M y s 2 (1w) *
7. M a s 2 (1w) *
125. 1. M o *
2. F ma w 1
3. M a s 1, 2
4. M c s 1, 2
5. M a s 2 (1h)
126. 1. M ma ***
2. F ma w 1
3. M c s 1, 2
4. M c s 1, 2
5. M ma b 1 ***
6. F ma w 5
7. M a s 5, 6
8. M c s 5, 6
9. M c s 5, 6
10. M c s 5, 6
11. M c s 5, 6
12. M a s (si) 6
13. M c s (si) 6
127. 1. F o wd *
2. F ma dv d 1
3. F a d 2 (h)
4. F ma d b 1

5. M ma h 4
6. M c s 4, 5
7. F c d 4, 5
8. F c d 4, 5
9. M ma b 1
10. F ma w 9
11. M c il s s 9, 10
12. M ma s 9, 10
13. F ma w 12 *
14. F c d 12, 13
15. F c d 12, 13
16. M c s 12, 13
128. 1. M o *
2. F ma w 1
3. M y s 1, 2
4. M a s 1, 2
5. M a s 1, 2
6. F y d 1, 2
7. M y ot h 6
8. M y dv s 1, 2
129. 1. M ma **
2. F ma w 1 *
3. F a d 1, 2
4. F c d 1, 2
5. F c d 1, 2
6. F c d 1, 2
7. M c s 1, 2
130. 1. F o *
2. M ma s 1
3. F ma ot w 2
131. 1. M o *
2. F ma w 1
3. M a s 1, 2
4. M c s 1, 2
5. M y s 1, 2
6. F y w 5
7. F c d 5, 6
132. 1. M ma ***
2. F ma w 1 *

3. F c d 1, 2
4. M a s 2 (1h) *
5. F a d 2 (1h)
6. F m a dv rel 2

133. 1. M y ***
2. F y w 1 *
3. F c d 1, 2
4. M c s 1, 2
5. F c d 1, 2
6. M ma dv b (m) 2 **

134. 1. M o **
2. F o w 1 *
3. M y s 1, 2
4. M y s 1, 2
5. F a d 1, 2
6. F y d 1, 2
7. M c il s 6 f

135. 1. M ma **
2. F ma w 1
3. M c s 1, 2
4. F c d 1, 2
5. F y d (b) 2
6. F y ½si 2

136. 1. M o ***
2. F o w 1
3. F ma w 1
4. M y s o 2
5. M a s 1, 2
6. F a d 1, 2
7. M a s 1, 3
8. F y d 1, 2
9. M y h 8 **

137. 1. M o *
2. F ma w 1
3. M y s s 1 (w) **
4. F y w 3
5. M a s 1 dv white w
6. F a il d 4 f

138. 1. M o *

2. F ma ot w 1
3. F a d (d) 1 (w)
4. F y d 1, 2
5. M y h 4
6. M a s 5 dv white w
7. F c d 5 dv white w
8. M c s 4, 5
9. F c d 4, 5

139. 1. M o ***
2. F ma w 1
3. M y s 1, 2
4. F a w 3
5. F a d 1, 2
6. M a h 5

140. 1. M y
2. F ma *
3. F a d 3 (3h)

141. 1. M ma *
2. F ma ot w 1
3. F c d 1, 2
4. M a s 1 (si) 2
5. F a d 1 (si) 2
6. M a s 1 (si) 2
7. F a d 1 (si) 2
8. F c d 1 (si) 2
9. M c s 1 (si) 2

142. 1. M ma ***
2. F ma ot w 1
3. M a s 1, 2
4. M a s 1, 2
5. F a d 1, 2

143. 1. M ma *
2. F ma *
3. F a d 1, 2
4. F c d 1, 2
5. F c d 1, 2
6. M c s 1, 2

144. 1. F ma *
2. M ma ot h 1 **

3. M a s 1, 2
4. F a d 1, 2
5. M a s 1, 2
6. F c d 1, 2

145. 1. M o
2. F o w 1 *
3. M a s 1, 2 **
4. M y s 1, 2 **
5. F y w 4
6. F c d 4, 5
7. M c s 4, 5

146. 1. M ma ***
2. F ma w 1
3. M y s 1, 2

147. 1. M ma ***
2. F ma w 1
3. F y dv d 1, 2
4. M c s 3 ot dv h

148. 1. F o wd *
2. F ma st d 1
3. M ma h 2
4. M a s 2, 3
5. M a s 2, 3
6. M a s 2, 3
7. M a s 2 (h) *
8. F a w 7

149. 1. M y ***
2. F y w 1 *
3. M ma b 1 ?

150. 1. M o **
2. F o w 1 *
3. M a s 1, 2
4. F a d 1, 2
5. M a s 1, 2
6. F a d 1, 2
7. M a s 1, 2
8. F ma d 1, 2
9. M ma h 8
10. F c d 8, 9

11. M a s 8 (h) ?

151. 1. M ma *
2. F ma w 1
3. M y s 1, 2
4. M a s 1, 2
5. F c d 1, 2
6. F c d 1, 2
7. M y s 1, 2 **
8. F y w 7

152. 1. M y *
2. F y w 1 *
3. M c s 1, 2
4. F c d 1, 2

153. 1. M ma **
2. F ma *
3. F a il d 2 f

154. 1. F o wd *
2. F y d (d) 1
3. F c il 2 white man
4. M y s (d) 1
5. F y w 4
6. M c s 5 dv h
7. M y s (d) 1
8. F ma ot w 7 *
9. F c d 7, 8
10. F c il d 8 f
11. F c il d 8 f
12. F a d (d) 1
13. M a s 8 (s) 1
14. M a s 8 (s) 1
15. F c d 8 (s) 1
16. F c d 8 (s) 1
17. M c s 8 (s) 1

155. 1. M y **
2. F ma *
3. F c d 1, 2

156. 1. M ma **
2. F ma w 1
3. M a s 1, 2

4. F a d 1, 2
5. M c s 1, 2
6. F c d 1, 2
7. F c d 1, 2
8. M c s 1, 2
9. F c d 1, 2

157. 1. F o wd *
2. F ma d (b) 1
3. M ma h 2
4. F a d 2, 3
5. F c d 2, 3
6. M c s 2, 3
7. F c d 2, 3
8. M c s 2, 3
9. F y dv d 2 (1h)
10. M c il s 9 f

158. 1. M ma ***
2. F ma w 1 *
3. M c s 1, 2
4. F c d 1, 2

5. F c d 1, 2

159. 1. M ma ***
2. F ma w 1
3. Ma s 1, 2
4. F a d 1, 2
5. F a d 1, 2
6. M c s 1, 2
7. M c s 1, 2
8. F c d 1, 2
9. M y s 1, 2
10. F y w 9
11. M c s 9, 10
12. F y d 1, 2
13. F c il d 12, f

160. 1. M o wd
2. F ma d 1
3. M ma h 2
4. F c d 2, 3
5. F a d 2 dv h
6. F c il d 2 (white man)

WANDERERS: PEOPLE WHO ARE MEMBERS OF NO HOUSEHOLD FOR ANY LENGTH OF TIME

W 1. 1. M ma *
2. F ma w 1
3. M c s 1, 2
Recently have lived with:
(a) father's sister of 1
(b) mother's brother's
sons of 2
Own a car.

W 2. 1. M y *
2. F y w 1
Recently have lived with:
(a) mother's sister of 1
(b) mother's father of 1
(c) parents of 2

W 3. 1. M y * recent money
inheritance

2. F y wi 1 (ot) *
3. F c d 1, 2
4. M c s 1, 2
5. F c d 1, 2
Recently have lived with:
(a) father of 1
(b) brother of 2
Now rent a house in Radner.
Own a car.

W 4. 1. M y recent land sale
2. F ma w (?) 1 *
3. F c il c 2 f
4. M y b 2 *
5. F y si 2 *
This is a temporary group-

ing of four wandering people. 1, 2, 4, and 5

W 5.   1. M ma wd *
       2. F ma wd w (?) 1
          5 children of 1 (1w)
          at government school
       Recently have lived with:
          (a) sister of 1
          (b) mother of 2
          (c) daughter of 2
          (d) sister of 2

W 6.   1. M ma
       †2. F y w (?) 1
       Recently have lived with:
          (a) father's sister of 1
          (b) old man who is no
              relation
       †She periodically returns to her
       former husband.

W 7.   1. M ma
       2. F ma w (?) 1 *
       3. F c d 1 (h)
       4. M c s 1 (w)
       5. F c d 1 (w)
       Recently have lived with:
          (a) mother's brother of
              1
          (b) father of 2
       Now living in house in
       Radner she inherited
       from her dead husband.

W 8.   1. M ma
       2. F y w 1
       3. M c s 1, 2
       4. F c d 1, 2
       Recently have lived with:
          (a) father of 1
          (b) mother's sister of 2

W 9.   1. F wd *

W 10. 2. M c il s 1 f
       Lives in a hotel in Bergen.
       Promiscuous.   Income
       from oil land inherited
       from dead husband.

W 10. 1. M y *
       Recently has lived with:
          (a) father's   brother's
              sons
          (b) friend
          (c) friend
       Has rent of 160.

W 11. 1. M o wd
       Recently has lived with:
          (a) daughter
          (b) sister's daughter
          (c) son

W 12. 1. M y *
       Recently has lived with:
          (a) father's sister's son
          (b) sister
       Owns a car and is dissipat-
       ing recent money inher-
       itance.

W 13. 1. M o wd
       Recently has lived with:
          (a) sister's son
          (b) brother

W 14. 1. M y dv
       Recently has lived with:
          (a) in jail
          (b) with a promiscuous
              woman
          (c) with former mis-
              tress who bore him
              an illegitimate child

W 15. 1. F ma *
       2. M ma ot h 1

Away visiting relatives of
1.

W 16. 1. M o **
2. F o w 1 (mixed
blood)
Away working temporarily.

W 17. 1. F ma
2. M ma (white) h 1
3. M y s 1, 2
4. M y s 1, 2
Away in a show.

W 18. 1. M y

On another reservation visiting.

W 19. 1. M ma *
On another reservation visiting.

W 20. 1. M ma wd
Working in a near-by city.

W 21. 1. M y
Away with a show.

W 22. 1. M ma (negro)
2. F ma w 1
Casual laborer.

SUMMARY OF DATA ON 160 HOUSEHOLDS

Size of family	Number of families	Total number of individuals	Average household
2	8	1,041	6.5
3	21	(473 adults	
4	13	568 children)	
5	27		
6	30		
7	14		
8	9		
9	14		
10	6		
11	7		
12	3		
13	2		
14	0		
15	1		
16	2		
17	2		
18	0		
19	1		

Chapter XII

MARITAL SITUATION

(1) Status of 202 Married Couples, Showing Previous Marriages, How Terminated, and Number of Living Offspring

Symbols and Scheme According to Columns:

Household number, numbers of husband and wife in household, 1, 2, indicating main couple, higher numbers indicating subsidiary position.

Number of marriages.

Terminated, by death — d, divorce — dv, by divorce from ex-spouse now deceased (dv).

Number of children in first column marked children is number by male and indicated spouse.

Number of children in second column is number of female and some spouse other than husband indicated by number.

House-hold no.	Husband no.	No. marriages of husband	How terminated	No. of living children	Wife no.	No. marriages of wife	How terminated	No. of living children
2	1	1		2	2	1		
3	1	1		2	2			
4	1	1	dv		2	1	d	2
5	3 (ot)	1		3	2	1		
6	1	1	d	2	2	1		
		2			1			
	5	1	d	4	4	1	dv	1
		2			2			
7	2	1		2	3	1		
8	1				2	1	d	2
						2	d	1
						3		
	3	1			4	1		
9	1	1		8	2	1		
10	1	1		3	2	1		
11	1	1	d	1	2	1	d	
	4	1			3	1	d	3
	2					2	d	
12	1	1		2	2	1	d	1
		2				2		
	4	1	dv	2	5	1		
		2						
13	1	1	d			2	1	
		2	d(1)					
	4	1				3	1	

House-hold no.	Husband no.	No. marriages of husband	How terminated	No. of living children	Wife no.	No. marriages of wife	How terminated	No. of living children
	7	1			8	1		
14	1	1			2	1	d	3
						2		
	3	1			4	1		
	10	1			9	1	dv	
				3		2		
15	2	1	d		1	1	d	3
		2	dv	1				
		3				2		
	8	1	dv	3	7	1	dv	8
		2				3		
	11	1			10	1	dv (?)	
						2	dv	
						3		
16	1	1	d	2	2	1	dv	2
		2	d			2		
		3		3				
17	1	1	dv		2	1	dv	2
		1		3		2		
	8	1		1	9	1		
18	1	1			2	1		
19	1	1	d	1	2	1	d	
		2	d	1		2		
		3		5		2		
	9	1	d		8	1	dv	1
				1		2	dv	1
						3	dv	2
		1	dv			4		
20	2	2		2	3	1		
21	1				2	1		
22	3	1		2	2	1		
	9	1			8	1		
23	1	1		5	2	1		
24	1	1			2	1	dv	
	3	1	dv		4	1		il. child
		2	dv			1		
		3				1		
25	1	1		5	2	1		
	2	1		6	2	1		
26	3	1		2	2	1		
	7	1	d		2	1		
		2		3				
27	1	1			2	1		
28	1	1	dv	1	2	1		
		2		4				
30	1	1		4	2	1		
31	2	1	dv		3	1	dv	

House-hold no.	Husband no.	No. marriages of husband	How terminated	No. of living children	Wife no.	No. marriages of wife	How terminated	No. of living children
		2	dv	1				
		3'			2	2	dv	
	4	1			5	1	dv	4
				2		2		
32	1	1			2	1		
	3	1			4	1	(dv)	
						2		
33	1	1		8	2	1		
	9	1			10	1		
34	2	1	d		1	1	(dv)	
						2	d	1
						3		
	4	1	d	5	3	1		
		2		1				
	9	1	dv	1	8	1		
		2		2				
	17	1	d		16	1	d	8
		2				2		
35	1	1	dv		2	1	dv	
		2	dv			2		
		3		4				
36	1	1	dv		2	1	dv	1
		2	dv			2		
		3		2				
	6	1		1	5	1		
	9	1	d	1	8	1	dv	
		2	dv	3				
		3	dv					
		4						
	13	1		3	14	1		
37	1	1			2	1	(dv)	1
				1		2		
38	1	1			2	1	(dv)	2
		1				2		
39	1	1		7	2	1		
	9	1		2	10	1		
40	1	1		3	2	1		
	5	1			6	1	d	1
				1		2		
42	1	1		3	2	1		
43	1	1		1(3)	2	1		
	7	1			6	1	d	1
						2	d	
						3	dv	
						4	dv	1
						5		
44	2	1		2	3	1		
45	1	1		5	2	1		

House-hold no.	Husband no.	No. mar-riages of husband	How termi-nated	No. of living children	Wife no.	No. mar-riages of wife	How termi-nated	No. of living children
	7	1			8	1		
46	1	1		1	2	1		
	3	1			4	1	dv	1
						2		
48	1	1	dv		2	1	d	1
		2				2		
	4	1		3	2	1		
49	1	1		1	2	1		
	5	1		2	4	1		
50	1	1		3	2	1		
51	1	1		4	2	1		
		1	dv					
52	1	2		3(1)	2	1		
	5	1		3	4	1		
53	1	1		5	2	1		
54	1	1		5	2	1		
55	1	1			2	1	dv	
						2		
56	1	1			2	1		
	4	1		1	2	1		
57	1	1			2	1	d	
				1		2		
58	1	1	d	2	2	1	d	5
		2				2		
59	1	1		4	2	1		
60	3	1		(1)3	2	1		
	7	1			2	1		
61	1	1		1	2	1		
62	1	1	dv	2	2	1		
		2		2				
	5	1	d		2	1		
		2						
63	1	1			2	1		
	4	1		4	2	1		
64	1	1		2	2	1		
65	1	1		4	2	1		
	6	1		2	5	1		
66	1	1	dv		2	1	d	
		2				2		
67	1	1			2	1	dv	
				3		2		
	8	1	dv	1	7	1	d	1
		2	dv	1		2		
		3		2				
69	1	1	(dv)		2	1		
		2		5				
70	1	1		5	2	1		
71	1	1		4	2	1		

House-hold no.	Husband no.	No. marriages of husband	How terminated	No. of living children	Wife no.	No. marriages of wife	How terminated	No. of living children
72	1	1		2	2	1		
73	1	1			2	1		
74	1	1		1 (3)	2	1		
75	1	1	d	3	2	1	dv	2
		2		5		2		
76	2	1		4	2	1		
77	1	1	d	1	2	1		
		2		1				
78	1	1	d	3	2	1		
		2						
79	1	1		1	2	1		
	15	1			14	1		
	16	1	dv		17	1	d	1
		2		1		2		
80	1	1		1	2	1		
82	1	1		1	2	1	dv	
						2		
83	1	1			2	1		
85	1	1			2	1	dv	
						2		
86 (?)	2	1	dv	3	1	1	dv	1
						2	d	1
						3	d	
						4	d	
						5		
87	1	1		2	2	1		
88	1	1	dv		2	1	d	1
		2				2	d	5
						3		
	8	1		2	7	1		
89	1	1			2	1	dv	1
				3		2		
90	1	1		4	2	1		
91	1	1	d	5	2	1	d	2
		2	dv			2		
		3						
92	1	1		7	2	1		
93	1	1			2	1	(dv)	5
				1		2	d	1
						3		
94	1	1		3	2	1		
95	1	1	d	1	2	1	d	1
		2		4		2		
96	1	1		7	2	1		
	8	1			9	1	d	1
				1		2		
97	1	1			2	1		
99	1	1	dv	1	2	1	dv	3

House-hold no.	Husband no.	No. mar-riages of husband	How termi-nated	No. of living children	Wife no.	No. mar-riages of wife	How termi-nated	No. of living children
						2		
100	1	1	d	3	2	1		
		2		2				
101	1	1	dv	2	2	1		
		2		7				
102	1	1			2	1	dv	
		2		2				
103	1	1	d	1 (1)	2	1	dv	2
		2				2		
104	1	1	dv	1	2	1	dv	1
		2		1		2		
105	1	1	d		2	1	d	
		2				2	dv	
	3	1		2	4	3		
106	1	1		1	2	1		
107	1	1		1	2	1		
108	1	1		6	2	1		
109	1	1			2	1	d	4
						2		
110	1	1		3	2	1		
111	1	1			2	1		
112	1	1	dv	1	2	1		
	2			1				
113	1	1		3	2	1		
114	1	1	dv	1	1	1	d	1
	2			1		2		
115	1	1		3	2	1	d	
	7	1	dv	6		1	d	
	2					2		
116	1	1		2	2	1		
117	1	1	d		2	1	d	1
	2			3		3		
120	1	1			2	1	dv	
						2	d	
						3		
121	1	1		4	2	1		
122	1	1		2	2	2		
123	1	1		1	2	1		
124	2	1	dv	2	3	1		
		2		2				
125	1	1	dv		2	1	d	3
				2		2		
126	1	1		2	2	1		
	5	1		5	2	1		
127	5	1	dv	1	4	1	dv	
	2			3		2		
	9	1		4	10	1		
	12	1		3	13	1		

House-hold no.	Husband no.	No. marriages of husband	How terminated	No. of living children	Wife no.	No. marriages of wife	How terminated	No. of living children
128	1	1		5	2	1		
	7	1	dv		6	1		
		2						
129	1	1	dv	1	2	1	d	
		2		5		2		
130	2	1			3	1		
131	1	1		4	2	1		
	5	1		1	6	1		
132	1	1	d		1	1	d	2
		2		1		2		
133	1	1	d		2	1	dv	
		2		3		2		
134	1	1		4	2	1		
135	1	1			2	1	d	4
				2		2		
136	1	1		3	2	1		
				1	3	1		
137	1	1	d	2	2	1	d	4
		2	dv	(1)		2		
		3	dv	1				
		4						
		1	dv	1	4	1	d	
						2		
138	1	1	d	1	2	1	d	
		2				2		
	5	1	dv	2	4	1		
		2		2				
139	1	1		2	2	1		
	3	1			2	1		
	6	1			5	1		
140	1	1	dv		2	1	dv	
		2				2	dv	
						3	d	1
						4		
141	1	1		6	2	1		
		2		2				
142	1	1	d		2	1		
		2		3				
143	1	1	dv		2	1	dv	
		2		4		2		
144	2	1		4	1	1		
145	1	1	d	1	2	1		
		2		2				
	4	1		2	5	1		
146	1	1		2	2	1		
147	1	1		4	2	1		
148	3	1			2	1	d	1
				3		2	d	

House-hold no.	Husband no.	No. marriages of husband	How terminated	No. of living children	Wife no.	No. marriages of wife	How terminated	No. of living children
						3		
	7	1			2	1		
149	1	1			2	1		
		1	dv		2	1		
150	1	2		6	2	1		
	9	1			2	1	d	1
				1		2		
151	1	1		2	2	1		
152	1	1	d		2	1		
		2		2				
153	1	1	dv	2	2	1	dv	1
		2				2	dv	1
						3		
154	4	1	dv		5	1	dv	1
		2				2	dv	
						3		
	7	1	dv		8	1	d	
		2		1		2		
155	1	1		1	2	1	d	
						2		
156	1	1	dv	2	2	1		
		2		7		1	d	2
157	3	1		5	2	2		
158	1	1		3	2	1		
159	1	1		8	2	1		
	9	1			2	1	dv	
				1, 2		2		
160	3	1			2	1	dv	
				1		2	dv	
						3		

Allowing for repetitions in table when two divorced people have remarried, there were sixty-seven divorces recorded, and ninety-four divorced individuals.

(2) STATUS OF 202 MARRIED COUPLES, SHOWING ECONOMIC ARRANGEMENTS, RESIDENCE, INCOME, OR OCCUPATION OF EACH SPOUSE

The following table is an analysis of 202 married couples showing: (a) Principal or subsidiary position; (b) Husband's property or income; (c) Whether husband works or not; (d) Wife's property or income; (e) Whether wife works or not; (f) Residence arrangement; (g) Age of husband.

SYMBOLS

Column 1:

Number of household followed by couple numbers
1. First couple — principal position in household
2. Other couples — subsidiary position in household

Column 2:
 Numeral means number of acres
  Followed by r — rented (e.g. 40 r — 40 acres rented)
  Followed by hm — homestead right
  p — pension
Column 3-5:
  f — farms
  l — works as a laborer; paid domestic labor for women
Column 6:
  W — residence on wife's property or with wife's relatives, sometimes
   misleadingly called matrilocal
  H — residence on husband's property or with husband's relatives, equally
   misleadingly called patrilocal
Column 7:
  y — twenty to thirty
  ma — thirty to fifty
  o — over fifty

Household number	Husband's property	Husband works?	Wife's property	Wife works?	Res- idence	Age of husband
1 —	—	—	—	—	—	—
2 (1, 2)	40r	—	—	—	H	ma
(9, 10)	o	f	—	—	W	ma
3 (1, 2)	40r	f	—	—	H	ma
4 (1, 2)	40r	—	—	—	—	y
5 (2, 3)	—	l	o	—	W	y
6 (1, 2)	40r	o	—	—	H	ma
(5, 6)	120r	—	—	—	W	ma
7 (2, 3)	—	—	—	—	H	ma
8 (1, 2)	30	f	—	—	H	ma
(3, 4)	—	—	—	—	H	y
9 (1, 2)	80	f	o	—	H	ma
10 (1, 2)	—	Gambling den	—	—	—	ma
11 (1, 2)	$80 pen- sion	—	$10	—	—	o
(3, 4)	8or	—	—	—	W	ma
12 (1, 2)	30r	—	—	—	H	o
(3, 4)	8or	—	—	—	—	y
13 (1, 2)	40r	o	40r	—	W	o
(7, 8)	40r	—	—	—	H	y
(3, 4)	—	—	—	—	W	y
14 (1, 2)	40	f	10r	—	H	o
(3, 4)	—	—	120	—	H	ma
(9, 10)	8or	—	—	—	W	y
15 (1, 2)	—	f	40r	—	W	ma
(7, 8)	—	f	—	—	W	o
(10, 11)	—	—	—	—	H	y
16 (1, 2)	8or	—	—	—	H	ma
17 (1, 2)	—	f on rented land	—	—	H	ma

Household number	Husband's property	Husband works?	Wife's property	Wife works?	Res-idence	Age of husband
(8, 9)	—	f a little	—	—	W	y
18 (1, 2)	40	f	—	—	H	ma
19 (1, 2)	—	—	80	—	W	o
(8, 9)	40r	f	—	—	W	y
20 (2, 3)	—	—	—	—	H	ma
21 (1, 2)	40	f	133	—	H	ma
22 (2, 3)	—	—	—	—	W	y
(8, 9)	—	—	—	—	W	y
23 (1, 2)	10r	—	—	—	H	ma
24 (1, 2)	—	—	40r	—	W	o
(3, 4)	—	f, land rented by mother	—	—	H	ma
25 (1, 2)	10r	f	—	—	H	ma
(8, 9)	40r	—	—	—	W	ma
26 (2, 3)	40r	—	—	—	W	ma
(7, 8)	—	—	—	—	H	ma
27 (1, 2)	40	—	—	f (white)	H	ma
28 (1, 2)	land sale	—	—	—	H	ma
29 —	—	—	—	—	—	—
30 —	40	f	—	—	H	ma
31 (2, 3)	—	—	—	—	H	y
(3, 4)	—	—	children's allowance, divorced husband in jail	—	H	y
32 (1, 2)	40	—	200r	—	H	o
(3, 4)	—	f	—	—	H	y
33 (1, 2)	$60 a month	Interpreter	—	—	H	ma
(9, 10)	—	—	—	—	H	y
34 (1, 2)	40r	—	80r	—	W	ma
(3, 4)	—	—	—	—	W	ma
(8, 9)	—	—	—	—	W	y
(16, 17)	—	—	—	—	W	ma
35 (1, 2)	80r	—	—	—	H	ma
36 (1, 2)	40r	—	—	—	.H	ma
(5, 6)	—	—	—	—	W	y
(8, 9)	40r	—	—	—	W	y
(16, 17)	—	f on shares	—	—	H	y
37 (1, 2)	80r	—	—	—	H	ma
38 (1, 2)	40r	—	—	—	H	ma
39 (1, 2)	40	f	—	—	H	ma
(9, 10)	—	f	—	—	H	y
40 —	40	f	—	—	H	ma
(5, 6)	—	f	—	—	H	y
41 —	—	—	—	—	—	—
42 (1, 2)	40	f	—	—	H	y
43 (1, 2)	40	f	—	—	H	y

Household number	Husband's property	Husband works?	Wife's property	Wife works?	Residence	Age of husband
(6, 7)	—	f	—	—	W	ma
44 (2, 3)	40r	—	—	—	H	y
45 —	—	—	—	—	—	—
46 (1, 2)	40	—	—	—	H	o
(3, 4)	—	f	—	—	H	ma
47 —	—	—	—	—	—	—
48 (1, 2)	—	f	80	—	W	o
(3, 4)	—	—	—	—	W	ma
49 (1, 2)	40	f	—	—	H	ma
(4, 5)	—	f	—	—	H	y
50 (1, 2)	—	—	320r	—	W	ma
51 (1, 2)	—	f	40	—	W	ma
52 (1, 2)	—	—	—	—	H	o
(4, 5)	—	l	—	—	H	y
53 (1, 2)	—	l	house in Bergen	—	W	ma
54 (1, 2)	40	Interpreter		—	H	ma
55 (1, 2)	11r	f	—	—	H	y
56 (1, 2)	40	—	—	f	H	ma
(4, 5)	—	f	—	—	H	y
57 (1, 2)	40r	—	80r	—	—	ma
(3, 4)	—	—	—	—	H	y
58 (1, 2)	80	f	—	—	H	ma
59 (1, 2)	160 farmed by white man	—	40	—	H	ma
60 (2, 3)	—	f	30r	—	W	ma
(6, 7)	80	—	—	—	W	ma
61 —	40r	f rented land	—	—	H	ma
62 (1, 2)	—	—	40 (f)	—	W	ma
(4, 5)	40r	f	—	—	W	y
63 (1, 2)	40	f	80r	—	H	ma
(3, 4)	—	f	—	—	W	ma
64 (1, 2) ot	—	—	50r	—	W	ma
65 (1, 2)	—	—	40r	—	W	ma
(5, 6) ot	—	Chauffeur for wife's father's brother	—	—	W	y
66 —	—	—	80r	—	W	ma
67 (1, 2)	40, in another state	f	80	—	W	ma
(7, 8)	—	l	Share in unsettled estate	—	W	ma
68 —	—	—	—	—	—	—
69 (1, 2)	10 woodland	l carpenter	—	—	H	ma
70 (1, 2)	—	caretaking	—	—	—	ma
71	40r	—	—	—	H	ma
72 (1, 2)	80	—	—	—	H	ma

Household number	Husband's property	Husband works?	Wife's property	Wife works?	Residence	Age of husband
73 (1, 2)	120r	—	—	—	H	ma
74 (1, 2)	—	—	—	—	W	ma
75 (1, 2)	—	1	—	1	H	o
76 (2, 3)	—	—	—	—	H	ma
77 (1,2) ot h	40r	—	—	Stenographer	W	ma
78 —	—	—	—	—	—	—
79 (1, 2)	—	—	40	—	W	ma
(14, 15)	—	f	—	—	W	y
(16, 17)	—	—	—	—	H	ma
80 (1,2) ot h	—	1	—	1	H	ma
81 —	—	—	—	—	—	—
82 —	—	—	40r	—	W	ma
83 —	40	f	—	—	H	o
84 —	—	—	—	—	—	—
85 (1, 2)	—	—	40r	—	W	ma
86 (1, 2?)	—	—	house	—	W	o
87 (1, 2)	—	1	40	—	W	ma
88 (1, 2)	—	—	40r	—	W	ma
(7, 8)	40r	—	—	—	W	y
89 (1, 2)	—	f rented land	—	—	H	ma
90 (1,2) ot w	40	f	—	—	H	ma
91 (1, 2)	40r	—	8or	—	H	o
92 (1, 2)	40	f	—	—	H	ma
93 (1, 2)	—	—	40r	—	W	ma
94 (1, 2)	40	f	—	—	H	ma
95 (1, 2)	40	f	—	—	H	ma
96 (1, 2)	40	f	—	—	H	ma
(8, 9)	—	f	1or	—	H	y
97 (1, 2)	—	f rented land	Woodland	—	H	ma
98 —	—	—	—	—	—	—
99 (1, 2)	—	—	40	—	W	o
100 (1, 2)	40r	—	—	—	H	ma
101 (1, 2)	$20 month pension	—	200r	—	W	ma
102 (1, 2)	16or	—	80	—	W	ma
103 (1, 2)	16or	—	—	—	H	ma
104 (1, 2)	40r	—	—	—	H	ma
105 (1, 2)	80 shares	—	—	—	H	o
(3, 4)	—	—	—	—	H	o
106 (1, 2)	40r	—	$\frac{1}{3}$ oil 80 another state	—	H	o
107 (1, 2)	30r	1	—	—	W	y
108 (1, 2)	16or	—	30	—	W	o
109 (1, 2)	—	—	40r	—	W	y
110 (1, 2)	Share $\frac{1}{2}$ 40	f	—	—	H	ma
111 (1, 2)	40	f	—	—	H	y
112 (1, 2)	—	Janitor	—	Seamstress	H	ma

Household number	Husband's property	Husband works?	Wife's property	Wife works?	Residence	Age of husband
113 (1, 2)	—	Farms mother's 40	40r	—	H	ma
114 (1, 2)	—	1 a little	$25 a month	—	—	y
115 (1, 2)	—	f	—	—	W	ma
(6, 7)	—	—	—	—	W	y
117 (1, 2)	—	1	40r	—	H	ma
118 —	—	—	—	—	—	—
119 —	—	—	—	—	—	—
120 (1, 2)	Oil land ot	Interpreter	80r	—	H	ma
121 (1, 2)	40r	—	40r	—	W	ma
122 (1, 2)	—	—	40r	—	W	ma
123 (1, 2)	—	—	40r	—	W	ma
124 (2, 3)	—	—	—	—	H	ma
125 (1, 2)	40r	—	—	—	H	o
126 (1, 2)	Land sale	f on mother's estate	—	—	H	ma
(5, 6)	—	rope spinner	—	—	H	ma
127 (4, 5)	—	—	—	—	W	ma
(9, 10)	—	—	—	—	H	ma
(12, 13)	—	—	80r	—	H	ma
128 (1, 2)	—	—	—	—	H	o
(6, 7)	—	—	—	—	W	y
129 —	—	f rented land	10 woodland	—	W	ma
130 (2,3) ot w	120r	—	—	—	H	ma
131 (1, 2)	5	—	—	—	H	o
(5, 6)	—	—	—	—	H	y
132 (1, 2)	120r	f	40 hm	—	W	ma
133 (1, 2)	60 Shared	—	80	—	H	y
134 (1, 2)	—	1	House	—	W	o
135 (1, 2)	House and $50 pension	1	—	—	H	ma
136 (1, 2)	40	Fishes	—	—	H	o
(8, 9)	—	1	—	—	H	y
137 (1, 2)	120r	—	—	—	H	o
(3, 4)	—	f	—	—	H	y
138 (1,2) ot w	160r	—	—	—	H	o
(4, 5)	—	—	—	—	W	y
139 (1, 2)	40r	f	—	—	H	o
(3, 4) c	—	—	—	—	H	y
(5, 6)	—	—	—	—	W	ma
140 (1, 2)	—	—	80r	—	W	y
141 (1,2) ot w	40r	—	—	—	H	ma
142 (1,2) ot w	40	f	—	—	H	ma
143 (1, 2)	40r	—	Sale of 80 40 rented	—	W	ma
144 (ot w)	—	1	House	—	W	ma
145 (1, 2)	—	—	40	—	W	o

Household number	Husband's property	Husband works?	Wife's property	Wife works?	Residence	Age of husband
(4, 5)	—	f	—	—	H	y
146 —	20r 20	f	—	—	H	ma
147 (1, 2)	—	Works for other tribe	—	—	H	ma
148 (2, 3)	—	—	—	—	W	ma
(7, 8)	16or	—	—	—	H	ma
149 (1, 2)	40	f	Radner property	—	H	y
150 (1, 2)	—	f	40	—	W	o
151 (1, 2)	40	—	Claim in un-settled estate	—	H	ma
(7, 8)	—	f	—	—	H˙	y
152 (1, 2)	40r	—	16r	—	W	y
153 (1, 2)	—	l	40	—	W	ma
154 (4, 5)	—	—	—	—	H	y
(7,8) ot w	—	—	160 hmr	—	H	y
155 (1, 2)	40r	—	10r 40	—	W	ma
156 (1, 2)	10r	f	20 ($\frac{1}{4}$40)	—	W	y
157 (2, 3)	—	—	—	—	W	ma
158 (1, 2)	40r	f	40	—	W	ma
159 (1, 2)	40	f	—	—	H	ma
(9, 10)	—	—	200r	—	H	y
160 (2, 3)	—	—	—	—	W	ma

(3) MARITAL SITUATION AMONG THOSE WHO LIVE OFF THE RESERVATION

Number living off the reservation — 134

    77 males

    57 females

    25 full-bloods

    38 more than quarter Antler

    71 less than quarter Antler

Marriages

	Males	Females
Indians of other tribes	17	14
White	24	30
Antlers	8	4
?	3	
Total	52	48

Total married — 100

Marriages to whites

	Males	Females
Full-bloods	1	1
More than quarter Antler blood	3	4
Less than quarter Antler blood	20	25
Total	24	30

Total — 54

Number of single persons

25 males   9 females

Of these:

7 are off reservation in institutions

39 are in same state

57 are in territory where there are other Indian groups

31 are in localities where there are no Indian groups

There is only one instance of a large family group settled in one spot off the reservation.

(4) ANALYSIS OF INTERTRIBAL AND INTERRACIAL MARRIAGES

FB — full-blood   — — less than quarter Antler blood
+ — more than quarter Antler blood

Tribe	Intertribal males FB	+	—	On reservation females FB	+	—	Intertribal males FB	+	—	Off reservation females FB	+	—
Same dialect, distant reservation	5		2	3			3	3		2	1	
Nearest tribe, different dialect					2		1	1			2	
Very similar dialect, distant reservation							3	1				
Two different dialects, distant reservation	1						1	2		2		
More distant tribe, different dialect	1							1			1	3
Other tribes, different languages (a)	1			1			1					
(b)												1
(c)										1		1
Negro		1		1				1				
Mexican								1				
White	3	1	4	1	5	12	1	5	20	1	4	25

(5) RECORDS OF LIVING ILLEGITIMATE CHILDREN

SYMBOLS

dv — divorced
wd — widowed
unm — unmarried
mo — mother

i — under two
c — two to ten
a — adolescent, over ten

No.	Age	Sex	Status of mother when born	Mother's present status	Living with which relative
1, 6	c	F	unm	wd	mo
15, 6	i	F	wd	Transitory union with father of illegitimate child	mo
29, 2		F	dv	Promiscuous	mo
29, 3		F	dv	Promiscuous	mo
24, 5	c	M	unm	Married	mo
43, 10	c	M	dv	dv, living about	Mother's parents
52, 3	c	M	unm	Dead	Maternal grandparents
	i	M	unm school girl	Married	mo
99, 6	a	M	wd	Married	mo
120, 3	a	M	unm	dv, living loosely in town	Legally adopted
127, 11	c	M	dv	Promiscuous	Father's parents
134, 7	c	M	unm	Living at home, unmarried, loose, syphilitic	mo
137, 6	c	F	unm	Married, has been wd and remarried	mo
154, 3	c	F	unm	Living loosely	mo
154, 10	c	F	wd	Married	mo
154, 11	c	F	wd (different fathers)	Married	mo
157, 10	c	M	unm	dv, promiscuous	mo
159, 13	c	F	unm	unm	mo
160, 6	a	F	dv	Married	mo
w-4, 3	c	F	dv	Married (?)	mo

(5) RECORDS OF LIVING ILLEGITIMATE CHILDREN
Continued

No.	Status of father when child was born	Status of father now
1, 6	dv	Divorced, lives on parents
15, 6	dv	Half living on place of mother of child, but they said he was to have none of the harvest so left
29, 2	Married	Divorced
29, 3	Married	Married
24, 5	Married	Married (father of two children by first wife and seven by second). Lives on his wife's money
43, 10	dv	Dead
52, 3	unm	Divorced and in penitentiary for running off with a young girl and stealing a car
	School boy	Returned to his tribe
99, 6	Married	Married
120, 3	White man	?
W 9, 2c	unm	Divorced
127, 11	unm	Divorced
134, 7	Married	Widowed and remarried
136, 6	dv	Married
154, 3	White man unm	?
154, 10	Married	Married
154, 11	dv	Divorced
157, 10	Married	Divorced
159, 13	unm	Married
160, 6	White man, married	Married
W 4, 3	Married	Dead

(6) ECONOMIC AND RESIDENTIAL STATUS OF WIDOWS

No.	Property	Residence	Dependent on	Dependents
1, 1	Hmst. 40r	Her hmst. land		Stepdaughter (dv) and four children
5, 1	House in Bergen deeded her by stepdaughter	Her house	ot. son-in-law for running expenses	Daughter, ot. son-in-law and three children live with her
17, 1	None	With daughter and with son who lives on his wife's money	Farming son-in-law	None
26, 1	Hmst. 40r	House in Radner with son-in-law	Daughter-in-law	Unmarried daughter, son, son's wife and three

(6) ECONOMIC AND RESIDENTIAL STATUS OF WIDOWS
Continued

No.	Property	Residence	Dependent on	Dependents
				children; she and her daughter's husband share support of these
31, 1	Hmst. 40r	Radner, rents one room		Son, his wife, dead husband's brother's son, and his wife. 4 stepchildren, 2 children
44, 1	80 allotment. 40r 40 farmed by son	On her allotment		Son, wife, and three children live with her and farm for her
45, 1	House in Bergen	In her house		Lives from gardening and casual slight earnings of her divorced dissolute son; cares for his two adolescent children
78, 2	Hmst. 40r	Son's house in Bergen		Keeps house for widowed son who works as a laborer, and his three children. They all go to boarding school
84, 1	$10 month pension, widow of ex-service man	With divorced sister who is given a house in return for services		One child of six
86, 1	Owns house in Radner	In her house	Receives some help from son-in-law who works in nearby city	Aged temporary drug-addict husband. Three grandchildren
98, 1	House in Radner. 80r and 40 farmed by son-in-law	In her house		Son, unmarried orphaned niece, 18. (daughter, son-in-law and grandchild depend upon use of her land)

(6) ECONOMIC AND RESIDENTIAL STATUS OF WIDOWS
Continued

No.	Property	Residence	Dependent on	Dependents
118, 1	40	On her 40		Three sons, one married, who farm her place for her
124, 1	2 houses and a lot in Bergen	In her house	2 grandsons aged 19 and 21 have rent of 40	Son, son's wife, and 2 grandchildren
127, 1	80r	House on 80		Divorced daughter and her sickly child, niece, niece's husband, and 3 children. Also a brother and his wife camp here and draw on her for food
148, 1	40r	Her house on 40	Stepgrandson has rent of 160 which adds money to her income	Stepdaughter, her husband, three children, stepgrandson and his wife, live in the household
154, 1	160r and house in Radner	Her house in Radner	She is blind, needs, but receives little care	15 people, grandchildren and their spouses, and great-grandchildren
157, 1	40r $30 a month pension	Rented house in Radner		Niece, niece's husband, and their five children

CHAPTER XIII

CASE HISTORIES OF TWENTY-FIVE DELINQUENT
GIRLS AND WOMEN

SCHEME OF PRESENTATION OF MATERIAL

CASE NO.   HOUSEHOLD NO.   PROPERTY
(For reference to household records, see Chapter XI)

1. Age?
2. Father?
3. Mother?
4. If reared by other relatives?
5. Relatives who furnished bad example?
6. Whether marriage preceded promiscuity or not?
7. Events which appear to have given initial impetus to delinquency?
8. Marital history?
9. Number of children and present whereabouts?
10. History of mental instability in family?
11. Conflicts with the law?
12. Drinks?
13. Venereal disease?
14. Relationship to other of these cases?
15. Present status and way of life?
16. Brothers? Number? Delinquent?
17. Extra comment?

CASE NO.   HOUSEHOLD NO.   PROPERTY
    1   (15, 1)   Hm. 40

1. 35.
2. Father living, divorced, has nothing to do with daughter.
3. Mother deserted father and eight children, period of promiscuity; within the last year has settled down with an old man on daughter's place.
4. ———

5. Mother furnished a bad example throughout adolescence and early twenties.
6. Married before any promiscuity.
7. Husband died, joined mother in loose life.
8. First marriage terminated by death of husband; period of promiscuity; pregnant; accused one lover who acknowledged responsibility for pregnancy; he went to live on her place, helped farm, she and her mother and new stepfather ejected him before harvest.
9. Three children, two by first husband, one illegitimate, all with her.
10. ——
11. Sent to woman's reformatory.
12. Drinks.
13. ——
14. ——
15. Living on inherited homestead land.
16. Four brothers; two delinquent.

CASE NO.	HOUSEHOLD NO.	PROPERTY
2	(W 9, 1)	Share in oil lands from ot husband

1. 28.
2. Father living, undistinguished.
3. Mother died when she was a child.
4. Reared by stepmother who was a promiscuous character.
5. Stepmother influenced her after her marriage.
6. Runaway marriage was opposed and broken up by parents.
7. Broken-up marriage and stepmother's example led to promiscuity; had an illegitimate child by a white man.
8. The one runaway marriage with ot. Indian who died and left property, and one rather long liaison with illegitimate child resulting.
9. One illegitimate child adopted by mother's brother; one illegitimate child now with her.
10. No history of mental disease.
11. No conflicts with law.
12. Drinks.

13. Positive.
14. F. f. b. d. No. 10; f. f. b. d. No. 11; f. f. d. d. No. 12.
15. In Bergen. Promiscuous.
16. None.

CASE NO.	HOUSEHOLD NO.	PROPERTY
3	(154, 2)	Will inherit from rich grandmother

1. 26.
2. Father committed suicide when child was five years old.
3. Mother died when child was six years old.
4. Reared by grandmother who was going blind.
5. No relatives who contributed particularly.
6. Has never been married.
7. Had illegitimate child by white man when she was fourteen.
8. Never married.
9. Has one child who is with her.
10. No mental history.
11. Arrested in nearby city for drunkenness and prostitution.
12. Drinks and is abusive and exhibitionistic.
13. Positive.
14. Parallel cousin No. 7; sister-in-law No. 20; second cousins nos. 15, 16, 17.
15. Living with blind grandmother. Promiscuous and heavy drinker.
16. One brother, delinquent.

CASE NO.	HOUSEHOLD NO.	PROPERTY
4	(135, 6)	No property

1. 22.
2. Father died when she was five.
3. Mother died when she was four.
4. Reared by grandmother.
5. No contributing relatives.
6. No promiscuity before marriage.
7. Married a Black Face who deserted her; married another Black Face who also deserted her; then became promiscuous.

8. Only two Black Face marriages.
9. No children.
10. No history of mental instability.
11. No conflict with law.
12. Drinks.
13. Positive.
14. Niece No. 5.
15. Living with married sister. Promiscuous.
16. No brothers.

CASE NO.	HOUSEHOLD NO.	PROPERTY
5	No household number, away	No property

1. 17.
2. Father has always been dissolute. Father of an illegitimate child by No. 13 and has been in the penitentiary for assault on a white man.
3. Mother deserted her and her father when she was two.
4. Reared by grandmother.
5. Aunt, No. 4, furnished bad example.
6. Has never married.
7. Bad influence of aunt was followed by a semi-kidnapping by a group of experienced elder boys and Case No. 12.
8. Never married.
9. No children.
10. Partially deaf.
11. Brought up before juvenile court after kidnapping incident and released, two months later committed to reformatory for continued promiscuity and conspicuous drunkenness.
12. Drinks excessively.
13. Negative.
14. Aunt No. 4.
15. In reformatory.
16. No brothers.

CASE NO.	HOUSEHOLD NO.	PROPERTY
6	(86, 4)	No property

1. 17.
2. Father is a widower, works in city near-by and sends home

some money for children's support.

3. Mother died when she was three.
4. Reared by grandmother.
5. Grandmother is at present having an affair with a sixty-year-old drug addict.
6. Merely promiscuous.
7. Delinquency result of ineffective chaperonage, and determined seduction by boy who kidnapped No. 5.
8. Never married.
9. No children.
10. Has tuberculosis developed in reformatory. (Sister died of tuberculosis.)
11. Sent to reformatory for drinking and promiscuity.
12. Drinks.
13. Negative.
14. No relatives on list.
15. Living with grandmother, too ill for much delinquency.
16. Two brothers, one younger, one delinquent.

CASE NO.	HOUSEHOLD NO.	PROPERTY
7	(75, 3)	None

1. 15.
2. Father virtuous, stern, a failure through bad luck.
3. Mother, white, sarcastic, ailing.
4. ——
5. No contributing relative.
6. Not married.
7. Ran wild in an attempt to obliterate mixed-blood antagonisms and identify herself with Indian group.
8. Not married.
9. No children.
10. No history of mental instability.
11. No conflict with law.
12. Doesn't drink.
13. Negative.
14. f. b. d. No. 14; f. f. b. s. d. No. 13; f. b. d. d. Nos. 15, 16, 17.
15. Living with parents, promiscuous.
16. One older brother, quiet, hard-working.

CASE NO.	HOUSEHOLD NO.	PROPERTY
8	(75, 3)	8or

1. 38.
2. Father reported to have been very strict.
3. Mother also very strict.
4. ——
5. No contributing relative.
6. Married against her will to a white man, ran away from him.
7. After forced marriage, eloped with an Antler, found Antler reservation much slacker than her own. Husband and baby died.
8. Married twice to Antlers, besides white marriage which was never consummated; first Antler husband died, second deserted her for her niece.
9. One child dead and one son, sixteen, living with her, on his money.
10. No mental instability history.
11. No conflict with law.
12. Drinks moderately.
13. Positive.
14. No relatives on list.
15. Lives extravagantly, and in rapid promiscuity, especially with young boys, also acts as a procuress.
16. Relatives unknown, other-tribal.

CASE NO.	HOUSEHOLD NO.	PROPERTY
9	(29, 1)	8or and land sale money

1. 35.
2. Father died in her infancy.
3. Mother died in her infancy.
4. Brought up by a series of relatives.
5. No contributing relative.
6. Married before any delinquency.
7. Deserted by first husband after first child's birth; went to live with another man; contracted syphilis from him and he deserted her when she was eight months pregnant; became completely promiscuous.

8. One legal marriage; widowed; one long association which she considered a marriage and tried to hold the man by recourse to law.

9. Four children, eldest legitimate, adopted by relatives, three younger illegitimate, one died and two living syphilitic.

10. ——

11. Has been in reformatory twice.

12. Drinks and becomes most quarrelsome.

13. Positive.

14. No relatives on list.

15. Out on parole and living promiscuously.

16. One brother who was recently charged with assaulting a child.

CASE NO.	HOUSEHOLD NO.	PROPERTY
10	(132, 2)	Hm. 40

1. 45.

2. Father was a violent tempered man, drank, gambled, stamped the illegitimate infant of his daughter to death, had been in prison for another murder.

3. Mother drank, died when child was six.

4. Reared by quiet stern stepmother.

5. Father was a bad example.

6. Lived circumspectly before marriage.

7. Deserted by her first husband, who was an alcoholic and had abused her; had an affair with a married man; returned to first husband, who died and left her a homestead right; when he died she became promiscuous again and is unfaithful to her present husband.

8. Married, had two children, first husband died, promiscuous, married present husband who is also promiscuous.

9. Three children, two by first marriage, with her (she and her second husband live on the children's income); one by second marriage.

10. No mental history.

11. No conflicts with law.

12. Drinks moderately.

13. Negative.

14. Sister, No. 11; niece No. 12; f. b. s. d. No. 2.

15. Married, leading an extravagant and unfaithful life.
16. One brother, a sober Peyote man.

CASE No.	HOUSEHOLD No.	PROPERTY
11	(160, 2)	No property

1. 43.
2. Sister of No. 10. Family history identical.
3. ——
4. ——
5. ——
6. Married before any promiscuity.
7. Married an unstable violent man, subject to epileptic-like seizures, (he is father of illegitimate child No. 154, 10); she left him; had an illegitimate child by a white man; husband of a mixed-blood cousin; accused an Indian; deserted oldest child in a public lavatory in near-by town.
8. Married twice only; deserted first husband and now married to a second; about eight years of promiscuity in between.
9. Three children, daughter No. 12 by first marriage, illegitimate by a white man; and a baby by present husband; oldest daughter in reformatory; two other children with her.
10. No mental history.
11. No conflicts with law.
12. Drinks.
13. Negative.
14. Sister No. 10; daughter No. 12; f. b. s. d. No. 2.
15. Married, still promiscuous, has a weak and unprotecting husband, both live with her father who lives mostly on charity.
16. One brother, a sober Peyote man.

CASE No.	HOUSEHOLD No.	PROPERTY
12	No household number, away	No property

1. 17.
2. Father violent, unstable, given to epileptic-like fits, nearly beat her to death recently.
3. Mother deserted father when she was three; No. 11.
4. Reared by paternal grandmother and then by two paternal aunts one of whom was promiscuous.

5. Aunt No. 10 and then Mother No. 11 both bad influences.
6. Promiscuity began without marriage.
7. Aunt's procuring started her into promiscuity, then involved in barn kidnapping with No. 5.
8. Not married.
9. No children.
10. ——
11. In reformatory.
12. Drinks.
13. ——
14. Mother No. 11; aunt No. 10, f. b. d. No. 26; m. f. b. s. d. No. 2.
15. In reformatory.
16. No brothers.

CASE NO.	HOUSEHOLD NO.	PROPERTY
13	(132, 6)	No property

1. 30.
2. Father an improvident waster, when his house was burned went to live on sister's place for the rest of his life.
3. Mother is quarrelsome and improvident.
4. Reared by parents.
5. Delinquent brothers, parallel cousin No. 23, close friend No. 10.
6. Promiscuity before marriage.
7. Had an illegitimate child by a married man; father of No. 5; period of promiscuity followed; marriage; youngest of three children died, she left him and a new period of promiscuity set in.
8. Married once after first period, a man with no property; they lived about with his relatives and hers, had three children and she left him when youngest died.
9. Four children, one illegitimate, three legitimate, one of these dead; illegitimate child with her parents; two legitimate children with husband's parents (95, 8, 9).
10. Father's sister's daughter epileptic.
11. No conflict with law.
12. Drinks.

13. Positive.
14. f. b. d. No. 23; sister-in-law No. 15.
15. Living as a nominal servant with No. 10; promiscuous.
16. Two brothers, past history of delinquency.

Case No.	Household No.	Property
14	(24, 4)	No property

1. 25.
2. Father had five wives; now divorced and almost stone deaf.
3. Mother died when she was four.
4. Lived about with a series of relatives.
5. Cousin No. 3.
6. Marriage after promiscuity.
7. Illegitimate child (24, 5) by a married man followed by promiscuity.
8. Later married present husband to whom she is unfaithful.
9. One illegitimate child with her.
10. ——
11. Case against married seducer was taken to court, but interpreter turned her down at the last minute because she was so impudent and she lost the case.
12. Drinks.
13. Positive.
14. Parallel cousin No. 7; second cousin No. 3; f. si. d's No. 15, 161, 17.
15. Married but promiscuous; husband away a good deal.
16. Two brothers; neither delinquent.

Case No.	Household No.	Property
15	(140, 8)	8or

1. 27.
2. Father had two wives; the former husband of mother was murdered; father suspected but never proved; father was murdered by a white man when she was six.
3. Mother permitted herself to be stolen from first husband; remarried immediately upon her husband's being murdered, and died in childbirth the following year when daughter was seven.

4. Reared by maternal grandmother until she was ten, then by father's brother whose wife was very strict and being other-tribal did not speak Antler.
5. Paternal aunt No. 19 bad example.
6. Promiscuous before marriage.
7. No. 19 and rebellion against authority of paternal uncle's wife resulted in a long period of promiscuity.
8. Only married once, to present complacent husband.
9. Three legitimate children.
10. f. b. is a congenital invert; cleft palate.
11. ——
12. Drinks.
13. Negative.
14. Sisters No. 16 and 17; half sister No. 18; paternal aunt No. 19; m. b. d. No. 14; m. b. d. No. 7; m. f. b. s. d. No. 3.
15. Married, promiscuous.
16. One brother, very delinquent. One half brother, very delinquent.

CASE NO.	HOUSEHOLD NO.	PROPERTY
16	(W 4, 2)	8or

1. 25.
2. Father (see No. 15); murdered when daughter was four.
3. Mother (see No. 15) died when she was five.
4. Maternal grandmother and other-tribal wife of paternal uncle (see No. 15).
5. Paternal aunt No. 19 bad example.
6. No promiscuity before first marriage.
7. Married and had a child; husband deserted her; period of promiscuity; settled down with a man who stole harness for a joy ride; he was put in penitentiary; another period of promiscuity; at present a long liaison with a man ten years younger.
8. Married once and two long liaisons.
9. One legitimate child (No. 96, 12) with paternal uncle; one illegitimate child by first long liaison, with her.
10. Paternal uncle congenital invert, cleft palate.
11. ——

12. Drinks.
13. Positive.
14. (See No. 15, who is her full sister).
15. Temporary liaison with a younger man who is living on her rents.
16. One brother delinquent; one half brother delinquent.

CASE No.	HOUSEHOLD No.	PROPERTY
17	(W 4m, 5)	8or

1. 23.
2. Father (see No. 15) was murdered when daughter was two.
3. Mother (see No. 15) died when daughter was three.
4. Paternal grandmother and other-tribal wife of paternal uncle.
5. Paternal aunt No. 19 bad example.
6. Promiscuous; never married.
7. Expelled from school after a sex episode; believed to be pregnant and put in a home for unmarried mothers; she was not pregnant. After several months she escaped from there in company with a white girl and came back to the reservation; became promiscuous.
8. Never been married, had one long liaison with a man who was and is again in the penitentiary.
9. No children.
10. Uncle a congenital invert; cleft palate.
11. She and lover stole a car; arrested in another state; she was sent to the reformatory.
12. Drinks.
13. Positive.
14. For relationship see No. 15.
15. Living promiscuously with No. 16.
16. One brother delinquent; one half brother delinquent.

CASE No.	HOUSEHOLD No.	PROPERTY
18	(157, 9)	10r

1. 22.
2. Father stole a second wife and was suspected of murdering second wife's husband; was murdered by a white man when daughter was a year old.

3. Mother married again and had five children; mother is regarded by community as unusually bad-tempered.
4. Reared by mother and an abusive stepfather.
5. Aunt No. 19, and half-sisters Nos. 15, 16, and 17, contributory.
6. Promiscuous before marriage.
7. Illegitimate child by man responsible for delinquency of No. 5, No. 6, and No. 12.
8. Mother bribed a Black Face-Antler mixed tribal to marry her by promising to deed him forty acres of land; after several years when both were promiscuous, he deserted her.
9. One illegitimate child with mother (157, 10).
10. Uncle congenital invert.
11. No conflict with law.
12. Drinks.
13. Positive.
14. Half sisters No. 15, 16, 17; paternal aunt No. 19; f. si. b. d. No. 7, 14; f. m. f. b. s. d. No. 3.
15. New and violent period of promiscuity begun with the return from jail and renewed relationship with first seducer.
16. One brother delinquent; one half brother delinquent.

CASE No.	HOUSEHOLD No.	PROPERTY
19	(140, 2)	80r

1. 40.
2. Parents, quiet and law-abiding, lived until after daughter was married.
3. Parents, quiet and law abiding, lived until after daughter was married.
4. Reared by parents.
5. No contributing relatives.
6. Married quietly and without any promiscuity.
7. She had four children, all but one died; then had operation and was told she could never have any more children; went completely to pieces, deserted her husband and child; a long period of promiscuity with two lengthy liaisons interspersed.
8. One legal marriage from which she ran away; three long liaisons including present one with a boy twelve years her junior.

9. One living child, a girl of fourteen, with mother, began running wild this summer.
10. Brother a congenital invert.
11. No conflict with law.
12. Drinks.
13. Positive.
14. Nieces, Nos. 15, 16, 17, 18; first cousin No. 9.
15. Keeping a younger man on her money in Bergen.
16. Dead brother father of Nos. 15, 16, 17, 18 suspected of murder; one living brother, procurer and invert.

CASE NO.	HOUSEHOLD NO.	PROPERTY
20	(154, 5)	No property

1. 25.
2. Father, drinks and is an inveterate gambler.
3. Mother, drinks and is an inveterate gambler.
4. Reared by parents.
5. No contributing relatives.
6. Married quietly.
7. Married a man who had already led a very loose life; he exchanged wives with another man; she disliked the exchange, left the new partner and became promiscuous.
8. One legal marriage; exchange liaison; present liaison with a casual young rake.
9. One child by first marriage, sometimes with her parents, sometimes with her.
10. No history of mental instability.
11. ——
12. Drinks.
13. Positive.
14. Sister-in-law No. 3.
15. Living in temporary liaison.
16. No brothers.

CASE NO.	HOUSEHOLD NO.	PROPERTY
21	(15, 8)	No property

1. 30.
2. Father is a casual drifter, just entered at sixty into a liaison with a woman almost as old as he (mother of No. 1), who has

lived promiscuously for years.

3. Mother died when daughter was sixteen.

4. Reared by parents.

5. No contributing relatives.

6. Married before promiscuity.

7. Eloped immediately after her mother's death with a Black Face, who deserted her; became promiscuous.

8. After first marriage has had two prolonged liaisons, one with brother of No. 18; one with present lover.

9. Has had two stillborn children, one legitimate from first marriage, one from liaison with brother of No. 18.

10. No history of mental instability, but she herself shows marked signs of sadism, chooses young immature lovers and subjects them to violent and brutal treatment; usually chooses lovers who are practising homosexuals.

11. Only conflict with law was accusation of infanticide after death of last child; exhumation proved no evidence.

12. Drinks.

13. Positive.

14. No relatives, f's wife's daughter No. 1.

15. Temporary liaison.

16. Brother very bad reputation, married and carrying on liaison with No. 25.

CASE No.	HOUSEHOLD No.	PROPERTY
22	No household number just returned from reformatory	No property

1. 20.

2. Father killed his father-in-law, with whom his legal wife took refuge in protest against a mistress; executed, when daughter was a small child.

3. Mother married again.

4. Reared by mother's brother, a drinking, gambling household; and father's brother, a quiet respectable household, in alternate periods.

5. Mother's brother's household contributory, learned drinking there.

6. Not married.

7. Pronounced alcoholism seems to have been chief cause.
8. No marital history.
9. No children.
10. Father's behavior only suggestion of mental instability.
11. Has been in girls' reformatory.
12. Drinks heavily.
13. Negative.
14. No relations on list.
15. Just returned from reformatory; promiscuity continuing, but alcoholism seems checked.
16. One brother very delinquent, responsible for first delinquency of No. 6.

Case No.	Household No.	Property
23	(147, 3)	No property

1. 26.
2. Ne'er-do-well father; earns living by tricking relatives, or sponges on Oil Indians.
3. Mother left father when No. 23 was at early adolescence, and ran around for a long time; then returned.
4. Reared by parents.
5. Mother, two delinquent brothers, delinquent cousin No. 13, all contributed bad example.
6. No promiscuity before marriage.
7. Deserted by a Black Face whom she had married; then had an illegitimate child by another Black Face; then a long period of promiscuity, during which she ran off with a white man to a near-by city.
8. Only one marriage, series of liaisons.
9. One illegitimate child (147, 4) lives with her parents.
10. F. s. d. an epileptic.
11. No conflicts with law.
12. Drinks.
13. Positive.
14. F. s. d. No. 13.
15. Promiscuous, living with parents and married sister as base.
16. Two delinquent brothers; one involved with No. 24.

CASE NO.   HOUSEHOLD NO.   PROPERTY
24   (71, 7)   No property

1. 40.
2. Father murdered in a drunken brawl when daughter was a small child.
3. Mother drunken in same brawl.
4. Reared by mother.
5. Dissolute mother.
6. No promiscuity before marriage.
7. Deserted by husband after one child was born; promiscuous period; then brother of No. 23 became partner to liaison, had a child; then a liaison with a Black Face, bore a child who was put on Black Face roll and placed in a school on Black Face Reservation; quarreled with Black Face husband, renewed promiscuity. Married an Antler who died, then promiscuous.
8. First marriage never legalized; two long liaisons each with a child; then two liaisons; then a legal marriage ended by death of husband; then liaison with former lover; then prolonged liaison with a boy of her daughter's age, who ran away to a show to get away from her; then liaison with brother of No. 22.
9. Three children, first stayed with father and is now married; second with paternal relatives; third on Black Face Reservation.
10. No history of mental instability except pronounced alcoholism.
11. ——
12. Drinks excessively.
13. Positive.
14. No relations on list.
15. Temporary liaison.
16. One brother, quiet.

CASE NO.   HOUSEHOLD NO.   PROPERTY
25   (134, 6)   No property

1. 26.
2. Father unstable; religious-minded, takes up each new religious craze; lazy, very poor.
3. Mother was pregnant before marriage, often taunted by father on this point; poor, proud, and lazy.
4. Reared by parents.

5. Paternal aunt bad influence.

6. Never married.

7. Illegitimate child by a married man followed by promiscuity; family attempted to accuse Indian with a rich wife and lost case; continued promiscuity with periods of religious conversion to Pentecostal faith.

8. No marital history.

9. One illegitimate child (134, 7) with her and her parents.

10. f, b, epileptic type, one sister died of epilepsy, f. f. b. d. s. epileptic.

11. Conflict with law in bastardy case, and when law invoked against her by wife of a man with whom she was caught in a rooming house in a near-by town; fined for disorderly conduct.

12. Drinks.

13. Positive.

14. f. b. d. No. 12.

15. Living with parents; promiscuous, present liaison with married brother of No. 21; works occasionally as waitress.

16. Two brothers, both timid, make no attempt to adjust themselves to society.

CASE NO.	HOUSEHOLD NO.	PROPERTY
26	(154, 8)	

This case cannot be presented in full as she is a member of the Short Robe tribe and background is not known. She is the niece of No. 8. Came to the Antler Reservation as a divorced woman. Had two illegitimate children, one by the father of No. 12 and one by the widower of the sister of No. 9. Then married the maternal uncle of No. 3. While married to him had a liaison with his sister's son, who was then nominally married to No. 8. Immediately on his death, married her present husband, who is brother of No. 3 and was No. 26's former husband's sister's son and No. 26's aunt's common-law husband.

SUMMARY

18 come from broken homes

6 cases mother died before girl was ten

2 cases father died before girl was ten

6 cases both parents died before girl was ten

4 cases of divorced parents

Records of fathers [1]
    14 drank
    1 notorious gambler
    2 murderers
    5 were murdered (one was father of four girls this makes total)
    2 were fathers of illegitimate children after marriage
    1 imprisoned for assault
    1 committed suicide
    9 fathers had no sort of known bad character

Records of mothers
    6 cases of deaths when girl was small, no record against mother
    7 mothers who lived until girl was adolescent or later, against
        whom there is no record
    4 cases where mothers were notorious drunkards
    5 mothers who deserted fathers
    3 daughters (sisters) of a mother who left her husband for
        their father and whose husband was believed to have
        been murdered by the girl's father

Record of children reared by relatives other than parents
    9 reared by mother or both parents
    7 reared by grandmothers
    2 by a whole series of relatives
    1 by maternal uncle's wife
    1 by paternal aunt
    1 by paternal uncle's wife
    2 by stepmothers

Record of which relatives contributed to delinquency
    3 mothers
    1 stepmother [2]
    7 paternal aunts [2]
    2 fathers
    2 cousins (female)
    1 maternal uncle
    1 grandmother

[1] These are done from the standpoint of the cases, ignoring the fact that sister-hood would skew the results if done from the standpoint of the fathers.
[2] This is a case where two women were responsible for influencing eight girls, one as a stepmother of 2, and aunt of 12 and 25, the other as aunt of 15, 16, 17, and 18.

8 cases showed no contributing relatives

Analysis of whether promiscuity was preceded by marriage or not

13 married before any promiscuity

12 promiscuous before marriage

Most significant point: all those who were promiscuous without preceding marriage are under thirty.

6 of the 12 who were promiscuous before marriage were reared by grandmothers (7 cases in all were reared by grandmothers).

5 of those promiscuous before marriage had illegitimate children.

8 of those who were promiscuous after marriage had illegitimate children.

CAUSES OF DELINQUENCY

Among those promiscuous before marriage

Illegitimate child...5

Trouble at school, expulsion and reform school................1

Desire of mixed-blood to identify with Indian group....1

Influence of older female relatives....................................3

Ineffective chaperon and skilled seduction.........................1

Among those who were married before they became promiscuous

Desertion by husband...8

Marriage opposed and broken up by father (example of stepmother)...1

Violent, epileptic-like husband, abusive............................1

Operation followed by statement that no more children could be borne...1

Forced marriage to a white man by parents [3]..................1

Death of husband and example of mother.........................1

Relation to intertribal and interracial problem

7 involvements with Black Faces (3 of the causatives desertion in promiscuity after marriage; 2 illegitimate children)

4 involvements with white men (3 illegitimate children)

1 mixed-blood girl

1 other-tribal (Short Robe woman)

[3] This case is an other-tribal Short Robe.

Chapter XIV

SUPPORTING DATA FOR EARLIER STATEMENTS

(1) Data on the Amount of English Spoken [1]

Analysis of 148 cases of men over 40
   76 speak creditable English.
   13 spoke absolutely no English.
   17 spoke practically no English.
   4 speak no Indian and 1 more practically none.

When 130 married couples over 40 are considered
   69 husbands and 38 wives spoke creditable English.
   7 husbands and 31 wives spoke absolutely no English.
   17 husbands and 6 wives spoke practically no English.

When 101 [2] married couples, all of the husbands under 40 are considered
   4 husbands and 13 wives spoke absolutely no English.

(2) Details of Domestic Economy

The attached budgets will give some idea of the simplicity of Antler housekeeping. The majority of the family sleeps on the floor, and in the morning the bedding, quilts, blankets, pillows (sheets may or may not be present) are simply hung out on a line or piled on the porch. Rugs and curtains are luxuries and are not missed. Tablecloths are seldom used, nor are napkins a necessity. The simplest common cutlery and white porcelain dishes are the rule. During the summer most cooking and living are done out-of-doors. The small number of clothes necessitates very little sewing, but a considerable amount of time has to go to mending. The average

---

[1] Based upon testimony of official interpreters.
[2] The fact that more married couples are mentioned here than in the analysis is due to the fact that the linguistic census was based upon census material before this material was corrected for divorce and death.

Antler man is patched upon patches, but his clothes are clean and neatly mended. Bedding also is constantly patched and mended. But if she does not make a garden nor gather and preserve wild fruits, nor help her husband farm, the work of an Antler household is no longer enough to occupy a woman more than three hours a day. Formerly, three or four hours a day were taken up by grinding corn. Now this is done at a mill.

Women over fifty as a rule still pursue the following activities

> Making sweet corn and grinding it themselves
> Drying meat
> Making hominy
> Gathering gooseberries, blackberries, wild plums, nuts, and
> > preserving them
> Making moccasins

Women between thirty and fifty

> Make all the bread which is eaten
> Still make hominy
> Gather wild fruits to make pies, but do less preserving
> Make their own clothes

Young married women

> Make fried bread and boil meat, but do not know how to make
> > hominy or sweet corn
> Mend their clothes
> Wash and iron

Vegetables grown in a good garden

Sweet corn	Onions
Potatoes	Turnips
Squash	Tomatoes
Beans	Cabbage

Antlers' ideal clothes' budget

Man

> 1 store suit, or at least 1 pair of store trousers (1 old pair
> > store trousers also)

2 pairs of overalls

4 shirts

2 pairs of shoes

2 suits of winter underwear

4 pairs of socks, 2 winter, 2 summer (a winter coat is not regarded as a *sine qua non*, although a coat, or sweater is necessary if a man does not wish to go abroad in a blanket)

Woman

4 dresses, 1 of silk or sateen, 1 old one of silk or sateen, 2 cotton

2 pairs bloomers

2 cotton vests

3 pair summer stockings

3 petticoats, one white and embroidered, the others old dress skirts

3 pair winter stockings

3 pairs moccasins, or

2 pairs shoes

2 shawls, one cashmere and fringed, one plain

Boy

2 pairs overalls

3 shirts

1 pair shoes

2 pairs winter stockings

2 pairs winter underwear

Girl

4 dresses

2 pairs summer stockings

2 pairs winter stockings

2 pairs winter underwear

2 sets summer underwear

Antlers' ideal of household furniture

1 bed (a second bed for the parents, the first being for the oldest child, is desirable but not necessary)

1 dining table

6 straight chairs

1 rocking chair
1 bureau
1 stove
1 sewing machine
1 wash tub, board and wringer
3 lamps (small with glass base)
1 water bucket
1 wash basin
1 large kettle
2 frying pans
2 stew pans
1 large baking pan
  curtains at the living room window
1 mirror

Household luxuries

Rug
Framed enlarged photographs
Whatnot
Washing machine, which is seldom used
Kitchen cabinet
Brass bed
Oil stoves

Minimum food for a week for a family of seven

(This relies upon a garden from which cabbage, squash, beans, and corn have been stored.)

Staples

Sugar	5 lbs.	$ .50
Coffee	1 lb.	.40
Baking powder	1 lb.	.25
Flour	48 lbs.	2.00
Lard	2 lbs.	.40
Salt		.10
Soap		.10
Matches		.05

Extras

Beans		.25
Raisins		.25
Meat	2 lbs.	.50

$4.80

A menu based upon these expenditures

Coffee

Bread made with baking powder, either baked or fried

Stew of hominy or cornmeal, flavored with vegetables, raisins, or meat

Even when more food is available, the principal dish is always one stew.

Antler meal according to best "white" standards

Meat, boiled. Beef, fresh pork, or chicken

Soup of meat-water, served separately

Boiled potatoes

Two boiled vegetables

Stewed fruit or pie filled with fruit

Bread

Coffee

Feast menu

Boiled beef and chicken   Coffee

Bread   Soup

Small domestic feast for doctor or Peyote

Boiled beef or chicken   Hominy

Bread   Soup

Coffee   Fruit and store cake

(3) INDIAN COMMENTS ON UNPOPULAR FAMILIES

Household	Property	Size of family	Reasons given by Indians
3	4of	3	"Hard to get along with."
18	4of	2	"Place too near settlement."
			"He's gone white."
			"He's a Christian."
			"He likes to mix with the mixed bloods although he can't read or write."
			"He mixes too much with the whites."
27	4of	2	"He's married to a white woman."
			"*She* does all the work."
37	8or	3	"All their relatives are dead."
			"No relatives on either side."
55	4of (owns ⅓)	2	"Young folks, but they fight so much folks won't stand them around."
			"They did live with his father, then the old folks went away and her mother butted in. Then her brother accidentally shot his younger brother, so they left there. Then he lost all his horses, and so they stay out there."
			"They fight so they just have to live by themselves."
61	4or 4of tribal land	3	"He's gone white."
			"They live like white people. They never eat or sleep on the floor."
			"They are like white people though she does dress like an Indian."
			"Why he has a 40 rented and then he goes and farms some more land."
			"He wouldn't have relatives hanging around."
64	⅓ 16or	4	"He's a Short Robe and they are always running off to his reservation."
			"They don't stay here much."
			"She has that stingy Vincent blood in her." [1]
66	16or	3	"They haven't any relatives."
			"He has a terrible temper."
			"All their folks are dead."
72	8of on shares	4	"He had a lot of children."
			"He farms on shares so he won't have folks around to eat it up."
74	4of	4	"They are always trying to get people in but they make them work too hard."
			"If women go there she makes them stand over the stove all day."
			"This year he got his half brother to come and farm and promised him a share of the crop and then just before harvest he"

(3) INDIAN COMMENTS ON UNPOPULAR FAMILIES
Continued

Household	Property	Size of family	Reasons given by Indians
			mortgages the whole crop and buys an automobile and Jack won't get a thing."
			"She has Vincent blood in her too." [1]
83	35f	2	"They are usually broke."
			"Never anything to eat in the house and he is always sponging on his stepmother."
			"His stepmother helps feed them, for he doesn't really farm and she's cross."
97	f rented land	2	"He farms like a white farmer."
			"He has money in the bank."
			"He makes his farm pay."
			"If anyone goes there he is quite a hand to work them."
98	120r	3	"Vincent blood again." [1]
			"Samuel doesn't like to have people about." (Samuel is the berdache.)
			"She's too stingy."
102	240r	4	"No poor relations on either side."
			"He keeps to himself."
123	40r	3	"Folks just don't go there."
			"His wife is awful jealous of him."
146	40f	2	"Wife went East to school."
			"They are Christians."
			"Try to live like white people."
			"Their daughter is a trained nurse and she married a white man."
			"She has flowers in her garden."
149	40f	3	"Folks are afraid of that blood."
			"His brother was a murderer, they say."

[1] The Vincents are a family who are all supposed to be unbelievably stingy. It is said of them that they never give anything away except in the ring (*i.e.*, before all the people).

CHAPTER XV

NOTES ON THE POSSIBILITY OF STUDYING THE MIXED-BLOOD SITUATION

A fair body of material concerning the mixed-blood population was accumulated, but awaits analysis for later publication. Meanwhile, it may be appropriate to suggest here some of the problems which a partial analysis reveals. Until a few years ago, it was customary to record the exact amount of Indian blood in each mixed blood whose name appeared upon the tribal roll. This has recently been superseded by the less exact notations of "over a fourth," or "under a fourth," Indian blood. The tribal roll also gives the present address of all those who live off the reservation. It does not, however, provide data concerning marriage with whites or members of other tribes. Such information has to be gathered from informants. Information as to occupation of individuals listed, or of husbands of women listed, also has to be obtained from informants. The addition of information requirements on these two subjects would make possible an interesting analysis of several points under what conditions women left the reservation; whether men or women were more likely to enter into intertribal marriages; whether residence of such intertribal marriages tended to be wife-determined or husband-determined; what was the occupational adjustment of males in intertribal marriages compared with males in Indian-white marriages; what was the range of occupational adjustment of Indians off their own reservation, but near another reservation, in comparison with the occupational adjustment of Indians who had left the Indian country completely; and how the adjustment of these latter was related to intratribal, extra tribal, mixed-blood, or white marriage.

Such Antler data as are available suggest that comparisons between them and other tribes would possibly yield interesting results. An analysis of the genealogies of the present mixed-blood population yielded no results; some families tended to marry back into the tribe, others married out. There are an overwhelming number of mixed bloods among those adults who are listed as unmarried. The meager occupational data available suggest that quarter-breed children born of a mixed-blood mother and a white father have a better economic chance than quarter-breed children born of a mixed-blood father and a white mother. This conclusion is an obvious correlate of the greater tendency for mixed-blood women married to white men to leave the reservation completely, and the fact that white men can command better economic opportunities than can mixed bloods.

205 mixed bloods on the reservation, mostly in the small towns and more distant farms.

65 of these had been reassimilated to the full-blood tradition, through original upbringing or marriage.

180 mixed bloods living off the reservation kept their names on the roll:

52 adult males.

47 adult females.

Remaining upon the roll should be interpreted as an economic, rather than a sentimental, point, although in many cases sentiment may play a part. But retaining membership in the tribe carries with it: the right to a *pro persona* share in any annuity or any bonus distributions to the tribe; a share in tribal lands; and the right to send children to the government Indian boarding schools.

ANALYSIS OF OFF-RESERVATION RESIDENCE, MARITAL STATE AND DEGREE OF MIXED BLOOD

SYMBOLS

FB — Full-blood (This is in terms of the roll. There are, however, many cases where Antlers with some white blood or Negro blood are listed as full-bloods. The designation cannot be taken as accurate.)

+ — More than a quarter Antler.

— — Less than a quarter Antler.

	Males				Females				Both sexes
	FB	+	—	Total	FB	+	—	Total	
Single	3	7	15	25	2	6	1	9	34
Married	12	16	24	52	8	9	31	48	100
Total				77				57	134

TYPE OF MARRIAGE AND DEGREE OF MIXED BLOOD

	Males				Females				Both sexes
	FB	+	—	Total	FB	+	—	Total	
ot	8	8	1	17	5	4	5	14	31
W	1	3	20	24	1	4	25	30	54
A	3	2	3	8	2	1	1	4	15*
Total	12	13	24	49	8	9	31	48	100

* Three unclassified, one married to a Negro, one to a Mexican, one unknown.

GENERAL SUMMARY

Married — 100   Single — 34
Full-bloods — 25; + one-quarter — 38; — one-quarter — 71
Males — 77   Females — 57
Married males — 49   Females — 48
Single males — 25   Females — 9
Married whites — 24 males   Females — 30
Married other tribes — 17 males   Females — 14
Married Antlers — 3 males

ANALYSIS OF OFF-RESERVATION MEMBERS OF TRIBE

THOSE REPORTING CHILDREN

Males				Females			
FB	+	—	Total	FB	+	—	Total
5	7	14	26	2	3	16	21

NUMBER OF CHILDREN REPORTED

By males		By females	
No. of Children	No. Reporting	No. of Children	No. Reporting
1	7	1	7
2	9	2	8
3	7	3	3
4	1	4	2
5	0	5	1
6	1		
7	1		
Total	26	Total	21

All of this material could, of course, be converted into percentages, in which case it would appear a great deal more significant than such small numbers can possibly be. I have preferred to leave it in a form which will make unmistakably clear the variety of material and its nonamenability to statistical analysis.

Tables Showing Analysis of Adult Members of the Tribal Roll Living Away from the Reservation

Correlation Between Residence and Type of Marriage

I — Those who are off the reservation in institutions other than schools. Includes prisons, homes, insane asylums.

V — Those who live off the reservation, but within a hundred miles of it in the same state or in the immediately adjoining state.

R — Those who live off the Antler reservation, but on or near other Indian reservations.

O — Those who live completely out of the Indian country, e.g. in Chicago or Los Angeles.

ot — Other tribal marriage.

W — White marriage.

A — Antler marriage.

MARRIED ADULTS

	Males					Females				
	I	V	R	O	Total	I	V	R	O	Total
ot	1	4	11	1	17		2	10	2	14
W	2	8	7	7	24		13	7	10	30
A		2*	4*	2	8			2	2	4
†		2		1	3					
Totals	3	16	22	11	52		15	19	14	48

UNMARRIED ADULTS

	I	V	R	O	Total	I	V	R	O	Total
ot	2	6	11	6	25	2	2	5		9
Totals	5	22	33	17	77	2	17	24	14	57

SUMMARY FOR BOTH SEXES

Off reservation in institutions, 7

Off reservation in other Indian territory, 57

Off reservation in adjoining territory, 39

Off reservation away from all Indian territory, 31

Total, 134.

* One has a wife on list.

† Three unclassified, one married to a Negro, one to a Mexican, one unknown.

CHAPTER XVI

SAMPLE CONVERSATIONS

SELECTIONS FROM AN INTERVIEW WITH A WIDOW, C, AND HER NEPHEW, B, DURING A MORNING SPENT AT HER HOUSE

C. "No, I'm not busy, I just finished cleaning up. They had meeting yesterday and decided on powwow. They can't put the committee out. Spending money like that. When my father and mother was alive they used to be treasurer and have enough money to make something as big as a pillow and my father would put it under his head. And he'd be just as careful, he wouldn't even let a nickel go out of it.

"I went to school four years. I was just in the fourth grade. I was tough and my father wanted me to go to school all the time. I used to tease my brother Jack and pull his hair all the time. Now he has a little kid that is just like he was, and I say, 'don't beat him up, he's just like you were, a tomboy,' as we say.

"That's the picture of my husband. He was in the war but he didn't go over. He was just in the war. I had another little girl, she was as big as Sue. She was smarter than Sue. She was lighter too. But I losed her. We used to tease her and say, 'She'll put a hand-kerchief on her head and be first in the dance.' That made her father cross.

"Jim's wife is awful mean to him. He's young, just nineteen. I didn't make him do no work when he stayed with us. Anna'd try to make him work and say, 'Jim, get some water.' And he'd say, 'Aunt Cathy's nice, but Aunt Anna's awful cross. I didn't like to make him work as if he had to earn his dinner. I'd just feed him. There was an awful nice little girl, that's her picture in the corner (of a frame of snapshots) that wants to marry him. We wanted him to marry her too. She's Bill Truman's daughter."

B. "He's about the biggest man on the reservation. Broad."

C. "She sent him a letter, but I tore it up. That wife of his is mean. She was married before. She beats him up. She's jealous of that girl. She knows about her waiting to get him and she watches him all the time. He came here, and gee, we was awful sorry for him. His arm was all cut. She broke two pictures like that on him. He sat here and cried and we cried and then I said, 'Well, there's no use our crying so, for he'll go back to that woman,' I said. And we washed the cut with linaments and got it all well, and in about three days she was back after him. Here he don't have to work, but she makes him do everything. If her shoes is there, she makes him bring them to her. That woman. We don't want him to stay with her. She's old and she's run around so much. No, they ain't married right."

B. "She's the legal wife of Jack Cobb. The Cobb boys sure is wild."

C. "Yes, we've had awful dry weather. This little rain won't do any good. Old Lady Baker she has a big pipe, a great big pipe, that one at the feast was just a little one, but this is a great big one. If you pour water on it, it rains. Her father taught her. She's been awful worried whether she ought to make rain or not. But she doesn't know how to stop the rain. She's afraid it might rain for a week and all the beans would be spoiled and people would be cross. She has a whole houseful of holy things down there that she takes good care of. There's one gang too if you pour water on them it rains and rains and won't stop. That's May's gang.

"Next Sunday we're going to have the feast. It ain't good to put it off that way. Last time old Lady Baker had things all collected and people had chickens cleaned and everything and here they didn't have it and they have to eat the chickens and collect new ones for next time. That Bob Crane, his wife's awful sick and he didn't ought to put it off like that. It's dangerous; she might die. The feast isn't no common thing like a hand game. You can't put it off that way.

"Matt Tyson is a doctor. He bleeds people and gets all the bad blood out of them. He bled one woman and her blood was just like milk, that's the last stage, you know. And she got well. Tom Tyson's wife is a real citizen. But her arm got all numb, and her fingers and she couldn't move it and he said, 'Well, I guess we'll try Uncle Matt,' and he bleeded it and she got well. She can work just like a man now."

B. "He's drunk all the time too."

C. "He cured one man who had paralysis. That Fred Cook. Yes, he's kind of silly. He kept holy things in his house. You oughtn't to do that. Indians oughtn't to keep them; they don't look after them right. They ought to send them away to the white people. You're likely to get sick."

B. "You're likely to go insane."

C. "Yes, Henry Burns' all right, but he makes hot water and kinnikinnick for his holy things real often. You have to take a little steak, just a little one like this (about 5 or 4 inches long) and cut it all up in strips and cook it real fine with gravy until its all soft. Then you sprinkle a little corn in it. Not a lot, just a little, and you don't have to cook it until it's soft, just cook it, you know. Then you take it out and pour it out with some kinnikinnick. If you do that real often, you're all right.

"There was a woman was sick and the doctor said, that other doctor, Doctor Jones, said she had something worrying her. He looked at her appendix and that was all right and he said she had something worrying her. She wondered what that could be. They brought her little girl home from school but that didn't seem to be it. Then they had a big Peyote meeting and that filled her all up and brought it all out. That woman that just died used to be a great one to take peyote. They used to have Peyote meetings and sometimes she'd not like someone who was there, and she'd want them to not come, so they'd tell them their influence would make her sick and they'd not come next time. Real nice men too, she'd say."

(I tell story from morning paper of girl come back to life.)

C. "Yes, they say that Jess Thompson when he was a real little fellow did that. He was dead, they thought, and they was all ready to bury him and he sat up, so now they keep the body for four days. Used to they used to wrap them up in one of those (parfleche) and put them right in the ground, my mother used to tell me. Just the relations. 'But now', she said, 'You have a nice casket to lie in and it's nice,' she said. All this meeting business is new. They used to just have the relations. They had a Peyote meeting there last night."

B. "Arthur Smith was master of ceremonies. My father was there. They invited him. They just invite some of them. Not everybody goes different ones. [I cite Peyote series for Bess Tate and the one at Henry Burns.] Yes, all three of those are different gangs.

They have to be invited. This is the fourth one. Yes, they always
have four, but this is the fourth.

"I'm in that Peyote. My father has a fireplace and I have right
to be there because I'm his son. Yes, it will surely come to me. Yes,
I've a brother, but he couldn't make it right. They are going to
change things in the Peyote now. They are going to have buttons
and everyone has to pay two dollars for them. And everyone has to
decide which way they are going to go, Peyote way, or gambling,
and drinking and running around with no mens. (I instance Bob
Crane) Yes, well they're going to get after him, that's all. He's
head of the feast and he's high up in the Dance and he ain't doing
right; he's doing wrong. He'll have to choose. It's a hard thing to
choose. I've got to make up my mind myself. I think if I were
married and settled down why then I'll go Peyote but now that's
I'm single, I don't know what I'll do." (I suggest Peyote weddings
as well as Peyote funerals, to make weddings sacred, and comment
on old-fashioned weddings, instancing Harry Siler's daughter's
wedding.)

C. "Yes, she had two hogs. That was about a month ago. Indian weddings was different. But nowadays, it's hard. People don't
have much. When my mother and father was living it was different.
They had everything then, hogs and cows and everything."

B. "Sometimes they used to give away horses, as many as seventeen horses." (I again suggest a Peyote wedding to stabilize
marriage.)

B. "The P tribe done something like that. There was a P
woman was drinking and running around with other men and she
realized that she was doing wrong and she gave a meeting and said
she was going to build her life anew. And she did. It worked. A R
was up here and told us about it.

"I've been working over to X. There's a lot of young fellows
ought to be working over there. Instead, they're all up at the Black
Face powwow. I was going back to X today but I didn't go yet.
I was up to the Black Face powwow last night. It was pretty good.
They pay us thirty-five and forty cents an hour. Most of them
work ten hours because they serve a lunch in the afternoon. I'm
not going to camp, I'm going to work with some Germans over
there and board with them. Awful nice people, them Germans,
real Indians, plenty to eat."

(I bring up subject of Frank Mathews.)

B. "Yes, he's got his last payment. Pretty soon he'll be living around with his car."

C. "He's got an awful nice wife and she'd like to have a home."

B. "I ain't got no money and none's ever coming to me. I never had use of none. I was in school when they had money. But I work, like this. We're through working over at Perry's now. Finished the house. But he's going to build a garage too. Gonna get a new car. He wants to have everything nice. I always worked. Not a lot, enough to get something to eat. My wife and I never did get along. She said she wanted to marry me, but we never did get along. She's too jealous."

C. "She's high-tempered. They was married when they was still going to school, and they tried to part them but they couldn't; when they come back from school, they went right together again."

B. "I never went with her at school. I went with other tribes. Seems like I couldn't please her. I tried, but I couldn't. I don't want to get married again. I know what marriage is like. Before I was married I used to work in the city. But my wife wouldn't go down there. She wanted to stay right beside her mother. We used to live down at her folks. My little girl's down there now. And her sister's little boy. Her sister's parted from her husband too. She's running around and living with Jane. But that won't last long. Jane will get jealous of her. Jane's still jealous of me. The other day I was in the store and Jane was there. And I started to go out after Maggie Webb and she said, 'There you are running around with the dogs,' and I turned around and said, 'Jane, I'm not having anything to do with you,' and she hit me with her hand game dishes and I knocked Dick Hobbs down. He's carrying a stick now on account of me. He's afraid of me. He's not man enough to stand up to me. Jane said she was going to ride about in a car and be fine, and now Dick Hobbs has deeded all that money over to his children."

C. "That's the land that Fanny's grandmother has too. Oh, she'll be disappointed. We told B. to dress up like a fine gentleman and she'd be coming back to him quick enough."

B. "But I'm through. I didn't want her to do it and now she's done it. I'm through. I've filed my papers and the divorce will be finished in October. Yes, I've paid for it. I ain't going to take my little girl either. I'll let her see." (Earlier he had remarked he was going to send his little girl away to school.)

(I ask: "Do you think the grandparents take good care of her?")

B. "No, I seen how they treated that little boy, her sister's child, but I'm going to let her see now."

C. "She'll be sorry. With five of them little kids. I watched her the other night at the hand game, she had them all there asleep on the blankets, she sat next to me, and she didn't know how to do nor nothing; she stood them up while they was still asleep and slapped them."

(I bring the conversation around to Philip and Marie.)

B. "He's broke now. He's mortgaged his car. Soon he'll be walking."

C. "Marie's been staying there taking care of Sarah." (Whose baby was born about three weeks ago).

B. "Marie told me about two weeks ago she ain't living with Philip. Just friendship, she said. I brought her home from a hand game about two weeks ago. She asked me to — I didn't ask her. She says pretty soon she'll leave Philip."

C. "She's got a little Black Face kid and she's been all over. They say she was in the city with a white man, a big white man who worked in a bank and she left him flat."

Random Comment

B. "Everybody laughs at Nancy Brown. We call her broomstick."

C. "George Harper's awful mean. His wife was sick but she was fat and he told her she was just lazy and she died. He used to hit her because he said she was lazy."

B. "Yes, I'd like to have lived in the buffalo days. Plenty of meat."

C. "Maybe I'd have liked it, I like most things, but it was hard work then. My mother used to tell me how hard it was to raise us. But now we have machines and easy life. That George Harper belongs to another band, they're niggers, we don't like to have anything to do with them. We don't like even to talk to them."

MEMORIES OF THE OUTING SYSTEM AT CARLISLE

(MAN OF SIXTY)

"I used to work in Y county Pennsylvania near Y —— thirty years ago. Yes, sir, I worked for an Englishman by the name of S ——. He'd been some kind of professor in one of those big colleges and he'd retired. Yes, I remember the D —— Park. Used to have big dances there every Saturday night and sometimes two or three months in a time [times in a month]. I couldn't dance, for we wasn't allowed to dance at school and everything I done was marked down on a card every month just like I was at school. So they put me at the gate. They had the floor roped off and there was two gates, and between dances I had to sweep up the floor and put candle shavings on the floor to make it smooth. So I stood there at the gate and I could see across to the other gate and pretty soon I seen a fellow come in all by himself and start along the floor. Now you ain't allowed on that floor unless you got a girl; single fellows ain't allowed there. So I hollered to the fellow on the other gate, but he says he's busy. Now you know everybody's going around on that floor and soon's you get on there you have to dance. And this fellow moved along to one side and a couple came around the corner and just then I seen him go up to her and run his knife — one of the eagle pen knives, you know, right into her heart. They stopped the dance and everybody rushed around, and I didn't know anything about the law in them days and I picked up the knife all bloody the way it was and brung it home. I was going to keep it and bring it out here as a souvenir. I showed it to Mr. S —— and he said 'all right, but you'll have to be a witness.' And sure enough they call me for a witness. So Mr. S —— said, 'You'll have to go. You want some money while you're in Philadelphia?' But I said, 'No, I got a friend in Philadelphia works for John Wanamaker. I'll stay with him.' So I went to the trial and they pretty near got me on the time. Then I happened to remember that that train leaves Y —— at eleven o'clock had just gone by. So I said that that train must get to L —— about 11:10. So I got that right too. But I told Mr. S. I wasn't going to go to any more dances if I got mixed up in things like that. [N. B., His wife had never heard this story.]

"Mr. S. had to go back to Europe because his mother was sick and he asked me what I'd like to do while he's gone. So I say I've been looking at the rubber boot factory and I believe I'll work there. I had a little thing and the rubber was in it to make a heel and all I had to do was to take that out with a long thing I hold in my hand and throw it over there and then another fellow takes it and fixes it, and I take another one with my other hand. First three or four days my arms surely did ache, but I got used to it. I worked there three months. I used to work around and try different places. I worked for a man named Frank P——. But he and his wife didn't get along very good and she was always going off to her folks, and I had to hitch up no matter what time of night it was. They had buckboards there, and surreys, and buggies, one horse rigs. Everything was different from here. All the milk used to be kept nice and cool in the spring house and you had to remember to take the milk can fartherest from the door. That was most cool, the others was just fresh. There was a lot to that too. And when you came into the dining hall had to put on different shoes and different clothes. Out here you just come in anyhow. First time I came back from school I was so homesick I only stayed two weeks and then I said, 'I'm going back to Carlisle.' I got back there and stayed about a week and then I went out to work. I brought seven hundred dollars back with me when I finally come home."

His wife: "The boys mostly went to Y county, but the girls was scattered down in Maryland and Delaware and all over. I always hoped that one time I'd get to see the sea before I came back out West, and sure enough the last summer I went to work at the seashore. We used to get up early in the morning and go out and gather the shells. Everybody'd try to get there first to get them. I brought some out here with me when we come but I don't know what became of them now. [Typical, like her casual acceptance of her son's cutting up the picture of Hiawatha to make a dance costume, and only remarking "Oh, that was my favorite picture."] We had a house right close to where the excursion trains came in."

Woman (forty-two years ago): 'I used to live on South Eleventh Street in Philadelphia. I worked for a woman named Smith. Her husband used to get up late in the morning and she ordered me to wait on him but never to speak to him. So one morning I was waiting on him and he spoke to me, but I didn't answer him, and he yelled at me and said, 'Answer me, girl' and tried to grab hold of me and I ran out in the street. And a neighbor met me and asked me where I was going and I told her and she said, 'Go on back in the house.' And she told me 'that man was a drunkard.' "

Woman (trips back East): "When I was East I got into a taxi-cab and the driver said, 'Excuse me, lady, but I've gotta smoke' and I said, 'Go ahead.' Didn't say I was dying for one myself. When I told my sister-in-law she said, 'Why didn't you tell him to give you one?' but I said, 'He called me a lady so I tried to make him keep on thinking I was one.' "

COMMENTS OF FOUR WHITE PEOPLE UPON AN INDIAN FUNERAL, COMPOSITE RECORD

Do you know two little babies died at once over at that Joe Gordon's place? You know that old fellow — he wears long hair and he's lousy. His daughter said she wouldn't have him in her house any more, he was so lousy. He's a morphine fiend too. Every time he gets any money he goes over to that doctor in Decatur who'll do anything for money, though they say that a doctor's allowed to give a shot of morphine in his office if it will do them any good, but he's not allowed to sell it to them. He gives this old fellow a shot in the heel, and that gets him home. Them children of his are just as poor as dirt. What'd the babies die of? Oh, after-effects of the measles. I suppose they never had no doctor. Oh, they did? Took them to X, did they and brung 'em home, I suppose just as they was gettin' better. Oh, the doctor said they was going to die and let 'em go, did he? Well, they do that — they'd ruther they'd die at home if they're going to die. And they had a regular funeral, did they? A feast? Where'd they get the money? I seed that old Joe this morning, and he was drunk then. The mother of the children's a big, fat, ugly squaw, ain't she? And the house where they had the funeral? Like all Indian houses — no screens, hardly any furniture. They sell all their furniture powwow time so they can go to powwow. Just a dirty little frame house, nothing in it, just a few big pictures of Indians on the wall, and a picture stuck full of the funniest snapshots — one of some boys with a pennant in front of them and some of the real old squaws. And it took them hours and hours, of course. They never start anything when they say they will. The men spent a whole day at it, I suppose, when they ought to have been at work. Took five men to dig the grave, did it? Oh, it would — aren't they lazy? Did you ever notice how short an Indian's arm is? Well, he never raises it except from his plate to his mouth. They got caskets from a near-by city. Paid thirty-five dollars each for them. Why, for little kids like that they could have gotten them for twelve or fifteen dollars. They never went over to the agency and asked for one of the war coffins, I suppose. Oh, of course, trust an Indian — they always want to do everything in style. When he's got money, it's just the best he wants. Does he pay five dollars for a hat? No — twenty-five dollars, and fifteen dollars for a pair of shoes. They had them poor little babies laid out on chairs — didn't even have a decent bed for them. They was dressed awful funny — in dresses made of shirting, and artificial flowers on them — roses and nasturtiums. Think of an Indian doing that! Shows they have some feeling anyhow. But they don't take good care of their children — just sling 'em around on those boards, and then the women go to a feast and just throw the little babies down in a row on the floor, and one of 'em will have measles or whooping cough or small-pox, and then they all get it. The little baby had pricks on his forehead? Bled it. Say, somebody ought to stop this bleeding. There's an Indian doctor goes around here and he takes a quart of blood out of them. Cures them all right. Next day they have to send for the undertaker. Somebody ought to stop that fellow. Where was those pricks? Oh, in the forehead. That ain't bleeding, that's for a headache. You watch lots of them and you'll see them all scratched up. What did they have to eat? Chicken! Oh, they did? Could you eat it? Oh, I couldn't touch any of that stuff they cook. They cook the meat until it's just as stringy. And what kind of bread? Store bread. Oh, yes, they're too lazy to bake. And what's that — they sprayed Flit over the casket! Isn't that too disgusting! Keep the bodies so long that they smell! But I don't suppose they mind. And then they stuck some of the food on a plate beside the bodies. Well, of all the funny ignorant things! And a lot of speeches, and then a lot of wailing — not real grief. I looked and hardly any of them had any tears in their eyes — just yelling away to get their dinners, I suppose. They didn't have the hearse. D'rather have the feast, I suppose, and they took the bodies up in an old wagon.

When they got there, no one had a screw driver, and they had to screw the lid down with knives and an old shovel. It took forever. And then an old squaw sat down and started to yell over another grave and they had to wait for her."

CONVERSATION OF A YOUNG MOTHER WHOSE BABY HAD DIED

"It had summer complaint. And it got just as thin. I took it to the hospital and the doctor made me wean it right when it was so sick. And then I couldn't make it eat anything. It seems as if that doctor were losing babies all the time that summer. He lost four in a month. There was another little baby sick in the next room to mine. Finally, my mother-in-law came up and she said, 'You better bring that baby home. It's certainly not going to live very long.' I didn't know, you know. I'd never lost a baby before. But the doctor wasn't there and I didn't like to go without being regularly discharged. So my mother-in-law went home and I said I'd come tomorrow. Then the baby in the next room died. And I talked to the mother and said, 'Beatrice, your baby didn't look nearly as sick as mine. What do you think I'd better do?' And she said, 'Alice, you'd better take it home. Don't let them keep you here and keep telling you it will get well like they did me.' I wanted to take it home for I knew if the baby died I could never stand it alone. Then the doctor came in and I said, 'Doctor, is my baby going to die like the one in the next room?' And he said, 'Oh, did it die?' And I said, 'Yes, and all the time you were telling that poor woman it would get better; now don't talk to me like that, tell me the truth about my baby.' And he said, 'I don't think it will live until morning.' So I sent for my husband and we came home and took it out to the old man's place. Old man said we'd have a Peyote meeting. It may be too late, we mustn't expect too much, but we'll try it. So we sat there, my husband and I, and what my baby couldn't drink, I drank. They oughtn't to have had us sit there because we didn't believe, you know, and we didn't know nothing about it. And my baby had been so sick it could hardly move and it got up and took two steps towards the drummers until the old man reached over and pulled it back. His face went just as white. You see she was named for his sister, and when the drummers sang, he heard his sister singing. And I guess she came back there because she had her name. My baby got a little better and took a little milk, but she was too weak. Towards morning that time I saw a white mist like over her so I knew she wasn't going to live long. When they had the Peyote meeting over her casket, I didn't take any for whatever I saw or heard, I wanted to see and hear without the influence of any drug. She had a pink silk handkerchief over her face, and I saw it move, and her little breast rose and fell, and her little hands moved. And then after she was gone and buried they had the last Peyote meeting. And when they'd put a little bit of all the food on a dish and set it down, a little whirlwind came and went right around the dish. I guess that was my baby. She'd been to all the other meetings so I guess she thought she'd come to the next one. I never believed in ghosts or nothing, but I think that was my baby."

INDEX

INDEX